Sourcebook of Texts
for the
Comparative Study of the Gospels

SOCIETY OF BIBLICAL LITERATURE
SOURCES FOR BIBLICAL STUDY

edited by

WAYNE A. MEEKS

Number 1

SOURCEBOOK OF TEXTS

FOR THE

COMPARATIVE STUDY OF THE GOSPELS

by

David L. Dungan
and
David R. Cartlidge

SCHOLARS PRESS
Missoula, Montana

SOURCEBOOK OF TEXTS
FOR THE
COMPARATIVE STUDY OF THE GOSPELS

Literature of the Hellenistic and Roman Period
Illuminating the Milieu and Character of the Gospels

by

David L. Dungan
and
David R. Cartlidge

Fourth Edition, Corrected

Published by

SCHOLARS PRESS

for

The Society of Biblical Literature

Distributed by

SCHOLARS PRESS
University of Montana
Missoula, Montana 59801

SOURCEBOOK OF TEXTS

FOR THE

COMPARATIVE STUDY OF THE GOSPELS

by

David L. Dungan
and
David R. Cartlidge

Library of Congress Cataloging in Publication Data

Dungan, David L   comp.
    Sourcebook of texts for the comparative study of
the Gospels.

    (Sources for Biblical study ; no. 1)
    Bibliography: p.
    1. Bible. N.T. Gospels — Extra-canonical
parallels. I. Cartlidge, David R. II. Title.
III. Series.
BS2555.5.D86   1975   226'.06   75-43845
ISBN 0-89130-068-6

PRINTED IN THE UNITED STATES OF AMERICA

4 5
Edwards Brothers, Inc.
Ann Arbor, Michigan 48104

To Helmut Koester,

Our friend and mentor,

Whose example in the elucidation

of Christian origins

Is hopefully reflected in this book.

Δόξα σοι, πολύμορφε Ἰησοῦ, σοὶ δόξα,
Ὁ φαινόμενος κατὰ τὴν μετρίαν ἡμῶν ἀνθρωπότητα.

Acta Thomae 153

TABLE OF CONTENTS

PREFACE TO THE THIRD EDITION

This *Sourcebook* is designed especially for history-of-religions study of the gospels written in the first and second centuries of the Common Era. What sets it apart as a textbook on the gospels is its attempt to move away from the horizons and limitations of studying primarily the New Testament Gospels, as is still the case with most introductory books on Christian origins which treat the contemporary world as some sort of un-related "background" against which to view New Testament Christianity. This handbook seeks to understand Christian origins within an area studies approach, namely, as an integral part of the Mediterranean culture in the Hellenistic and Roman periods. It is axiomatic to this approach to avoid the customary distinc-tion between the four New Testament Gospels as "orthodox" and all others as "heretical." This is necessary for two reasons. First, in the area studies approach, one does not operate with such notions as "standard Christianity" or "normative Judaism"; one does not use any abstract prescriptive definitions of this sort. Instead, all religious claims are taken at face value, so that the widest variety, and even conflict, within a given religion is recognized and allowed to remain "in full bloom," as it were. Thus "orthodoxy" or "heresy" are used only with respect to this or that particular sub-group, i.e., in the way it actually used it. As is well known, what is heretical to one group or age is orthodox to another, and vice versa. This cer-tainly applies to the more than *three dozen* gospels the early Christians produced at one time or another.

In the second place, there is overwhelming evidence to prove that, in the earliest period, our four New Testament Gospels were hardly accepted as orthodox by everyone and were not at all seen as the final, standard set. In fact, the very idea of a standard *set* of gospels does not appear until well

after the middle of the second century, while the decision to
elevate precisely these four gospels to that elite circle was
carried out by one sub-group of later Western Christendom, which
then succeeded, with the Emperor's indispensable assistance, in
forcing its decision upon all dissident factions. Therefore, to
carry *this* sub-group's choice as to "heretical" and "orthodox"
gospels back up into the first or second centuries is simply
anachronistic. Indeed, it may be that our habit of always
thinking only of these four writings, whenever the term "gospel"
is used, and assuming that the gospels most familiar to us must
have been the ones the earliest Christians all preferred, such
habitual assumptions as these may be our most serious handicap
in seeking to gain a less biased picture of Christianity's
earliest period.

        Given this approach, the idea has been to provide a
collection of sources for college and seminary students to use
in searching for answers to such questions as, what were the
religious and literary precedents the early Christians used in
order to tell the Greco-Roman world about their Savior, Jesus
of Nazareth? What old, potent religious symbols and images
inspired the early Church to portray Jesus in the ways that it
did, so as to communicate so powerfully to its age? What kinds
of writings were these gospels? For it is obvious that they
are not all the same sort of thing. What kind of writing would
a first-century, Hellenized, Syrian magistrate, living in Antioch,
have taken Matthew or Luke-Acts to be? What then would he have
thought of the Coptic Gospel of Thomas on the one hand, or the
Gospel of Philip on the other? Of what other similar kinds of
literature would they have reminded him?

        The material included in this *Sourcebook* does not
presuppose any particular answer to these questions. Rather,
it is intended to be something like a lab-manual, a varied
collection of writings and excerpts of many different kinds,

which student and teacher can discuss together in class and in
term papers. This handbook format has been especially chosen
to facilitate note taking in and around the texts, during class
discussions and while working in the library.

The collection of materials included in this edition
does not pretend to be complete, particularly on the side of
contemporary Jewish and pagan literature. As far as the gospel
literature is concerned, it is fairly well represented. The
many gospels which have been omitted are either extant in such
fragmentary form, or are so late, that they throw little light
on the earliest period of gospel-producing activity, when the
basic lines for all later gospel writing seem to have been laid
down, in one way or another.

We have arranged the material in two ways. In *Part I*,
there are excerpts and fragments illustrating specific oral and
literary forms, as well as biographical motifs and narrative
conventions, taken from the literatures of many different
national and religious traditions. *Part II* is an attempt to
present whole writings or whole stories in order to enable the
student to focus on the question of genre and compositional
analysis. The selections from Part II listed in the various
sections of Part I are an aid to this type of investigation.
This indispensable line of inquiry seeks to discover the ways
in which the above-mentioned forms, motifs, and traditional
theological images have been combined into a completed work
which, as a whole, was intended to convey a definite interpretation of its chief figure to the reader, whether it be about
Jesus, or Moses, or Apollonios of Tyana, or someone else.

All selections are new translations provided with
brief introductions intended to orient the beginning student.
Notes and comments on the texts have been kept to a minimum,
it being considered wiser to leave that up to the individual
instructor and student. Exceptions to this rule are the Gospel

of Philip, The Life of Apollonios and The Life of Moses, which
have brief notes scattered through the text. Wider exploration
of the Hellenistic-Roman environment may continue to suggest
other literature to include in this collection. Any suggestions
concerning the format of the collection as a whole, or pertinent
new materials to put into future editions of the *Sourcebook*,
will be gratefully received.

   The editors are glad for this opportunity to express
to the Society of Biblical Literature Publications Committee
their thanks for including the *Sourcebook* among its new publications. We heartily share its conviction that the commercial
publishing industry has long since grown unbearably expensive,
time-consuming, and restrictive on what shall be printed and
how it must look, given the technological advances of the past
few years. We strongly hope that the Society's example will
encourage other learned societies to imitate the kind of inex-
pensive, flexible, and gratifyingly rapid publication process
that the Society of Biblical Literature, under the leadership
of its superb former Executive Secretary, Robert W. Funk, has
afforded us.

   Special thanks are due to Dean Boyd L. Daniels, of
the College of Liberal Arts, University of Tennessee (Knoxville),
for making available to us his translation of the *Protevangelium
Jacobi*; to Prof. Thomas B. Curtis, Department of Classics, of
the same institution, for his translation of Cicero's "Dream of
Scipio" and also checking the Asklepios inscriptions from
Epidauros; to Prof. Elaine H. Pagels, Department of Religion,
Barnard College, for her introduction and commentary on the
Gospel of Philip; and to Prof. Eldon J. Epp, Department of
Religion, Case-Western Reserve University, for the bibliography
on Mystery Religions of the Greco-Roman World. The author of
each of the selections is indicated in parentheses below the
title, while the introductions and notes, except where otherwise

indicated, are all by D. L. Dungan, who also edited the whole
work. Our thanks for assistance in preparing this third edition
are due to Ms. Jayne Mitchell, of the Department of Religious
Studies, University of Montana, who directed the preparation of
the manuscript for the "Sources for Biblical Study" series, and to
Ms. Joann Armour, of the same department, who typed the final
copy. Lastly, we wish to express our gratitude to Professor F.
Stanley Lusby, Chairman of the Department of Religious Studies,
University of Tennessee (Knoxville), for his constant encouragement and support.

David R. Cartlidge   David L. Dungan
Department of Religion   Department of Religious Studies
Maryville College   University of Tennessee
Maryville, Tennessee 37801   Knoxville, Tennessee 37916

December 1973

PART I

EXCERPTS FROM PAGAN, JEWISH,

AND CHRISTIAN WRITINGS

1. THE BIRTH OF ALEXANDER THE GREAT

(Plutarch, *Parallel Lives, Alexander* 2.1-3.2;
trans. D.R. Cartlidge)

(Introduction: Within Alexander's own lifetime, it
was widely believed that Olympias, Alexander's mother, had
conceived him through the agency of one of the Gods, namely
Zeus. Not the ordinary Zeus of the Greek homeland, however,
but the exotic Zeus-Ammon, whose world-famous shrine was in
far-away Siwa, Cyrene, deep in the Sahara. Writing some 400
years after his death, Plutarch records the generally accepted
account concerning Alexander's true divine origin, but he also
included the skeptical minority viewpoint.)

2.   Alexander was a descendant of Herakles, on his

father's side, through Karanos; on his mother's side he was

descended from Aikos through Neoptolemos; this is universally

believed. It is said that Philip (Alexander's father) was

initiated into the mysteries at Samothrace with Olympias (his

mother). He was still a youth and she was an orphan. He fell

in love with her and conjoined a marriage, with the consent of

her brother, Arumbas.

        The bride, before the night in which they were to

join in the bridechamber, had a vision. There was a peal of

thunder and a lightning bolt fell upon her womb. A great fire

was kindled from the strike, then it broke into flames which

flashed everywhere, then, they extinguished. At a later time,

after the marriage, Philip saw a vision: he was placing a seal

on his wife's womb; the engraving on the seal was, as he thought,

in the image of a lion. The men charged with interpreting

oracles were made suspicious by this vision and told Philip to

keep a closer watch on his marital affairs. But Aristander of

Telmessus said (the vision meant that) her husband had impreg-

nated her, for nothing is sealed if it is empty, and that she

was pregnant with a child whose nature would be courageous and

7

lion-like.

On another occasion, a great snake appeared, while Olympias was asleep, and wound itself around her body. This especially, they say, weakened Philip's desire and tenderness toward her, so that he did not come often to sleep with her, either because he was afraid she would cast spells and enchantments upon him, or because he considered himself discharged from the obligation of intercourse with her because she had become the partner of a higher being.

3.   ...After the vision (of the snake), Philip sent Chairon of Megalopolis to Delphi (to learn its meaning). He brought an oracle to Philip from Apollo: Philip was henceforth to sacrifice to Zeus-Ammon and worship that God especially. Furthermore, he was to put out the eye which spied through the crack in the door on the God who, in the form of a serpent, had lain with his wife. And Olympias, as Erastosthenes says, when she sent Alexander on the campaign (against the Persians), told him alone the forbidden secret of his conception, ordering him to act worthy of his birth. But others say that she just dismissed him remarking (to her friends), "Alexander never stops lying about me to Hera" (i.e., by claiming Zeus had been unfaithful to Hera, his wife).

2. THE BIRTH OF PLATO

(Diogenes Laertius, *Lives of Eminent Philosophers* 3.1-2, 45;
trans. D.L. Dungan)

(Introduction: This author, more a collector of
opinions about the philosophical schools than a philosopher
himself, lived during the first half of the third century C.E.,
possibly in Alexandria. His account of the life and teachings
of Plato (ca. 429-347 B.C.E.) reflects the enormous veneration
felt toward this philosopher in Diogenes' day, including this
belief in Plato's miraculous (but hardly virgin) birth, an
account which can be found in many other writers from the Roman
period.)

Plato, the son of Ariston and Periktione or Potone,
was an Athenian. His mother's family went back to Solon. He
was, moreover, a brother of Dropides, the father of Kritias,
the father of Kallaischros, the father of Kritias (one of the
Thirty) and Glaukon, the father of Charmides and Periktione,
who with Ariston were the parents of Plato, the sixth generation
from Solon. Solon, moreover, traced his ancestry back to Neleus
and Poseidon. And they say his father's ancestry goes back to
Kodros the son of Melanthos, who, according to Thrasylos'
account, are descended from Poseidon.

Speusippos,[1] in his writing "The Funeral Feast of
Plato," and Klearchos, in his "Encomium on Plato," and Anaxil-
aides, in the second book "On the Philosophers," all say that
there was at Athens a story that when Periktione was ready (to
bear children) Ariston was trying desperately but did not succeed (in making her pregnant). Then, after he had ceased his
efforts, he saw a vision of Apollo. Therefore he abstained
from any further marital relations until she brought forth a
child (from Apollo).

---

[1]Plato's nephew, and close friend.

9

And Plato was born, as Apollodoros says in his
"Chronology" in the 88th Olympiad, on the seventh day of
Thargelion, which was the day the Delians say Apollo was born...

> (Plato's genealogy is here traced back to divine
> ancestors, through one of the preeminent fathers of
> Athens. Note also the fixing of the date of birth
> according to general Greek history (cp. Lk. 3:1f.).
> To show that Diogenes Laertius fully intends his
> reader to understand that Plato was the son of Apollo,
> let us hear one of the "epitaphs" he composed for
> Plato:)

3.45   "If Phoebus[1] did not beget Plato in Greece,

           How did he heal men's souls with words?

           For as Asklepios, also begotten by Apollo, is a
             physician

           Of the body, so Plato makes the soul immortal."

---

[1]Phoebus Apollo was worshipped as a God of divine wisdom and
bodily health.

3. THE GOSPEL OF JAMES (*PROTEVANGELIUM JACOBI*)

(Text collated and translated by B.L. Daniels)

(Introduction: The Gospel of James (*Protevangelium Jacobi*) has been one of the most influential of all the Christian apocrypha. Scholars have long agreed that at least the major portion of it was written in the second century. It is one of the earliest expositions of the idea of the virgin birth, and contains also the story of the birth of Mary and the circumstances of her betrothal to Joseph. In addition, there has come from the Gospel of James a great deal of the imagery which Christian artists have used in portraying the birth of Jesus. This translation is based upon a fresh collation of the latest manuscripts (especially Papyrus Bodmer V, a 3rd century complete text of the Gospel of James) and therefore supersedes all other translations.)

1.1   According to the histories of the twelve tribes of Israel, Joachim was a very wealthy man. He brought his

2   offerings two-fold to the Lord, saying to himself: "This from my abundance will be for all the people, and this which I owe as a sin offering will be for the Lord God as a propitiation for me."

3   Now the great day of the Lord drew near, and the children of Israel brought their offerings. Reuben stood up

4   against Joachim, saying: "It is not permissible for you to bring your offerings first, for you did not produce offspring in Israel."

5   Joachim was greatly distressed, and he went to the

6   book of the twelve tribes of Israel, saying to himself: "I will look at the records of the twelve tribes of Israel to determine whether I alone did not produce offspring in

7   Israel." He searched, and he found that all the righteous

8   had raised up offspring in Israel. Further, he remembered the patriarch Abraham, that near his last day the Lord God gave to him a son, Isaac.

9   Joachim was very sorrowful; he did not appear to his
wife, but betook himself into the desert and pitched his
10   tent there. Then he fasted for forty days and forty nights,
saying to himself: "I will not return, either for food or
drink, until the Lord my God considers me. Prayer will be
my food and drink."

2.1   Now his wife Anna sang two dirges and beat her breast
in a two-fold lament, saying: "I will mourn my widowhood,
and I will mourn my barrenness."
2   The great day of the Lord drew near and Euthine, her
maid, said to her: "How long will you humble your soul?
Behold, the great day of the Lord has come, and it is not
3   proper for you to mourn. Rather, take this headband which
the mistress of work gave to me; it is not permissible for
me to wear it, because I am your servant-girl and it has a
4   mark of royalty." Then Anna said: "Get away from me! I
have not done these things; the Lord God has humbled me
5   greatly. Perhaps someone gave this to you deceitfully, and
now you have come to make me a partner in your sin."
6   Euthine, her maid, said: "What am I to you, since you do
not listen to my voice? The Lord God closed your womb in
order not to grant you fruit in Israel."
7   Anna was very grieved, and she took off her mourning
garments and cleansed her head and put on her bridal garments.
8   About the ninth hour she went down into her garden to walk,
and she saw a laurel tree and sat down beneath it; and she
9   entreated the Lord, saying: "O God of my fathers, bless me
and hear my prayer, even as you blessed the womb of Sarah
and gave to her a son, Isaac."

3.1   Anna looked up toward heaven and saw a nest of
sparrows in the laurel tree; and she sang a dirge to herself,
saying:

2   "Woe is me! Who gave me birth? What sort of womb

brought me forth? For I was born a curse among the children
of Israel. I was made a reproach, and they derided me and
banished me out of the Temple of the Lord my God.

3   "Woe is me! To what am I likened? I am not likened
to the birds of heaven, for even the birds of heaven are
fruitful before you, O Lord.

4   "Woe is me! To what am I likened? I am not likened
to the wild beasts of the earth, for even the wild beasts of
the earth are fruitful before you, O Lord.

5   "Woe is me! To what am I likened? I am not likened
to the voiceless creatures, for even the voiceless creatures
are fruitful before you, O Lord.

6   "Woe is me! To what am I likened? I am not likened
to these waters, for even these waters are fruitful before
you, O Lord.

7   "Woe is me! To what am I likened? I am not likened
to this earth, for even the earth brings forth her fruit in
its season and blesses you, O Lord."

4.1   And behold, an angel of the Lord appeared, saying:
"Anna, Anna, the Lord God heard your prayer, and you will conceive and give birth, and your offspring shall be spoken of
2   in the whole inhabited world." Anna said: "As the Lord my
God lives, if I give birth, whether male or female, I will
present it as a gift to the Lord my God, and it shall be a
3   ministering servant to him all the days of its life." And
behold, two angels came, saying to her: "Behold, your husband Joachim is coming with his flocks."

4   Now an angel of the Lord had come down to Joachim,
saying: "Joachim, Joachim, the Lord God heard your prayer.
5   Go down from here; for behold, your wife Anna is pregnant."
Joachim went down, and he summoned his shepherds, saying:
"Bring here to me ten female lambs, spotless and without
6   blemish, and the ten lambs shall be for the Lord my God; and
bring to me twelve choice calves, and the twelve calves shall

be for the priests and the council of elders; and a hundred
year-old he-goats, and the hundred he-goats shall be for all
the people."

7   And behold, Joachim came with his flocks, and Anna
stood at the door and saw Joachim coming with his flocks.

8   Anna ran and threw her arms around his neck, saying: "Now
I know that the Lord God has blessed me very greatly, for
behold, the widow is no longer a widow, and she who was

9   barren has conceived!" Then Joachim remained in his house
for the first day.

5.1   On the next day he brought his offerings, saying to
himself: "If the Lord God has had mercy on me, the golden
plate of the priest's headdress will make it apparent to

2   me."[1] Joachim brought his offerings, and he observed the
priest's golden plate intently as he went up to the altar of

3   the Lord; and he did not see sin in himself. Joachim said:
"Now I know that the Lord God has had mercy on me and for-

4   given me all my sins." Then he went down from the Temple
of the Lord, justified, and came into his house.

5   Now her time was fulfilled, and in the ninth month
Anna gave birth. She said to the midwife: "What have I

6   borne? The midwife said: "A girl." Then Anna said: "MY
soul is exalted this day;" and she laid herself down.

7   When the required days were completed, Anna cleansed
herself of the impurity of childbirth, and gave her breast
to the child. She called her name Mary.

6.1   Day by day the child grew strong. When she was six
months old her mother stood her on the ground to see if she
could stand. Walking seven steps, she came to her mother's

2   bosom. Her mother caught her up, saying: "As the Lord my

---

[1]It is not known how the High Priest's headdress would make
known God's forgiveness. See below, p. 338.

God lives, you shall not walk on this earth until I bring

3 you into the Temple of the Lord." Then she made a sanctuary
in her bedroom, and prohibited everything common and unclean
from passing through it; and she called the undefiled daughters of the Hebrews, and they served her.

4   Now the child came to be a year old, and Joachim gave
a great feast; he invited the high priests, the priests, the
scribes, the elders of the council, and all the people of

5 Israel. Joachim brought the child to the priests and they
blessed her, saying: "O God of our fathers, bless this child,
and give to her a name famous forever in all generations."

6 All the people responded: "So let it be. Amen." Then he
brought her to the high priests and they blessed her, saying:
"O God of the high places, look upon this child, and bless
her with the highest blessing which has no successor."

7   Her mother picked her up and brought her into the
sanctuary of her bedroom, and gave her breast to the child.

8 Then Anna sang a hymn to the Lord God, saying: "I will sing
a sacred song to the Lord my God, because he considered me

9 and took away from me the reproach of my enemies; and the
Lord my God gave me a fruit of his righteousness, one yet
manifold before him. Who will report to the sons of Reuben
that Anna gives suck?"

10   She laid the child to rest in the bedroom, in her

11 sanctuary, and she went out and served them at the feast.
When the meal was finished, they went down rejoicing and
they glorified the God of Israel.

7.1   Months passed. The child became two years old, and

2 Joachim said: "Let us take her up into the Temple of the
Lord, in order that we may fulfill the pledge which we have
made; lest the Lord send to us for it and our gift be

3 unacceptable." Anna said: "Let us await the third year,
lest the child long for her father and mother." And Joachim
said: "So let it be."

4   When the child was three years old, Joachim said:
"Let us call the undefiled daughters of the Hebrews, and let
5   each one take a torch, and let them be burning, in order that
the child not turn back and her heart be misled out of the
Temple of the Lord." Thus they did, until they had gone up
into the Temple.
6   The priest received her, and kissing her he blessed
her and said: "The Lord God has magnified your name in all
generations; in you, at the end of days, will the Lord God
7   manifest his deliverance to the children of Israel." He set
her on the third step of the altar, and the Lord God gave
grace to her; and she danced with her feet, and all the
house of Israel loved her.

8.1   Her parents returned, marveling and giving praise and
glorifying the Lord God that the child did not turn back.
2   Now Mary was in the Temple of the Lord like a dove being fed,
and she received food from the hand of an angel.
3   When she was twelve years old there took place a conference of the priests, saying: "Behold, Mary has become
4   twelve years old in the Temple of the Lord our God. What,
therefore, shall we do with her, lest she defile the sanc-
5   tuary of the Lord?" The high priests said to Zacharias:
"You stand at the altar of the Lord. Enter and pray concerning her; and whatever the Lord God may reveal to you,
this let us do."
6   The priest entered the Holy of Holies, taking the
vestment with the twelve bells, and he prayed concerning her.
7   And Behold, an angel of the Lord appeared, saying: "Zacharias
Zacharias, go out and call together the widowers of the
people, and let each of them bring a rod; and to whomever
8   the Lord God shows a sign, to this one shall she be wife."
The heralds therefore went forth through the whole Jewish
countryside and sounded the trumpet of the Lord, and all came
running.

9.1   Now Joseph, casting down his adze, came himself into
their meeting. When they all were gathered together, they
2   came to the priest, taking the rods. He, having received
the rods of all of them, went into the Temple and prayed.
When he finished the prayer he took the rods and came out
3   and returned them; and there was no sign on them. Joseph
received the last rod, and behold, a dove came forth from
4   the rod and settled on Joseph's head. Then the priest said:
"Joseph, Joseph, you have been designated by lot to receive
the virgin of the Lord as your ward."

5   Joseph refused, saying: "I have sons, and I am an old
man, but she is a young maiden -- lest I be a laughing stock
6   to the children of Israel." The priest said: "Joseph, fear
the Lord your God! Remember what God did to Dathan and
7   Abiram and Korah, how the earth was split in two and they
were all swallowed up on account of their disputing. And
now, Joseph, beware lest these things be also in your house."
8   Joseph, frightened, received her as his ward; and
Joseph said to her: "Mary, I have received you from the
9   Temple of the Lord. Now I am leaving you behind in my house,
and I am going away to build houses; later I will return to
you. The Lord will guard you."

10.1   There took place a council of the priests, saying:
2   "Let us make a veil for the Temple of the Lord." The priest
said: "Call the undefiled virgins from the tribe of David."
3   The attendants went out and sought (them), and they found
4   seven. Then the priest remembered the child Mary, that she
was of the tribe of David and was pure before God; and the
attendants went forth and brought her.

5   They brought them into the Temple of the Lord, and the
priest said: "Assign by lot for me here someone who will
spin the gold thread and the white and the linen and the silk
and the hyacinth-blue and the scarlet and the genuine purple."
6   The genuine purple and the scarlet were assigned by lot to

Mary, and taking them she went into her house. Now at that
7   time Zacharias was dumb, and Samuel replaced him until the
8   time when Zacharias spoke. Mary, taking the scarlet, spun it.

11.1   She took her pitcher and went out to fill it full of
water; and behold, there came a voice saying: "Hail, highly
favored one! The Lord is with you; you are blessed among
2   women." Mary looked about, to the right and to the left,
3   to see whence this voice might be coming to her. Filled
with trembling she went into her house; and putting down the
pitcher, she took the purple and sat down on a chair and drew
out the purple thread.
4   Behold, an angel of the Lord stood before her, saying:
"Do not fear, Mary, for you have found favor before the Lord
5   of all, and you will conceive by his Word." Mary, having
heard this, considered to herself, saying: "Shall I conceive
by the Lord, the living God? As all women do, shall I give
6   birth?" And behold, the angel appeared, saying to her: "Not
thus, Mary, for the power of God will overshadow you; therefore also that holy thing which is born shall be called Son
7   of the Most High. You shall call his name Jesus, for he
shall save the people from their sins." Then Mary said:
8   "Behold the servant-girl of the Lord is before him. Let it
be to me according to your word."

12.1   She worked the purple and the scarlet and brought them
to the priest; and the priest blessed her and said: "Mary,
the Lord God has blessed your name, and you will be blessed
among all the families of the earth."
2   Mary, full of joy, went to her kinswoman Elisabeth and
knocked on the door. Elisabeth, hearing (her), put down the
3   scarlet and ran to the door and opened it to her; and she
blessed her and said: "How is it that the mother of the Lord
should come to me? For behold, that which is in me leapt and
4   blessed you." But Mary forgot the mysteries of which the

angel Gabriel spoke; and she looked up toward heaven and said:
"Who am I that, behold, all the families of the earth bless
me?"

5   She remained three months with Elisabeth. Day by day
her womb became larger; Mary, becoming fearful, came to

6   her house and hid herself from the children of Israel. Now
she was sixteen[1] years old when these strange events happened
to her.

13.1   It came to be the sixth month for her, and behold,
Joseph came from his buildings; and he came into his house

2   and found her pregnant. He struck his face and threw himself to the ground on the sackcloth and wept bitterly, say-

3   ing: "With what sort of countenance shall I look to the
Lord God? What shall I pray concerning this maiden? For I
received her a virgin from the Temple of the Lord God, and

4   I did not guard her. Who is he who has deceived me? Who

5   did this evil thing in my house and defiled her? Is not the
story of Adam summed up in me? For just as Adam was in the
hour of his giving glory to God and the serpent came and
found Eve alone and deceived her, thus it has also come about
for me."

6   Joseph arose from the sackcloth and called Mary and
said to her: "Having been cared for by God, why did you do

7   this, forgetting the Lord your God? Why have you humbled
your soul, you who were nurtured in the Holy of Holies and
who received food from the hand of an angel?"

8   She wept bitterly, saying: "I am pure, and I do not
know a man." Joseph said to her: "Whence then is this

9   which is in your womb?" She said: "As the Lord my God lives,
I do not know whence it came to me."

---

[1]The MSS give Mary's age variously from twelve to seventeen
years. The oldest, as well as the largest number, of the MSS
have sixteen.

14.1   Then Joseph feared greatly and stopped talking with
2   her, considering what he would do with her. Joseph said:
     "If I should hide her sin, I will be found disputing with the
3   law of the Lord; if I show her to the children of Israel,
     I am afraid lest that which is in her is angelic and I shall
4   be found delivering innocent blood to the judgment of death.
     What therefore shall I do with her? Shall I put her away
     secretly from me?"
5   Night came upon him; behold, an angel of the Lord
     appeared to him in a dream, saying: "Do not fear this child,
6   for that which is in her is from the Holy Spirit. She will
     bear a son, and you shall call his name Jesus, for he will
7   save his people from their sins." Then Joseph arose from
     his sleep and glorified the God of Israel who had given to
     him this favor; he guarded the child.

15.1   Now Annas, the scribe, came to Joseph and said to him:
     "Joseph, why have you not appeared in our assembly?" Joseph
     said to him: "Because I was weary from my journey, and I
     rested the first day."
2   Annas turned and saw Mary pregnant; and he came running
     to the priest and said to him: "Joseph, to whom you have
3   borne witness, has acted very lawlessly." The priest said:
     "What is this?" Annas answered: "The virgin whom Joseph
4   received from the Temple of the Lord he has defiled; he mar-
     ried her secretly and did not reveal it to the children of
5   Israel." The priest said to him: "Joseph did these things?"
     Annas responded: "Send attendants, and you will find the
     virgin pregnant."
6   The attendants went forth and found her as he said; and
     they brought her into the sanctuary, and she stood at the
7   tribunal. The priest said to her: "Mary, why did you do
     this? Why did you humble your soul, forgetting the Lord
8   your God? You who were nurtured in the Holy of Holies, and
     received food from the hand of an angel, and heard their

9   hymns, and danced before the Lord -- why did you do this?"
    But Joseph said: "As the Lord God lives, I am pure regarding
11 her." Then the priest said: "Do not bear false witness, but
    tell the truth. You married her secretly and did not reveal
12 it to the children of Israel; you did not incline your head
    beneath the Mighty Hand so that your seed might be blessed."
    And Joseph was silent.

16.1   The priest then said: "Give back the virgin whom you
    received from the Temple of the Lord." Joseph began to weep.
2   The priest went on: "I will give you to drink the water of
    the Lord's testing, and it will make your sins manifest in
3   your eyes."[1] Taking it, the priest gave Joseph to drink and
    sent him into the desert; and he came back whole. He also
4   gave the child to drink and sent her into the desert; she
5   also returned whole. And all the people wondered, since
    their sin did not appear in them.
6   The priest said: "If the Lord God did not make your
    sin manifest, neither will I judge you;" and he released
7   them. Then Joseph took Mary and went into his house,
    rejoicing and glorifying the God of Israel.

17.1   Now there came an order from Augustus the emperor for
    all who were in Bethlehem of Judea to be enrolled. Joseph
2   said: "I will enroll my sons, but this child -- what shall
    I do with her? How shall I enroll her? As my wife? I am
3   ashamed to do so. As my daughter? The children of Israel
    know that she is not my daughter. This day of the Lord he
    will do as he wishes."
4   He saddled his donkey and set her upon it; his son
5   led, and Samuel followed. They drew near to Bethlehem --
    they were three miles distant -- and Joseph turned and saw
    Mary looking gloomy, and he said: "Probably that which is

----

[1]See Num. 5:11-31.

6   in her is distressing her." Once again Joseph turned and saw

7   her laughing, and he said: "Mary, how is it that I see your
face at one moment laughing and at another time gloomy?" She

8   said to Joseph: "It is because I see two peoples with my
eyes, the one weeping and mourning, the other rejoicing and
glad."

9   They were in the midst of the journey, and Mary said to
him: "Joseph, take me down from the donkey, for that which

10 is in me is ready to be born." He took her down from the
donkey and said to her: "Where shall I take you to shelter
your shame? For the place is desolate."

18.1   He found there a cave, and he brought her in and placed
his sons beside her. Then he went out to seek a Hebrew midwife in the country of Bethlehem.

2   ((Now I, Joseph, was walking about, and I looked up and
saw the heaven standing still, and I observed the air in

3   amazement, and the birds of heaven at rest. Then I looked
down at the earth, and I saw a vessel lying there, and work-

4   men reclining, and their hands were in the vessel. Those
who were chewing did not chew, and those who were lifting did
not lift up, and those who were carrying to their mouths did

5   not carry, but all faces were looking upward. I saw sheep
standing still, and the shepherd raised his hand to strike

6   them, and his hand remained up. I observed the streaming
river; and I saw the mouths of the kids at the water, but

7   they were not drinking. Then suddenly all things were
driven in their course.))[1]

---

[1]The paragraph enclosed in double parentheses (( )) is not
included in the oldest extant witness to the text, MS 31. Most
of the later MSS includes this account of the immobility of
nature, either in the version given or in a variant form in the
third person.

19.1   Finding a midwife, he brought her. They came down
       from the mountain, and Joseph said to the midwife: "Mary is
2   the one who was betrothed to me, but she, having been brought
       up in the Temple of the Lord, has conceived by the Holy
       Spirit." And she went with him.[1]

3   They stood in the place of the cave, and a dark cloud
       was overshadowing the cave. The midwife said: "My soul is
       magnified today, for my eyes have seen a mystery: a savior
4   has been born to Israel!" And immediately the cloud with-
       drew from the cave, and a great light appeared in the cave
5   so that their eyes could not bear it. After a while the
       light withdrew, until the baby appeared. It came and took
       the breast of its mother Mary; and the midwife cried out:
       "How great is this day, for I have seen this new wonder!"

20.1   The midwife went in and placed Mary in position, and
       Salome examined her virginal nature; and Salome cried aloud
       that she had tempted the living God -- "and behold, my hand
       falls away from me in fire." Then she prayed to the Lord.
2   Behold, an angel of the Lord appeared, saying to
       Salome: "Your prayer has been heard before the Lord God.
       Come near and take up the child, and this will save you."
3   She did so; and Salome was healed as she worshipped. Then
4   she came out of the cave. Behold, an angel of the Lord spoke

---

[1]The paragraph here given is the short version of MS 31. Most
of the MSS have a greatly expanded version of Joseph's encounter
with the midwife, either in the version given below or in a
variant form in the third person:
    And behold, there was a woman coming down the mountain, and
she said to me: "Sir, where are you going?" I said to her: "I
seek a Hebrew midwife." She said to me: "Are you from Israel?"
I said: "Yes." And she said: "Who is she who is giving birth
in the cave?" I said to her: "She is the one betrothed to me."
She said: "Is she not your wife?" I answered: "Mary is the one
brought up in the Temple of the Lord, and I was given her by lot
as wife. She is not my wife, but she has conceived by the Holy
Spirit." The midwife said to him: "Is this true?" Joseph said
to her: "Come and see;" and the midwife went with him.

saying: "Salome, Salome, do not report what marvels you have
seen until the child has come into Jerusalem."[1]

21.1   And behold, Joseph was prepared to go into Judea. Now
there arose a tumult in Bethlehem of Judea, for Magi came
saying: "Where is the king of the Jews? For we saw his star
2   in the east, and we have come to worship him." Herod, hearing this, was terrified. He sent attendants and summoned
them, and they explained clearly to him concerning the star.
3   The Magi departed, and behold, they saw a star in the
east, and it preceded them until they came into the cave and
4   stood at the head of the child. Then the Magi, seeing the
child with its mother Mary, brought forth gifts from their
leather pouches: gold, frankincense, and myrrh. But having
been warned by an angel, they went away by a different route
into their own land.

22.1   When Herod realized that he had been deceived by the
Magi, in his wrath he sent his murderers, telling them to kill

---

[1]There is also a more elaborate version of chapter 20 which is
found in most of the later MSS:

     The midwife went in and said: "Mary, get yourself in
position, for a great deal of controversy surrounds you." Then
Salome tested her virginal nature with her finger; and Salome
cried out and said: "Woe is my lawlessness and my faithlessness,
for I have tempted the living God. And behold, my hand falls
away from me in fire."
     Then she bowed her knees before the Lord, saying: "God of
my fathers, remember me, for I am seed of Abraham and Isaac and
Jacob. Do not expose me to contempt to the children of Israel,
but return me to the needy. For you know, O Lord, that I accomplished my healings in your name, and I received my pay from you."
     And behold, an angel of the Lord appeared, saying to Salome:
"The Lord heard your prayer. Bring your hand near to the child
and take him up, and it will be to you salvation and joy."
Salome, overjoyed, came to the child, saying: "I will worship
him, I will take him up, and I will be healed, for a great king
is born to Israel." Immediately Salome was healed; and she came
out of the cave justified. And behold, there came a voice saying
to her: "Salome, Salome, do not report what marvels you have
seen in Bethlehem until the child comes to Jerusalem."

2   all the babies two years old and under. Mary, hearing that
they were killing the babies, was frightened, and she took
the child and wrapped him and placed him in a cow stable.

3   Now Elisabeth, hearing that Herod sought John, took
him and went up into the mountain. She looked around for a

4   place where she might hide him, but there was no place. Then
Elisabeth groaned, saying in a loud voice: "Mountain of God,
receive a mother with her child" -- for Elisabeth was unable

5   to ascend. And immediately the mountain opened up and it
received her. That mountain appeared to her as a light, for
an angel of the Lord was with them, protecting them.

23.1   Herod sought John, and he dispatched attendants to the
altar to Zacharias, saying to him: "Where have you hidden

2   your son?" He answered, saying to them: "I am a ministering-
servant of God, and I serve in the Temple. How do I know
where my son is?" The attendants went away and reported all
these things to Herod.

3   Angered, Herod said: "His son is going to be king in
Israel." Again he sent the attendants, saying to him: "Tell
me the truth! Where is your son? You know that you are at

4   my mercy." The attendants went forth and reported these
things to Zacharias. In answer he said: "I am a witness of

5   God; pour out my blood. The Lord will receive my spirit,
for it is innocent blood you are shedding at the doorway of

6   the Temple of the Lord." About daybreak Zacharias was
murdered, and the children of Israel did not know how he
was murdered.

24.1   But at the hour of the salutation, the priests went
in, and the blessing of Zacharias did not meet them as was

2   customary. The priests stood waiting for Zacharias to greet
them in prayer and to glorify the most high God. When he

3   failed to come they were all afraid. But a certain one of
them, getting up his courage, went into the sanctuary and

4   saw by the altar of the Lord dried blood; and a voice said:
    "Zacharias has been murdered, and his blood will not be wiped
    away until his avenger comes."
5   When he heard these words he was afraid, and he came
6   out and reported to the priests what he had seen and heard.
    They took courage and went in, and they saw what had taken
7   place; and the wall-panels of the Temple cried aloud, and
8   they split in two from top to bottom. They did not find
    his corpse, but they found his blood, which had become like
    stone.
9   They were filled with fear, and they went out and
    reported that Zacharias had been murdered. All the tribes
    of the people heard it, and they mourned and lamented him
    three days and three nights.
10   Now after the three days, the priests deliberated on
    whom they would set up in the place of Zacharias, and the
11 lot fell on Simeon. This was the one to whom it had been
    revealed by the Holy Spirit that he would not see death
    until he saw Christ in the flesh.

25.1   Now I, James, who wrote this history in Jerusalem,
    there having arisen a clamor when Herod died, withdrew
    myself into the desert until the tumult in Jerusalem ceased.
2   Now I glorify the Lord who gave to me the wisdom to write
    this history. And grace will be with all who fear the Lord.
    Amen.[1]

---

[1]There are innumerable variations in this closing statement.
Many MSS add doxologies of this nature: "To whom be the glory
and the power unto eternal ages." Some MSS have a trinitarian
statement: "The grace of the Father and the Son and the Holy
Spirit be with you all." The version given in this translation
is that of the earliest and most representative MSS.

4. THE BIRTH OF JESUS

(Selections from the Arundel manuscript of a Latin Infancy
Gospel; intro. and trans., D.R. Cartlidge)

(Introduction: This Gospel is, as it stands, a
medieval document which uses the *Pseudo-Matthew Gospel* and
Gospel of James as sources. However, there are passages which
are unique to this Gospel and which appear to use a source
which is probably from the Church's early years, and which has
a very interesting birth narrative. James (*Latin Infancy
Gospels*, p. ix) suggests a second century date for this unknown
source. However, one must be cautious here; see O. Cullmann's
remarks in E. Hennecke, *New Testament Apocrypha* Vol. I, pp.
406-7. We here present selections from a portion of the Gospel
which seems to reflect this earlier source.)

68.   ...The midwife said to Joseph, "Sir, where are you

going?" He replied, "I seek a Hebrew midwife." The woman said

to him, "Are you from Israel?" Joseph said, "I am from Israel."

The woman said to him, "Who is the young woman who will give

birth in this cave?" Joseph replied, "Mary, who was promised

to me, who was raised in the Lord's temple." The midwife said

to him, "She is not your wife?" And Joseph, "She was promised

to me, but was made pregnant by the Holy Spirit." The midwife

said to him, "What you say, is it true?" Joseph said to her,

"Come and see."

69.   They entered into the cave. Joseph said to the mid-

wife, "Come, see Mary." When she wished to enter to the inter-

ior of the cave, she was afraid, because a great light shone

resplendent in the cave, the light did not wane in the day nor

through the night as long as Mary stayed there....

(After the birth, the midwife utters this prayer.)

..."Lord, great God, have mercy, because never has this been

heard nor seen until now, nor even dreamed of, that the breasts

are full of milk and a male child should make his mother known
to be a virgin. There was no offering (*pollucio*) of blood in
the birth, no pain occurred in the parturition. A virgin conceived, a virgin has given birth and after she gave birth, she
remained a virgin."

70.   (The midwife is asked to relate what she had seen to
Symeon, Joseph's son. See Mt. 13:55; Mk. 6:3. The following
is, therefore, a "flashback.")

71.   When I entered to the maiden, I found her face looking
upward and intently and secretly speaking to Heaven. I truly
believe that she prayed to and blessed the Most High. When I
had come to her, I said to her, "Daughter, tell me, do you not
feel some pain or is not some part of your body gripped with
pain?" She, however, as if she heard nothing, remained immobile
like solid rock, intent on Heaven.

72.   In that hour, a great silence descended with a great
fear. For even the winds stopped, they made no breeze; there
was no motion of tree leaves, nor sound of water. The streams
did not flow; there was no motion of the sea. All things produced in the sea were silent; there was no human voice sounding;
there was a great silence. For the pole (or people) itself
ceased its rapid course from that hour [Latin uncertain here].
Time almost stopped its measure. All, overwhelmed with great
fear, kept silent; we were expecting the advent of the most
high God, the end of the world.

73.   As the time drew near, the power of God showed itself
openly. The maiden stood looking intently into Heaven; she
became as a grapevine [or, she became snow-white]. For now the
end of the events of salvation was at hand. When the light had
come forth, Mary worshipped him to whom she saw she had given
birth. The child himself, like the sun, shone brightly, beautiful and most delightful to see, because he alone appeared as

peace, soothing the whole world. In that hour, when he was
born, the voice of many invisible beings in one voice proclaimed
"Amen." And the light, when it was born, multiplied and it obscured the light of the sun itself by its shining rays. The
cave was filled by the bright light together with a most sweet
odor. The light was born just as the dew descends from heaven
to the earth. For its odor is fragrant beyond all the sweet
smell of ointments.

74.   I, however, stood stupefied and amazed. Awe grasped
me. I was gazing intently at the fantastically bright light
which had been born. The light, however, after a while, shrank,
imitated the shape of an infant, then immediately became out-
wardly an infant in the usual manner that infants are born.
I became bold and leaned over and touched him. I lifted him
in my hands with great awe, and I was terrified because he had
no weight like other babies who are born. I looked at him
closely; there was no blemish on him, but he was in his body,
totally shining, just as the dew of the most high God. He was
light to carry, splendid to see. For a while I was amazed at
him because he did not cry as new-born children are supposed
to. While I held him, looking into his face, he laughed at
me with a most joyful laugh, and, opening his eyes, he looked
intently at me, and suddenly a great light came forth from his
eyes like a great flash of lightning.

ADDITIONAL SELECTIONS IN PART II

5. Apollonios of Tyana (Philostratus, *Life of Apollonios of Tyana* I.4-5), see pp. 260-262.

6. Herakles (Diodorus Siculus, *Library of History* 4.9.1-10.4), see pp. 347-349.

7. THE BIRTH AND CHILDHOOD OF PYTHAGORAS

(Iamblichus, *The Life of Pythagoras*, 3-10; trans. D.R. Cartlidge)

(Introduction: It has been said that, one hundred years after his death, around 497 B.C.E., hardly anyone at Athens still remembered anything of Pythagoras of Samos; seven hundred years later, his followers knew everything about him including the secret recipe of his favorite honey-cakes. The author of this account of Pythagoras' ancestry and birth, the Neo-platonic, Syrian philosopher Iamblichus, was just such a follower. Living in the fourth century C.E., he was a vigorous opponent of the newly emerging Christian religion, writing many books on Pythagoras and his teachings.)

3.   It is said that Ankaios, who lived in Samos, in Kephallenia, was begotten by Zeus. Whether he received this repute because of virtue or a greatness of soul, he exceeded the wisdom of the other Kephallenians. An oracle was given about him by the Pythian oracle (Apollo of Delphi) to gather a colony from among the Kephallenians and the Arcadians and the Thessalians.... 4. They say that Mnesarchos and Pythais, who were the parents of Pythagoras, were descended from this house and were of the family of Ankaios.... 5. Once when this nobility of birth was being celebrated by the citizens, a certain poet from Samos said he (Pythagoras) was begotten by Apollo....

(Iamblichus goes on to show that this is really simply rumor, at least as far as Apollo's physically being the father of Pythagoras is concerned, i.e., by impregnating the philosopher's mother. However,....)

8.   However, the soul of Pythagoras came from the realm of Apollo, either being a heavenly companion or ranked with him in some other familiar way, to be sent down among men; no one can deny this. It can be maintained from his birth and the manifold wisdom of his soul. 9. ...He was educated so that he was the most beautiful and god-like of those written about in

histories.   10. After his father died, he increased in nobility
and wisdom.   Although he was still a youth, in his manner of
humility and piety he was counted most worthy already, even by
his elders.   Seen and heard, he persuaded everyone (to his way
of thinking), and to everyone who saw him he appeared to be
astonishing, so that, reasonably, he was considered by many to
be the son of a God.

8.   GOSPEL OF PSEUDO-MATTHEW (Selections)

(Trans. D.R. Cartlidge)

(Introduction: This is a third or fourth-century
Gospel. It is based to a great extent upon The Gospel of James.
We include it because it demonstrates the tendency to ascribe to
Jesus the aura of the "divine man" miracle-worker, and it also
demonstrates the use of prophecy-fulfillment as a narrative
device, which is also found in the canonical Matthew. From this
trait, it apparently was given its title, which might be translated, "Imitation-Matthew".)

1.   In those days, in Jerusalem, there was a man named
Joachim from the tribe of Judah. And he was a shepherd of sheep,
honoring God by his simplicity and his goodness. He had no
concern other than his flocks. From their fruit he offered all
to honor God, offering double service in fear of God...He divided
what he possessed into three parts: he gave one part to the
widows, orphans, strangers, and paupers; another part to those
who truly served God; the third part he kept to himself and his
household. Because of this action, God increased his flocks,
so that there was no one like him among the people of Israel...
When he was twenty he married Anna, Issachar's daughter; she was
from his tribe, that is from the race of David. While he lived
with her for twenty years, he begot neither sons nor daughters
from her.

2-5.   (Anna, who complains of her childless state and the
five month absence of her husband (who has gone to the hills with
his flocks), is visited by an angel who promises her a daughter.
Mary is born (4) and Anna gives thanks (5).)

6.   (Mary was held in admiration by all the people. She
is beautiful, pious, and speaks beautifully. She was fed each
day by angels and "while she was taught by virgins senior to her
no one exceeded her in watchfulness, no one more erudite in the
wisdom of the law, more humble, more elegant in singing the

psalms of David, more graceful in charity...more perfect in virtue.")

7.   (Abiathar, the priest, offered her uncountable gifts to marry his son. Mary swears that no man has known her and none ever will.)

8-9.   (Mary is betrothed to Joseph and the annunciation takes place. She is in Joseph's house accompanied by five other virgins.)

10.   ...Joseph was in the coast town Capernaum at his job; he was a carpenter. He stayed nine months. He came back to his house and found Mary pregnant. He trembled all over and was in anguish. He cried out: "Lord God, take my spirit, because it is better for me to die than to live." The virgins who were with Mary said: "I say, Lord Joseph. We know that a man has not touched her; we know that her faithfulness and virginity are preserved immaculate..." Joseph however said: "Will you persuade me that I should believe (confess to you) that an angel of the Lord impregnated her?..."

11.   (The angel comes and convinces Joseph of the truth. Joseph says to Mary: "I have sinned because I suspected you.")

12.   (Further demonstrations of Mary's virginity.)

13.   (Jesus' birth.)

14.   On the third day after our Lord's birth, Mary went out of the cave; she went into the stable and placed the child in a manger, and an ox and a donkey worshipped him. Then that which was spoken through Isaiah the prophet was fulfilled: "The ox knows his owner and the donkey his lord's manger."[1] These animals had him between them; they unceasingly worshipped him.

---

[1]Isaiah 1:3.

Thus that which was spoken through the prophet Habbakuk was
fulfilled: "You are known between the two animals."[1] Joseph
and Mary stayed there with the child three days.

15-17.   (They go to Bethlehem. Jesus is circumcised. The
presentation at the Temple (see Luke 2). The coming of the Magi.
The massacre of the Jewish children.)

18.   When they came to a certain cave and wanted to rest
in it, Mary got down from the pack horse, and, sitting down,
held Jesus in her lap. There were three boys with Joseph and
some girls with Mary on their journey. And behold, suddenly,
many dragons came out of the cave. When the boys saw them in
front of them they shouted with great fear. Then Jesus got down
from his mother's lap, and stood with his feet before the dragons. They, however, worshipped him, and, while they worshipped,
they backed away. Then what was said through the prophet David
was fulfilled: "The dragons of the earth praise the Lord, the
dragons and all creatures of the depths."[2] Then the infant Jesus
walked in front of them and ordered them not to harm any men.
But Mary and Joseph were very afraid lest the child should be
harmed by the dragons. Jesus said to them: "Do not be afraid,
nor consider me a child; I always have been a perfect man and
am so now, and it is necessary that all the wild beasts of the
forest be tame before me."

19.   Similarly, lions and leopards worshipped him and
accompanied them in the desert. Wherever Mary and Joseph went,
they preceded them; showing the way and inclining their heads,
they worshipped Jesus. However, the first day that Mary saw
the lions and other types of wild beasts around them, she was
very frightened. The child Jesus with cheerful face looked back

---

[1]Habbakuk 3:2 LXX

[2]Psalm 148:7

and said: "Do not be afraid, mother, they did not rush here to
hurt you but to obey you." When he said this he cut off the
fear in her heart. The lions traveled with them and with the
oxen and donkeys and the pack animals which were necessary to
carry them, and they hurt none of them while they remained.
They were tame among the sheep and rams which they brought with
them from Judea and had with them. They traveled among wolves
and they were not frightened; there was no harm to the one from
the other. Then that which was said by the prophet was fulfilled:
"Wolves shall pasture with lambs, the lion and the ox shall eat
fodder together."[1] There were two oxen and the wagon, in which
they had to travel, which the lions guided on their journey.

20.   It so happened, that on the third day after their
departure, that Mary was fatigued by the excessive heat of the
sun in the desert and seeing a palm tree said to Joseph: "I want
to rest a bit under its shadow." Joseph quickly led her to the
palm and let her get down from the animal. While Mary sat, she
looked at the top of the palm and saw it full of fruit. She said
to Joseph: "I wish, if it is possible, that I have some fruit
from this palm." Joseph said to her: "I am astonished that you
say this, when you see how high this palm is, that you think to
eat from the fruit of the palm. I think more of the lack of
water, which already fails us in the water bags; we now have
nothing by which we can refresh ourselves and the animals."
Then the infant Jesus, who was resting with smiling face at his
mother's bosom, said to the palm: "Bend down, tree, and refresh
my mother with your fruit." And immediately, at this voice, the
palm bent down its head to the feet of Mary, and they gathered
fruit from it by which all were refreshed. After they had
gathered all its fruit, it remained bent down, waiting so that
it should raise up at the command of him who had commanded it to

---

[1]Isaiah 11:6f.

bend down. Then Jesus said to it: "Raise up, palm, and be
strong, and be a companion of my trees which are in my father's
paradise. Open a water course beneath your roots which is
hidden in the earth, and let flow waters from it to satisfy us."
And the palm raised itself at once, and fountains of water, very
clear and cold and sweet began to pour out through the roots.
When they saw the fountains of water they rejoiced with great
rejoicing, and they and the beasts of burden were all satiated
and gave thanks to God.

21.   The next day they went on from there. At the time
they began the journey, Jesus turned to the palm and said: "I
give you this privilege, palm, that one of your branches be
carried by my angels and planted in my father's paradise. I
confer upon you this blessing, that all who win in any contest,
it shall be said to them: 'You have attained the palm of
victory.'" When he said this, behold an angel of the Lord
appeared and stood above the palm tree. He took one of its
branches and returned to Heaven with the branch in his hand.
When they saw this they fell on their faces and were just as if
they were dead. Jesus spoke to them, saying: "Why has fear
gripped your hearts? Do you not know that this palm, which I
have had carried into paradise, will be ready for all the saints
in the place of delight, just as it was ready for you in this
desert place?" They were all replete and filled with great joy.

22.   While they traveled on, Joseph said to him: "Lord,
the excessive heat is cooking us; if it pleases you, let us go
by the sea, so that we can travel with ease through the coastal
towns." Jesus said to him: "Fear not, Joseph, I will shorten
your journey, so that what you were going to travel across in the
space of thirty days, you will finish in one day." While they
were speaking, behold, they began to see the mountains and cities
of Egypt.

Rejoicing and exulting they came to the region of
Hermopolis, and went into one of the Egyptian cities called

Sotinen. Since they knew no one from whom they could ask for
hospitality, they went into the temple which was called "the
capitol of Egypt." There had been placed in this temple 365
idols, to which, on appointed days, honor was given to the Gods
in sacrilegious ceremonies.

23.   It happened that, when the blessed Mary with her
child had entered the temple, all the idols fell on the ground,
so that all lay flat, convulsed and with their faces shattered.
Thus they revealed openly that they were nothing. Then that
which was said by the prophet Isaiah was fulfilled: "Behold,
the Lord shall come on a swift cloud and enter Egypt, and all
the idols made by Egyptians shall be moved from his face."[1]

24.   When this had been announced to Afrodosius, the
governor of the city, he came to the temple with his whole army.
When the priests of the temple saw that Afrodosius hastened to
the temple with his whole army, they supposed to see his revenge
on those because of whom the Gods were overthrown. He entered
the temple and when he saw that all the idols lay prostrate on
their faces, he went to Mary and worshipped the child whom she
carried at her bosom, and while he worshipped him, he said to
his whole army and his friends; "If he were not the God of our
Gods, our Gods would not have fallen before him on their faces,
nor would they lie prostrate in his presence. They thus silently
confess he is their Lord. If we do not do with prudence all that
we see our Gods do, we shall possibly incur his indignation and
all come into destruction, just as happened to Pharoah, king of
Egypt, who did not believe in such marvels and was drowned with
his whole army in the sea." Then all the people of that city
believed in the Lord God through Jesus Christ.

25.   After a little time the angel said to Joseph: "Return
to the land of Judah; they who sought the life of the boy are dead.

---

[1]Isaiah 19:1.

9. THE INFANCY GOSPEL OF THOMAS

(Trans. D.R. Cartlidge)

(Introduction: One of the earliest (ca. 125 A.D.) writings devoted to "filling the gap" left by some of the other Gospels -- namely, what happened to Jesus before his twelfth year, this Gospel became very popular, being translated into numerous languages. It is a classic example of the influence of the Hellenistic "divine man" concept on a Christian description of Jesus Christ. Only here it might be more appropriate to speak of a "super-boy" concept.)

1.   I, Thomas the Israelite, announce and make known to all the brethren of the Gentiles the childhood and great deeds of our Lord Jesus Christ, which he did when he was born in our country. This is the beginning.

2.1.   When this child Jesus was five years old, he was playing at the ford of a stream. He made pools of the rushing water, and made it immediately pure, and he ordered this by word alone. 2. He made soft clay and modeled from it twelve sparrows. It was the Sabbath when he did this. There were many other children playing with him. 3. A certain Jew saw what Jesus did while playing on the Sabbath; he immediately went and announced to his father, Joseph, "See, your child is at the stream, and has taken clay and modeled twelve birds; he has profaned the Sabbath." 4. Joseph came to the place and seeing what Jesus did he cried out, "Why do you do this on the Sabbath, which is not lawful to do?" Jesus clapped his hands and cried to the sparrows, "Be gone." And the sparrows flew and went off chirping. 5. The Jews saw this and were amazed. They went away and informed their leaders what they had seen Jesus do.

3.1.   The son of Annas the scribe was standing there with Joseph. He took a branch of a willow and scattered the water

41

which Jesus had arranged. 2. Jesus saw what he did and became
angry and said to him, "You unrighteous, impious ignoramus,
what did the pools and the water do to harm you? Behold, you
shall also wither as a tree and you shall not bear leaves nor
roots nor fruit." 3. And immediately that child was all
withered. Jesus left and went to the house of Joseph. The
parents of the withered one bore him away, bemoaning his lost
youth. They led him to Joseph and reproached him, "What kind
of child do you have who does such things?"

4.1.   Then, he was going through the village and a child
who was running banged into his shoulder. Jesus was angered
and said to him, "You shall go no further on your way." And
immediately the child fell down dead. Some people saw this
happen and said, "From whence was this child begotten, for his
every word is an act accomplished?" 2. The parents of the dead
boy went to Joseph and blamed him, "Because you have such a boy,
you cannot live with us in the village; or, teach him to bless
and not to curse, for he is killing our children."

5.1.   Joseph took the child aside privately and warned him,
saying, "Why do you do such things? These people are suffering
and they hate us and are persecuting us!" Jesus said, "I know
that these are not your words, but on account of you I will be
silent. However, they shall bear their punishment." Immediately,
those who cursed him were blinded. 2. Those who saw were very
frightened and puzzled, and they said about him, "Every word he
speaks, whether good or evil, happens, and is a miracle." When
he saw what Jesus had done, Joseph arose and took hold of Jesus'
ear and pulled it hard. 3. The child was angry and said to him,
"It is fitting for you to seek and not find. You have acted
very stupidly. Do you not know I am yours? Do not anger me."

6.1.   A man named Zaccheus, a teacher, was standing there
and he heard, in part, Jesus saying these things to his father.

He was greatly astonished that he said such things, as he was a child. 2. And after a few days he approached Joseph and said to him, "You have a smart child, and he has a mind. Come, hand him over to me so that he may learn writing. I will give him all understanding with the letters, and teach him to greet all the elders and to honor them as grandfathers and fathers, and to love his peers." 3. He told him all the letters from the Alpha to the Omega plainly, with much discussion. But Jesus looked at Zaccheus the teacher, and said to him, "You do not know the Alpha according to nature, how do you teach others the Beta? You hypocrite! First, if you know it, teach the Alpha, then we will believe you about the Beta." Then he began to question the teacher about the first letter and he could not answer him. 4. Many heard as the child said to Zaccheus, "Listen, teacher, to the order of the first element, and pay attention to this, how it has lines, and a central mark which goes through the two lines you see, (they) converge, go up, again come to head, become the same three times, subordinate, and hypostatic, isometric ...[The text is unreliable.] You now have the lines of Alpha."

7.1.   When the teacher Zaccheus heard so many things and such allegories of the first letter spoken by the child, he was puzzled about such expoundings and his teaching. He said to those present, "Woe is me, I am wretched and puzzled; I have shamed myself trying to handle this child. 2. I beg of you, brother Joseph, take him away. I cannot bear the severity of his glance. I cannot understand his speech at all. This child is not earthborn; he is able to tame even fire. Perhaps he was begotten before the world's creation. What belly bore him, what womb nurtured him, I do not know. Woe is me, friend, he completely confuses me.[1] I cannot follow his understanding.

---

[1]Tischendorf translates: *stupefacit me* for an uncertain verb here.

I have fooled myself; I am thrice wretched. I worked anxiously
to have a disciple, and I found myself with a teacher. 3. Consider my shame, friends; I am an old man and have been conquered
by a child. And I have lost heart and die because of this child,
for at this hour I cannot look into his gaze. When they all say
that I have been conquered by this little child, what will I be
able to say? What can I discuss about the lines of the first
element he spoke to me? I do not know, O friends, for I do not
know its beginning and end. Therefore, I beg you, brother
Joseph, take him into your house. He is something great, a God,
an angel, or what I should say I do not know."

8.1.   While the Jews were comforting Zaccheus, the child
gave a great laugh, saying, "Now let what is yours bear fruit,
and the blind in heart see. I am from above in order that I
may curse them and call them into the things which are above,
because He who sent me on your account ordered it." 2. And
as the child ceased talking, immediately all those who had
fallen under his curse were saved. And from then no one dared
to anger him, lest he should curse him and he should be crippled.

9.1.   After some days Jesus was playing upstairs in a certain
house, and one of the children playing with him fell from the
house and died. And when the other children saw, they ran away,
and Jesus remained alone. 2. The parents of the dead child
came and accused Jesus of throwing him down. Jesus replied, "I
did not throw him down." But still they accused him. 3. Thereupon Jesus leaped down from the roof and stood by the body of
the child and cried out in a great voice, saying "Zenon!" (that
was his name) - "Rise up and tell me, did I throw you down?" He
immediately rose up and said: "No, Lord, you did not throw me
down, but you raised me." Those who saw this were astonished.
The parents of the child glorified God because of this sign
that happened, and they worshipped Jesus.

10.1.   After a few days a young man was splitting wood in
the vicinity; the axe fell and split the bottom of his foot,
and he was bleeding to death. 2. There was an outcry and
people gathered. The child Jesus ran there. He pushed through
the crowd, and seized the injured foot of the youth; immediately
he was healed. He said to the youth, "Now get up, split your
wood and remember me." The crowd, seeing what had happened,
worshipped the child, saying, "Truly, the Spirit of God lives
in this child!"

11.1.   When he was six, his mother sent him to draw water
and to bring it in the house, giving him a pitcher. But in the
crowd, he had a collision; the water jug was broken. 2. Jesus
spread out the garment he had on, filled it with water, and
bore it to his mother. When his mother saw the miracle she
kissed him, and she kept to herself the mysteries which she saw
him do.

12.1.   Again, in planting time the child went with his
father to sow seed in their field. While they sowed, his
father sowed, and the child Jesus planted one grain of wheat.
2. When he had reaped and threshed it, it yielded one hundred
measures, and he called all the poor of the village to the
threshing floor and gave them the grain. Joseph took the
remainder of the grain. He was eight when he did this sign.

13.1.   His father was a carpenter and made at that time
ploughs and yokes. He received an order from a certain rich
man to make a bed for him. One beam came out shorter than the
other and he did not know what to do. The child Jesus said to
Joseph, his father, "Lay the two pieces of wood alongside each
other, and make them even at one end." 2. Joseph did as the
child told him. Jesus stood at the other end and grasped the
shorter beam; he stretched it and made it equal with the other.
His father Joseph saw and was astonished, and embracing the

child, he kissed him and said; "I am blessed, because God has
given this child to me."

14.1.   When Joseph saw the mind and age of the child, that
he was growing up, he again wished him not to be ignorant of
letters. And he took him and gave him to another teacher. But
the teacher said to Joseph, "First I will teach him Greek and
then Hebrew." For the teacher knew the child's learning and
feared him. Nevertheless he wrote the alphabet, and taught him
for many hours, but Jesus did not answer him. 2. Then Jesus
said to him, "If you really are a teacher, and you know the
letters well, tell me the power of Alpha and I will tell you
that of Beta." The teacher was angered and hit Jesus on the
head. The child was hurt and cursed him. Immediately the
teacher fainted, falling to the ground upon his face. 3. The
child returned to the house of Joseph. But Joseph was grief-
stricken and ordered his mother, "Do not let him go outside the
door, because anyone who angers him dies."

15.1.   After some time there was another teacher, a good
friend of Joseph. He said to him, "Bring the child to me at
school, maybe by flattery I can teach him letters." Joseph
said, "If you dare, brother, take him with you." He took him
with fear and much anxiety, but the child went with pleasure.
2. Jesus went boldly into the school and found a book lying on
the lectern and taking it, did not read the letters in it, but
opened his mouth and spoke by the Holy Spirit and taught the
Law to those standing around. A great crowd gathered and stood
listening to him. They were astonished at the beauty of his
teaching and the eloquence of his words, that being a babe he
could say such things. 3. Joseph heard and was frightened.
He ran into the school, wondering whether this teacher was also
without skill, but the teacher said to Joseph, "Know, brother,
that I took the child as a disciple, but he is full of much
grace and wisdom, and I beg you, brother, take him into your

house." 4. When the child heard this, immediately he smiled at him and said, "Since you spoke correctly and witnessed correctly, on account of you the one who was stricken shall be healed." And immediately the other teacher was healed. Joseph took the child and returned home.

16.1.   Joseph sent his son James to gather wood and to bring it into the house. The child Jesus followed him. While James was gathering the sticks, a snake bit James's hand. 2. He lay dying, Jesus came near and breathed on the bite. Immediately James ceased suffering, the snake burst, and James was healed.

17.1.   After this, in the neighborhood of Joseph a certain child took sick and died. His mother wept bitterly. Jesus, hearing the great mourning and clamor, ran quickly and found the child dead. He touched his breast and said, "I say to you, child, do not die, but live and be with your mother!" And immediately the child looked up and laughed. Jesus said to the woman, "Pick him up and give him milk and remember me." 2. The crowd standing around saw and was amazed, and they said, "Truly this child is a God or an angel of God, because his every word becomes a finished deed." And Jesus left there and played with the other children.

18.1.   After some time a house was being built and there was a great clamor. Jesus arose and went there. Seeing a man lying dead, he took his hand and said, "I say to you, man, arise, do your work!" And immediately he arose and worshipped him. 2. The crowd, seeing this, was astonished and said, "This is a heavenly child; for he saved many souls from death, and can save them all his life."

19.1.   When he was twelve his parents, according to custom, went to Jerusalem to the Passover with their companions. After the Passover they returned to their homes. While they were

going back home, the child Jesus went back to Jerusalem. His
parents thought that he was in the caravan. 2. When they had
gone a day's travel, they sought him among their kinfolk and
when they did not find him they were troubled. They returned
again to the city to seek him. After three days they found him
in the temple, seated in the midst of the teachers, listening
and questioning them. They all were attentive and amazed at
how he, being a child, could argue with the elders and teachers
of the people, solving the chief problems of the Law and the
parables of the prophets. 3. His mother, Mary, came up and
said to him, "How can you have done this to us, child? Behold,
we have looked everywhere for you, grieving." And Jesus said
to them, "Why did you look for me? Do you not know that I must
be in my Father's house?" 4. The scribes and Pharisees said,
"Are you the mother of this child?" She said, "I am." They
said to her, "You are blessed among women, because God has
blessed the fruit of your womb. We have never before seen or
heard such glory or such excellence and wisdom." 5. Jesus
arose and followed his mother and was obedient to his parents.
But his mother kept in her heart all that had happened. Jesus
grew in wisdom and stature and grace. Glory be to him for ever
and ever. Amen.

ADDITIONAL SELECTIONS IN PART II

10. Apollonios of Tyana (Philostratus, op. cit., I.7-8),
     see pp. 262-264.

11. Moses (Philo, *About the Life of Moses* I.20-29),
     see pp. 302-305.

12. HEALINGS PERFORMED BY ASKLEPIOS

(Epidauros inscriptions; trans. D.R. Cartlidge and T.B. Curtis)

(Introduction: The origin of the worship of Asklepios as a healing God is unclear, but it seems to have arisen after the time of Homer, who only spoke of him as a mortal physician. Later on, legends concerning his divine origin appeared (his father being considered to have been Apollo), and the central cult-temple for his healing activity was Epidauros on the Adriatic Sea, although there were many others. It was the custom for the person healed to record the basic facts of his case on a marble plaque, and leave this at the temple, as a memorial. The following accounts are taken from just such plaques, found in the temple at Epidauros. These were inscribed mostly during the fourth century, B.C.)

1.   Cleo was pregnant five years. She, already five years pregnant, was brought prostrate in bed to the God as a supplicant. Immediately as she came from Him and from the temple, she bore a boy; as soon as he was born, he washed himself in the spring and walked around with the mother. After she had accomplished this, she wrote about it on the votive offering. One should be amazed not at the greatness of the tablet, but at the God. Five years Cleo bore the burden in her womb until she slept in the temple and she became healthy.

3.   A man who had the fingers of the hand crippled except one came to the God as a supplicant. But seeing the tablets in the temple, he disbelieved in the healings and he sneered at the inscriptions. While sleeping he saw a vision. It seemed he was casting the bones (in the crypt) under the temple[1] and as he was about to cast the bones, the God appeared and seized upon the hand and stretched out its fingers. As it turned out, He seemed

---

[1] I.e., throwing the sacred dice to gain a favorable omen that he would be healed.

51

to bend the hand to stretch out the fingers one by one. When
He straightened all of them, the God asked him if he still disbelieved the inscriptions upon the tablets of the temple. He
said, "No." Asklepios replied, "Because formerly you did not
believe those things which are not unbelievable, may you henceforth be named 'Unbeliever.'" When it was day, he came out,
healthy.

4.   Ambrosia from Athens had one good eye. She came, a
supplicant, to the God. But, as she walked around the temple
of healings, she mocked some things as incredible and impossible,
that the lame and blind could be healed at only seeing a dream.
While lying there, she saw a vision. It seemed the God stood
over her and said to her that He would make her healthy, but it
was necessary that she set in the temple a silver pig as a
reward, that is, as a remembrance of her stupidity. While
saying these things, He cut into the place where her other eye
was diseased and poured in some medicine. When it was day, she
went out healthy.

5.   There was a child who could not speak. He came to the
temple for a voice. He sacrificed and performed the customary
rituals. After this, the child, while he was bringing a torch
to the God, was commanded, as he was looking at his father, to
wait one year, and when he had gotten what he wanted, to come
back and offer the thank offering. The child suddenly said,
"I will wait." And the father, astonished, ordered him to
speak again. He spoke again. From this time he was healed.

6.   Pandaros of Thessaly had brand-marks on his forehead.[1]
While he lay there, he saw a dream. It seemed the God bound
the brand-marks with a cloth and ordered him, since he was

---

[1]Customarily put on slaves by their owners as a means of
identification.

outside the holy ground, to remove the band as an offering to
the temple. In the morning, he went forth and removed the band,
and his face appeared empty of the brand-marks. He presented
the cloth band as an offering to the temple. It had upon it the
marks from his forehead.

7.   (This is how) Echedoros received brand-marks from (his
fellow-slave) Pandor as well as from his master. He took money
from Pandor to offer as a gift to the God in Epidauros for him.
But he did not make the offering. As he slept he saw a dream.
It seemed the God was standing over him and asking if he had
some money from Pandor in Athens as a gift to the temple. He
denied he received any such thing from him, but said that if He
would make him healthy, he would set up a statue to Him with an
inscription upon it. After this the God ordered him to wrap the
band of Pandor around his brand-marks, then go out from the holy
ground, remove the band and wash his face in the spring and to
look at himself in the water. In the morning he went out from
the holy place and took off the band; it did not have writing.
Looking down into the water he saw his face with its own brand-
marks still on it and it had also received the brand-marks of
Pandor.

8.   A good omen concerning a child of Epidauros. Suffering from a skin rash he went to sleep. It seemed the God stood
over him and said, "What will you give me if I make you well?"
He said, "Ten dice throwings." The God laughed and said, "Now
stop that!" In the morning he came out healed.

13. MIRACLES PERFORMED BY PYTHAGORAS

(Iamblichus, *Life of Pythagoras* 36, 60f., 134-136;
trans. D.R. Cartlidge)

(Introduction: See note at #7.)

36.　　　At that time he (Pythagoras) was going from Sybaris
to Krotona. At the shore, he stood with men fishing with nets;
they were still hauling the nets weighed down (with fish) from
the depths. He said he knew the number of fish that they had
hauled in. The men agreed to do what he ordered, if the number
of fish was as he said. He ordered the fish to be set free,
living, after they were counted accurately. What is more
astonishing, in the time they were out of the water being
counted, none of the fish died while he stood there. He paid
them the price of the fish and went to Krotona. They announced
the deed everywhere, having learned his name from some children.

60.　　　...It is said he mastered the Daunian bear, which had
severely harmed the inhabitants, stroking it with his hand for
a long time; he fed it with maize and acorns, compelled it by an
oath not to touch any living thing, and sent it away. The bear
went immediately into the mountain and the woods, into hiding,
and from that time was never seen to attack an irrational
creature (i.e., a lower animal). 61. Seeing an ox in Tarantum
eating green beans,[1] in a field, he approached the ox-keeper
and told him to tell the ox to refrain from eating the beans.
The ox-keeper laughed at him because Pythagoras said, "Tell
(the ox)," and said he did not know how to speak in "ox-
language," but if (Pythagoras) knew, it was in vain to order

---

[1] Considered sacred by the Pythagoreans.

the ox-keeper to speak, but fitting to him (Pythagoras) to
advise the ox. Pythagoras approached the ox and whispered in
its ear a long time. The ox then not only refrained from beans,
but never again, it is said, tasted them.

134.   ...Once, crossing the Nessos river with his companions,
he spoke to it by voice, and the river answered, loudly and
clearly so that all heard, "Hail, Pythagoras." Also, on one
and the same day, both in Metapontius of Italy and Tauromenius
of Sicily he was present and conversed in common with his companions in both places; this is asserted strongly by all (his
biographers), even though there are many miles between the two
cities by land and sea, and no one can pass from one to the
other in many days.... 135. ...myriad other divine signs and
wonders are recorded without error and uniformly by the historians about this man: infallible earthquake predictions; he
got rid of plagues rapidly and stopped strong winds; he caused
hail to stop at once; he calmed rivers and seas so that his
companions might cross over easily.... 136. ...it is said also
that he predicted an earthquake from well water which he
tasted, and that a ship sailing with a fair wind would sink.

14. VESPASIAN HEALS SOME ALEXANDRIANS

(Tacitus, *Histories* 4.81; trans. D.R. Cartlidge)

(Introduction: During the winter of 69 C.E. Vespasian, one of Rome's leading generals, was in Alexandria waiting out the period of civil war in Italy that had erupted after Nero's suicide in 68. His army was blockading Egypt's grain supply which Rome badly needed. Before long, he was able to gain control of the Empire.)

Throughout those months in which Vespasian was waiting in Alexandria for the season of the summer winds and a calm sea, many miracles happened, by which were exhibited the favor of Heaven[1] and a certain leaning toward the divine in Vespasian. One of the commoners of Alexandria, who was known for the loss of his sight, threw himself before his knees, praying to him with groans for a remedy for his blindness, having been so ordered by the God Serapis, whom the nation, being most pious, worships more than all others. And he prayed to the emperor that he should stoop to moisten with his spit his cheeks and the eyeballs. Another, whose hand was useless, ordered by the same God, prayed that Caesar should step on it with his foot. Vespasian at first laughed; then, at the same time, he was moved to fear by the thought of the infamy of failure and to hope by the prayers of the men and the voices of flattery. Finally he ordered it to be determined by physicians if such blindness and debility could be conquered by human strength. The doctors handled the two cases differently: in one, the power of sight had not been destroyed and would be restored if the obstructions were removed. In the other, the joints had fallen into deformity; if a healing force were applied, it would be possible to restore them. This was perhaps the wish

---

[1]As we might suppose, Tacitus was a "court historian."

of the Gods, and the emperor had been chosen for divine service.
At any rate, if the healing was achieved, Caesar had glory; the
onus of failure would belong to the poor beseechers. Therefore,
Vespasian, sure that his good fortune was able to achieve anything and that nothing was incredible, with smiling face, standing amid the excitement of the tense multitude, did what he was
asked. Immediately the hand was changed to a useful one and
the day shone again for the blind man.

15. A SYRIAN EXORCIST

(Lucian, *The Lover of Lies* 16; trans. D.R. Cartlidge)

(Introduction: This brief excerpt is taken from a satirical dialogue by the second-century C.E. Syrian author, Lucian of Samosata, dealing with the way people readily believe all sorts of things concerning the supernatural world.)

"You act ridiculously," Ion said to me, "by your constantly doubting everything. I would like to ask you what you say about those who free the demon-possessed from their terrors, thus plainly exorcising the ghosts. I hardly need to go into it -- everyone has heard of the Syrian from Palestine,[1] so skilled was he in these things. Whomever he received, those who were moonstruck and rolled their eyes and filled their mouths with foam, they arose, and he dispatched them away healthy, when they were free of the terror, for a large fee. When he stands by them as they lie there, he asks (the demons) from whence they came into the body. The sick man is silent, but the demon answers in Greek or some barbarian tongue, or in the language of the country from which he comes, how and from whence he came into the man. The Syrian then levels oaths at him (to drive him out), but if the demon is not persuaded, he threatens (even worse punishments) and expels the demon. I actually saw one coming out, black and smoky in color."

"It is nothing for *you* to see such things, Ion," I replied, "to whom the Eternal Forms plainly appear, which the father of your school, Plato, points out; but to us with weak eyes these things are rather vague!"

---

[1]The identity of this healer is unknown.

16. THE MIRACLES OF CHANINA BEN DOSA

(bBer. 34b, bTa'an. 24b/25a, bBer. 33a); trans. D.L. Dungan

(Introduction: Rabbi Chanina ben Dosa lived in Palestine in the mid-first century C.E., and was a friend and colleague of Yohanan ben Zakkai, the founder of the Academy at Yavneh (Jamnia). He was especially famous for his total piety, being considered a completely righteous man (bBer. 61b); "one for whose sake God shows favor to his entire generation" (bHag. 14a).)

1.   Chanina ben Dosa's healings through prayer (bBerakoth 34b.)

Our rabbis say, once upon a time Rabban Gamliel's son got sick. He sent two men of learning to Rabbi Chanina ben Dosa to beg him mercy from God concerning him. He saw them coming and went to a room upstairs and asked mercy from God concerning him. When he had come back down he said to them, "Go, the fever has left him." They said, to him, "What? Are you a prophet?" He said, "I am not a prophet nor am I the son of a prophet. But this I have received from tradition: if my prayer of intercession flows unhesitatingly from my mouth, I know it will be answered, and if not, I know it will be rejected." They sat down and wrote and determined exactly the moment he said this, and when they came back to Rabban Gamliel he said to them, "By the Temple service![1] You are neither too early nor too late but this is what happened: in that moment the fever left him and he asked for water!"

Once again when Rabbi Chanina ben Dosa was going to study Torah with Rabban Yochanan ben Zakkai, the son of Rabban Yochanan ben Zakkai became ill. He said to him, "Chanina, my son, ask mercy from God for him and he will live." He put his

---

[1]A kind of oath; "By God!"

head down between his knees[1] and asked mercy for him and he
lived. Rabban Yochanan ben Zakkai said, "Now if ben Zakkai
fastened his head between his knees all day long, there would
not be any attention paid to him." His wife said to him, "What?
Is Chanina greater than you?"[2] He replied, "Of course not, but
he is like a servant before the king and I am like a prince
before the king."[3]

2.   A humorous story: bread is miraculously given to ben
            Dosa's wife (bTa'anit 24b/25a.)

    Rab Judah[4] said (in the name of Rab),[5] day in and day
out a Heavenly Voice[6] goes forth from Mt. Horeb proclaiming,
"the whole world is preserved for the sake of Chanina my son
and all it takes to sustain *him* from the eve of one Sabbath to
the next eve of Sabbath is a handful of carōb-beans!"[7] (To show
you how poor he was,) his wife had a habit of burning a fire all
during the eve of Sabbath and throwing in leaves to avoid

---

[1]Indicating especially strenuous praying.

[2]At this time, ben Zakkai was the Ruler of the people, just
after the great rebellion 67-73 C.E.

[3]He can go in with requests anytime.

[4]A Palestinian sage who lived about 300 C.E.

[5]Rab, otherwise known as Abba Arika the Tall, died 247 C.E.,
was one of the most important of the early Babylonian rabbis.

[6]Or *Bath Qōl*, a constant aspect of rabbinic stories; cp. John
12:28, "Jesus said, 'Father glorify thy name.' Then a Voice
came from Heaven saying, 'I have glorified it,' etc. The Bath
Qōl provides Heaven's point of view in the stories.

[7]A hilarious exaggeration. The carōb was a kind of common
bean eaten only by the poverty-stricken. This story tells how
ben Dosa's proud wife tried to hide their abject poverty -- and
was unexpectedly helped.

disgrace.[1]   Well, there lived in the neighborhood a certain
malicious woman who said, "I know full well that they don't
have anything and that she is not cooking anything! What is
all that smoke for?" So she went and knocked on the door. The
wife of Chanina was ashamed (to let her neighbor find out) and
hid in the bedroom instead of answering the door. Suddenly a
miracle was done for her. Her neighbor peeked in the window
and (contrary to her expectations) saw the oven filled with
bread baking and the kettle filled with dough. She called out
to Chanina's wife, "Hey you! Get the spatula! Quick! Your
bread is burning!" Chanina's wife shouted back, "Why do you
think I went to the bedroom!"

3.   Chanina ben Dosa's complete sinlessness proves itself
             (bBerakoth 33a.)

         Our rabbis say, once upon a time a poisonous snake
was injuring people. They went and made it known to Rabbi
Chanina ben Dosa. He said to them, "Show me its burrow."
They showed him its burrow and he placed his heel upon the
mouth of the hole. It came forth and bit him -- and it died.
He put that snake on his shoulders, went to the House of Study
(*Beth ha-midrash*), and said to them, "See, my sons; it is not
the snake that kills but sin that kills." Then they said, "Woe
to the man a snake attacks and woe to the snake which Rabbi
Chanina ben Dosa attacks!"[2]

---

[1]The smoke would make it look as if she was cooking food
ahead in preparation for the Sabbath like everyone else. Since
the Sabbath was a day of rest, no housework could be done on it,
and all food had to be ready ahead of time.

[2]The same story is also found in Tosef. Ber 3.20, only there
it is a scorpion that bites him during prayer -- and dies.

17. A JEWISH BOY CALMS THE MEDITERRANEAN

(jBerakoth 9.1; trans. D.L. Dungan)

Rabbi Tanchuma[1] said, "Once upon a time a certain cargo ship belonging to Gentiles was crossing the Great Sea in which there was a certain Jewish boy. A great tempest rose up upon the seas, and every single one among them arose and bowed down taking his idol in his hand and crying out in prayer, but to no avail. Then, when they saw it was no use, they said to the Jewish boy, 'Come, my son. Call to your God. He will hear us, for He responds to you when you complain to Him, and He is strong.' So the boy got up and begged with all his heart, and God received his prayer and quieted the sea. Then as they came to the shore, they all went down to buy things they needed. They said to him, the little boy, 'Is there not anything you want to buy for yourself?' He said to them, 'Why do you ask this of me, a poor foreigner?'[2] They said to him, 'You, a poor foreigner? We are the poor foreigners! Some are here and their idols are back home in Babylon, others are here, but their idols are in Rome, and others are here who have their idols with them, but none of them is any help to anyone. But you know every place where you go, your God is with you, as it is written, 'What great nation is there that has a God so near to them as our God is whenever we call to Him?'" (Deut. 4:7).

---

[1]Lived ca. 350 C.E.

[2]Implying that he was penniless.

65

18. THE EXCOMMUNICATION OF ELIEZER BEN HORKANOS

(bBaba Mezia 59b; trans. D.L. Dungan)

(One day the sages at Yavneh were debating a legal question (*halachah*), namely whether an oven constructed in sections with sand between them was a "utensil" and therefore subject to the laws of household purity. A dramatic conflict erupted between Eliezer ben Horkanos who argued it was not a utensil but just pieces of tile, and all the other sages, who said it *was* a utensil because the outer shell of cement binding the whole together made it a unified entity used in daily chores. This seemingly insignificant issue became the occasion for a deadly conflict between the rabbis.)

On that day, Rabbi Eliezer replied with every legal argument in the world, but the rabbis would not accept them. Thereupon, he said to them, "If the halachah is on my side, let that carōb tree show it!" The carōb suddenly uprooted itself and flew through the air one hundred cubits -- some say four hundred cubits. They said to him, "No bringing of proof from a carōb tree!" He said to them, "If the halachah is on my side, then may that stream of water show it!" The stream of water turned around, and flowed backward. They said to him, "No bringing proof from streams of water!" He turned and said to them, "If the halachah is on my side, may the walls of the House of Study we are in show it!" The walls of the House of Study leaned inward, as if about to fall. Rabbi Yehoshua rebuked the walls, saying to them, "If the sages battle each other over halachah, why do you interfere?" They did not fall out of honor for Rabbi Yehoshua, nor did they straighten up out of honor for Rabbi Eliezer; they continue crookedly standing to this day. Again Eliezer said to them, "If the halachah is on my side, let Heaven show it!" A Voice from Heaven [*Bath Qōl*] cried out, "What do the rest of you have against Rabbi Eliezer? The halachah is on his side in everything!" Rabbi Yehoshua leaped to his feet and quoted [Deut. 30:12], "'It is not in Heaven'".

What did Yehoshua mean by saying, "'It is not in Heaven'"? Rabbi Yeremiah explained, "Since the Torah has already been given from Mount Sinai, we do not pay heed any longer to a Heavenly Voice. You yourself, O Lord, wrote in the Torah given at Mount Sinai: 'turn aside after the multitude'".[1]

Later, Rabbi Nathan happened to see the Prophet Elijah. He asked him, "What did The Holy One, Blessed be He, do when we did not pay heed to any of Rabbi Eliezer's miraculous proofs, or the Heavenly Voice?" Elijah replied, "What did he do! God said, 'My sons have defeated me! My sons have defeated me!'"

They say that on that same day, after the debate, all the rabbis gathered everything Rabbi Eliezer had before pronounced clean and burned them with fire,[2] for they had all voted to "bless" him.[3] Then they said, "Who will go make it known to him?" Rabbi Akiba[4] said to them, "I will go, lest an unworthy man go and tell him and cause the destruction of the whole world completely."[5] What did Rabbi Akiba do? He put on black clothing and a black overgarment[6] and came to Rabbi Eliezer, sitting down nearby four cubits away. Rabbi Eliezer said to him, "Akiba, what happened today?" He said to him, "Master, it seems to me that

---

[1] I.e., "accept the majority view point" in matters of halachah. It is irrelevant to the rabbis' argument that the original meaning of this phrase from Ex. 1 ff. has to do with another subject altogether.

[2] Because they were unclean; i.e., all his decisions were now considered null and void.

[3] A euphemistic expression. They voted to excommunicate Rabbi Eliezer.

[4] The successor to Gamliel II and one of the most influential rabbis of this period (90-135).

[5] By provoking Rabbi Eliezer to anger, which he would convey to his God, who would in turn punish the world.

[6] A sign of mourning.

your brothers have separated from you."[1]   Then Eliezer tore his
clothing and took off his shoes and sat on the ground, tears
dropping from his eyes. Instantly, the world was blighted;
one-third of the olives, one-third of the wheat, and one-third
of the barley died (... A Tanna says, "A great disaster happened
on that day, for everything upon which Rabbi Eliezer's eye fell
burned up.")

Some days later, Rabban Gamliel was traveling in a
boat. A tempest rose up and threatened to sink his boat and
drown him. He said to himself, "It seems to me this is happening only because of what we did to Rabbi Eliezer ben Horkanos."[2]
So he stood up on his feet and cried out: "Master of the World!
It is obvious to all and well-known to you that it was not
selfishly for my honor that I acted, or for the glory of the
house of my father that I acted, but for your honor, in order
that divisions of opinion (*Torah*) not increase in Israel."[3]

The waters immediately calmed down.

(The account ends with the story of how Rabbi Eliezer's
wife, who was Rabban Gamliel's sister, was terrified what her
husband, Eliezer, might do to her brother. Thus she would not
allow her husband to pray, lest he pour out his grief to God, and
God would severely punish Gamliel. But one day not long after,
while her attention was diverted by a beggar's request for some
bread, Eliezer went upstairs and began to pray. Thereupon, the
story says, news came over from Gamliel's house that he had
suddenly died at that very moment.)

---

[1]Excommunicated you.

[2]R. Gamliel II was Ruler (*Nasi*) at the time, and he apparently
was the one primarily responsible for Eliezer's excommunication.

[3]R. Eliezer must have been at the head of a dissident faction
of some sort.

19. DIVINE SIGNS THAT ISRAEL'S GOD HAD LEFT HIS TEMPLE

(bYoma 39b; trans. D.L. Dungan

Our rabbis teach, the year in which Shimeon the Just[1] died, he said to them, "This year I will die." They said to him, "How do you know?" He said to them, "Every Day of Atonement there appears to me an old man in a white garment covered with a white outer garment. He would enter the Holy of Holies with me and go out with me. But today there appeared to me an old man in a black garment and a black outer garment. He went in with me and did not come out with me." After the Festival of Yom Kippur (Atonement) was over, he (Shimeon) was sick for seven days and died. Thereupon his brothers the priests stopped pronouncing the Name of God in the Blessing.[2]

Our rabbis teach, for 40 years before the destruction of the House of the Lord, the dice of the Lord did not come up in the right hand,[3] the crimson ribbon did not turn white,[4] the candle on the west end of the seven-branched candle-stick (*Menorah*) did not burn,[5] and the doors of the Inner Court kept opening by themselves, until Rabban Yochanan ben Zakkai[6] shouted,

---

[1]High Priest around 200 B.C.E.

[2]Because God's glory (Shekinah) was not in the Temple.

[3]Indicating an affirmative answer, that the sacrifice would be accepted by God.

[4]Which was tied between the horns of the sacrifice. If it became white, it signified God's forgiveness; "though your sins be as scarlet they shall be as white as snow" (Isaiah 1:18).

[5]I.e., longer than the rest. It was lit first and was said to burn longer than the other six, as a miracle to show when the Lord was in the Temple.

[6]Chief rabbi in the days prior to the destruction of the Second Temple by the Romans, 70 C.E.

saying to it, "Temple, Temple, are you going to give the alarm
yourself? I know that you will be destroyed, for already
Jeremiah...has foretold it concerning you."

20. PORTENTS ACCOMPANYING THE MURDER OF JULIUS CAESAR

(Vergil, *Georgics* 1.463-468, Suetonius, *The Lives of the Caesars*
1.88-89, Plutarch, *Parallel Lives, Julius Caesar* 69.3-5;
trans. D.R. Cartlidge)

(Introduction: Julius Caesar was assassinated in 44
B.C. by men who bitterly resented his flagrant trampling upon
the Senate's authority. But none of the following accounts of
miraculous signs of the Gods' sorrow at Caesar's death were
written by those men. Vergil and Suetonius, in particular,
belonged to the circle of writers dedicated to embellishing the
rising glory of Octavian, Caesar's nephew, and the Empire under
his control.)

1.   (Vergil, *Georgics*, 1.463-468)

...Of these the Sun shall give you signs, the story
told at evening,[1] the clear skies from whence the wind drives
the clouds, and what is the significance of the humid south-
wind. Who would dare to call the Sun a liar? He, in fact warns
that a secret insurrection is imminent and that deceit and
furtive battles are swelling. He expressed mercy for Rome when
Caesar was killed; he hid his shining head in gloom and the
impious age feared eternal night."

2.   (Suetonius, *The Lives of the Caesars*, 1.88-89)

(Julius Caesar) died when he was fifty-six, and he
was registered among the rank of the Gods, not only by means of
(the Senate) decree, but also in the conviction of the common
people. In fact, at the first games which were established for
him by his heir Augustus, a comet shone for seven straight days,
rising about the eleventh hour, and it was believed to be the

---

[1]Prediction of the next day's weather by the color of the
sunset.

soul of Caesar who had been received into Heaven.   It is because
of this that a star is placed on the crown of the head of his
statue....

    Hardly any of his murderers lived after him for more
than three years, nor did they die a natural death.   They were
all damned, and they died in various ways, some by shipwreck,
some in battle; some killed themselves by the same dagger with
which they assassinated Caesar.

3.   (Plutarch, *Caesar*, 69.3-5)
    (At Caesar's death) the most astonishing event of
human design concerned Cassius.   After he was defeated at
Philippi, he killed himself with the same dagger which he had
used against Caesar.   Concerning the events of divine design,
there was the great comet (for it shone seven nights after the
assassination of Caesar, then disappeared) and the blocking of
the sun's rays.   For throughout the whole year the sun rose pale,
and it had no radiance, and the heat which came from it was weak
and effete, so that the air lay heavy due to the feebleness of
the warmth which entered it.   The fruits, half-ripe and imperfect, faded and decayed because of the chill of the atmosphere.
But especially the ghost that appeared to Brutus showed that the
murder was not pleasing to the Gods....[1]

---

[1] Here Plutarch is referring to the well-known legend of his
time that a ghost appeared to Brutus the night before his final
battle.   This apparition predicted his defeat and death.

21. PLUTARCH EXPLAINS CERTAIN ALLEGED MIRACLES

(Plutarch, *Coriolanus* 37-38, *Cleomenes* 39, *Pyrrhus* 3;
trans. D.R. Cartlidge)

1.   (Plutarch, *Coriolanus* 37-38)

        (Introduction: Plutarch recounts a legend about a
statue, erected in honor of Roman women, which suddenly began
speaking as it was being set up. The words reported of it were,
"Dear to the Gods, O women, is your pious gift of me.")

        Those who tell this story say these words were spoken
two times, wishing us to believe what probably did not happen
and is difficult to credit. That statues have seemed to sweat
and shed tears and to release drops which are like blood, is not
impossible. For wood and stone often gather a mold which produces a moisture, and they make many colors and receive colors
from the atmosphere. There is nothing to hinder us from thinking that the Gods use these as signs. It is possible that
statues can emit a noise like a moan or a groan on account of a
split or a division, which is more harsh if it occurs in the
interior. It is, however, completely impossible that articulate
speech and language so clear and abundant and so cultured (as
reported of this statue) could come from a lifeless thing. For
not even the human soul, or a God, lacking a body put together
and equipped with vocal organs, can speak or converse. But
where history compels us with many and plausible witnesses, we
could say an experience unlike that coming from the senses
arises in the fantasizing portion of the soul and persuades the
belief, such as in a dream when we seem to hear (though we do
not hear) and see (though we do not see).

2.   (Plutarch, *Cleomenes* 39)

          After a few days, those who were guarding the hanging
body of Cleomenes[1] saw a large serpent wrapped around the head of
the body and hiding the face, so that no flesh-eating bird could
get at it. Because of this, superstition and fear suddenly fell
upon the king.[2] This, at first, gave to the women an opportunity
for (giving Cleomenes the necessary) purifying rites, as being a
man of a higher nature and dear to the Gods, who had been taken
up (to Heaven). And the Alexandrians and those who frequented
the place worshipped him, addressing Cleomenes as a hero and a
child of the Gods, until wiser men stopped them, telling them
that as rotting oxen put forth bees and horses wasps, and beetles
are engendered by asses in a like state, so human bodies give
forth snakes when the juices about the marrow gather and thicken.
And because they recognized this, the ancients associated the
snake more than any other animal with heroes.

3.   (Plutarch, *Pyrrhus* 3)

          To those who had a disease of the spleen, Pyrrhus[3]
seemed to be a help. He would sacrifice a white cock, and,
while the patient lay on his back, he would press the stomach
gently with his right foot. No one was so poor or unworthy
that, if he asked, he would not be given the healing. The king
would then accept the cock which was sacrificed, as an honor
which pleased him. It was said that the big toe of Pyrrhus'
right foot had divine power, so that after his death, when the

---

[1]The famous Spartan King (260-219 B.C.) who died in exile in
Alexandria.

[2]Cleomenes had fled to Ptolemy Euergetes for refuge, and his
successor, the king here referred to, imprisoned Cleomenes,
whereupon he committed suicide. The king exposed the body
instead of giving it an honorable burial.

[3]In Plutarch's age, Pyrrhus was considered with Alexander the
Great to be one of the greatest generals who ever lived; King
of Epirus on the Aegean (319-272 B.C.)

rest of the body had been cremated, it was found unharmed and
untouched by the fire.

22. THE WINE MIRACLE OF DIONYSOS

(Pausanius, *Description of Greece* 6.26.1f.;
trans. D.R. Cartlidge)

(Introduction: The author of this excerpt was a Greek
geographer and traveler who lived during the second century C.E.
He composed a lengthy account of his homeland, including especially religious sites, customs and practices. In describing
the province of Elis, he tells of an annual miracle that occurs
there in a temple dedicated to Dionysos.)

There is an old theatre and shrine of Dionysos between
the market place and the Menius. The statue of the God is the
work of Praxiteles. Of the Gods, the Eleans worship especially
Dionysos, indeed they say their God invades the Thyia[1] during
the annual feast.... The priests carry three kettles into the
building and set them down empty, when the town citizens and
strangers, if they happen to be there, are present. The priests,
and any others who wish, put a seal on the doors of the building.... In the morning they come to read the signs and when they
go into the building they find the kettles filled with wine.
These things most trustworthy men of Elis, and strangers with
them, swear to have happened. This is by word of mouth; I myself did not arrive at festival time. The Andrians also say
that every other year, in the feast of Dionysos, wine flows of
its own accord from the temple. If it is fitting that such
things should be believed by Greeks, then one ought to accept,
by the same reasoning, what the Ethiopians around Syene[2] say
about the Table of the Sun.[3]

---

[1]A temple to Dionysos.

[2]Aswan.

[3]Pausanius does not indicate what miraculous occurrences are
meant.

23. JESUS' MEDICAL CORRESPONDENCE WITH KING ABGAR

(Eusebius, *Ecclesiastical History* 1.13.1-10; trans. D.R. Cartlidge)

(Introduction: Around the year 300 C.E., the Christian historian Eusebius described the evangelization of eastern Syria, telling of Abgar, a former king of the region around Edessa. This Abgar became ill, and, hearing of Jesus' remarkable healing powers, sent a letter to him requesting him to come to Edessa and heal him. Eusebius then quotes Jesus' letter in reply. Of the authenticity of these letters, Eusebius was quite convinced, saying, "We have written evidence of these [epistles] from the archives of Edessa, then the capital city.")

(Abgar's letter.)

Abgar Ouchama, the Toparch, to Jesus, the good Savior who has appeared in the area of Jerusalem, greeting. I have heard all about you and about your healings which you do without medicines and plants. According to the report, you make the blind see, the lame walk; you cleanse those with leprosy, you exorcise unclean spirits and demons, you heal those tormented by chronic disease, and you raise the dead.

I heard these things concerning you and I decided you are one of two things: either you are God and you came down from Heaven to do these things, or you do them because you are a son of God. I, therefore, beg you to take the trouble to come to me and to heal the suffering I have. I also heard that the Jews are spreading evil rumors about you and wish to hurt you. My city is small and pious and there is room for both of us.

(This is Jesus' reply.)

Jesus to Abgar: You are blessed; you believe in me, and you have not seen me. It is written concerning me, "those who have seen me will not believe in me," and "those who have not seen me will believe and will be saved." Regarding what you wrote to me, i.e., to come to you, I have to complete everything I was sent to do and, after this fulfillment, to be taken up to Him who sent me. After I have been taken up, I will send to you

one of my disciples to heal your suffering and to provide life
for you and those with you.

ADDITIONAL SELECTION IN PART II

24. Apollonios of Tyana (Philostratus, op. cit., III.38-40; IV.10, 20, 45), see pp. 275-281, 282-283.

25. THE STOIC "SCOUT" SENT FROM ZEUS TO MANKIND

(Arrian, *Discourses of Epictetus* 3.22.19-25, 53, 81, 95;
trans. D.R. Cartlidge)

(Introduction: Epictetus was a famous Stoic philosopher, who lived during the late first and early second century in Rome. In this selection from his "Discourses," he describes different aspects of the divine mission of the Stoic "scout".)

19.   First, you must make pure the governing principle of
your life, and have this plan: "From now on, my mind is my raw
material, as wood is to the builder, as leather to the shoe-
maker. My job is to use my information correctly. 21. My body
means nothing to me; its parts are nothing to me. Death? Let
it come when it will, either the death of all or a part of me.
22. Exile? To where can anyone expel me? He cannot send me
outside the world. Wherever I go, there is the sun, there the
moon, there the stars, dreams, omens, communion with the Gods."
23. Next, after he is thus prepared, the true Stoic cannot allow
this to suffice, but he must know that he has been sent as a
messenger from Zeus to men to show them about good and evil
things, that they have strayed off and are looking in the wrong
places for the essence of the good and evil. They look where it
is not; where it is they have no idea. He must be a spy, as
Diogenes was when he was taken off to Philip after the battle
of Chaironeia. Truly, the Stoic spys out what is beneficial and
what is harmful to men. He must spy accurately and, when he
comes back, he must report truthfully. He must not become panic-
stricken, so that he identifies as enemies those that are not,
nor in any other way should he be troubled or mixed up about his
information.

53.   Consider carefully. Know yourself. Ask God. Without
God, do nothing. If He thus counsels you, be certain that He
wants you to become great, or to receive many beatings. For
mixed into the Stoic's life is this all too sweet refinement;

he must be beaten like a donkey, and, while he is beaten, he must love the floggers as if he were the brother or father of them all. Not you, however. If someone beats you, you go into the middle of the town and shout, "O Caesar, in your peaceful reign, why do I suffer? Let us go to the proconsul." But to a Stoic, what is a Caesar or a proconsul, or anyone else other than He who sent him and whom he serves, namely, Zeus? Does he call on anyone except Zeus?

81.   Friend, (the Stoic) is the father of all men; he has mankind as sons, womankind as daughters. This is the way he comes to all; thus he cares for all. Or do you think he chastises everyone because he is a meddler? He does this as a father, as a brother and father of us all, as a servant of Zeus.

95.   ...every thought he thinks is as a friend and servant to the Gods, as a sharer in the reign of Zeus. He always has this motto before him: "Lead me on, O Zeus and Destiny!" (Cleanthes).

26. POIMANDRES

(*Hermetic Tractates* 1; trans. D.R. Cartlidge)

(Introduction: This work, whose title might be translated, "Shepherd of Man," is a famous Gnostic initiation-vision,
which tells how the "I" of the writing gradually by stages
becomes one with Poimandres, the True Mind. Neither Christian
nor Jewish in any usual sense of the word, it has become famous
as the classic text illustrating the Gnostic conviction that
creation as such was evil, was due to some sort of "Fall" or
split within the Divine Being itself. We have included it
because of its conclusion; the speaker, now enlightened and
"given power," goes forth to preach the Gnostic "Gospel" to all
men.)

1.　　　　When my thoughts were turned toward the existence of
things, and my mind was heavy with drowsiness, my bodily senses
were subdued, as if they were weighed down in sleep from too
much food or from physical labor; it seemed that a great Being,
huge, of unmeasurable size, began to call my name and it said
to me, "What do you wish to hear and to see and when you have
understood, to learn and to know?"

2.　　　　I said, "Who are you?" "I am Poimandres," he said,
"the True Mind; I know what you wish, and I am everywhere with
you."

3.　　　　I said, "I want to learn the existence of things and
to know the nature of these things, and to know God." I said,
"I truly wish to hear." Again he spoke to me, "Hold in your mind
what you wish to learn, and I will teach you."

4.　　　　When he said this he changed his form, and in the
twinkling of an eye all things were opened to me, and I saw a
boundless vision, everything became light, pleasing and happy;
I saw it and loved it. After a little while there was a deep and
terrifying darkness which sank down, which was made bit by bit.
It coiled down, it seemed to me, like a snake. Then this darkness
changed into a certain wet substance, indescribably shaken, and
it gave off smoke as from a fire, and it gave forth a continuous

inarticulate cry. Then it gave a formless cry which was like a
voice of fire, it seemed to me.

5.   From the light.....a holy Logos came down upon the
nature, and unmixed fire leapt from the wet nature into the
heights above; the fire was light, fast, and at the same time,
active, and the air which was light followed in the ether going
up as far as the fire, away from the earth and water, so that it
seemed it was suspended above it. The earth and water remained
mixed together, so that one could not tell the earth from the
water. The mixture was moved because of the pervading spiritual
Logos which ordered it.

6.   Poimandres said to me, "Do you know what this vision
means?" "I shall know," I said. "The light, it is I, Mind, your
God, who is before the wet nature which appears out of the darkness. I am he who is from the shining Mind, the Logos, the Son
of God." "What does this mean?" I said. "Know this. That which
you saw and heard is the Logos of the Lord, the Mind, the Father
God. These are not distinguished from each other; Life is the
union of all things." "I thank you," I said. "Think about the
light and know this."

7.   When he said this he looked at me for a long time, so
that I was afraid because of his form. Looking up I saw in my
mind the light in unmeasurable powers, and it became a boundless,
ordered cosmos, though the fire was surrounded by a mighty force
and was held static. This is what I thought of as the Logos of
Poimandres helped me.

8.   I was amazed and again he said to me, "You see in
your mind the archetypal image, the pre-beginning of all beginnings, which are limitless." That is what Poimandres said to me.
"These things," I said, "are the materials of which nature is
made." Again he said, "From the counsel of God, which received
the Logos and saw the good world and imitated it, and made the
world through its own substance and begotten souls (or, "according to its fitting elements and products, the souls"...so Nock-
Festugière).

9.   The mind of God was both male and female; it was life
and light, and it begot by the Logos another Mind, the world
creator (*demiurge*). The demiurge, being God of fire and spirit,
created seven particular powers, which in ordered circles orbited
the sensible world. Their power is called Fate.

10.   At once the Logos of God leapt from the down-bearing
substance (of God) into the clean creation of nature and joined
to the world-creator Mind; they were of like substance. The
down-bearing substance of nature was left without Logos so that
it was merely stuff.

11.   The world creator Mind, joined with the Logos,
surrounded the circles and made them spin, and he turned his
creation and let it turn from an indeterminate beginning to an
unmarked end; their rotation begins where it ends. This rotation
of things, just as Mind willed it, brought forth, from the down-
bearing substance, irrational living beings, irrational because
they do not have the Logos. The air produces flying things, and
the water swimming things. Earth and water are now separate from
each other, just as Mind wished. And (the earth) produces from
herself living things, four-footed animals and snakes, wild and
tame beasts (cf. Gen. 1:24).

12.   The Father of All, Nous, who was life and light,
created Man in his own image: with whom he was pleased because
he was his own child. He was beautiful because he had the form
of his Father. God was truly pleased with his own image and he
made him Lord over creation (cf. Gen. 1:26-28).

13.   When he (=Man) saw the creation made by the World
Creator in the fire, he desired to create also, and the Father
gave him permission. He entered the created sphere having great
power, and he saw all the creations of his brother, and they
(the powers) were pleased with him and each gave to him his own
power. He learned their power and received their nature. He
then wished to break out of their orbits and to know the power
of the one who rules over the fire.

14.   He who had all authority over the world of mortal

things and irrational animals, leaned down through the world
spheres having broken through their circling and showed to down-
bearing Nature, the beautiful form of God. When Nature saw his
beautiful form and all the power of the rulers in him, she smiled
with love, for she had seen the beautiful form of Man reflected
in the water, and his shadow on earth. He saw his form in her
and in the water; he loved and wished to live in it. The will
and action were together, and he came to live in a form deprived
of Logos. Nature received her beloved and encircled him, and
they were united, they were in love.

15.   For this reason, alone of all things upon earth, man
has a double nature; he has a mortal body and is immortal because
of his common image with the Heavenly Man. Being immortal and
having authority over all things, he still suffers mortality,
submitting to Fate. Though he is above the cosmic system, he is
a slave to it; though he is bi-sexual, being from a bi-sexual
Father, and sleepless from the Unsleeping One......he is overcome
...(Here the text is unreliable. It is usually assumed that the
end of the sentence states that man, because of his fall which
is depicted above, is now a hetero-sexual animal, and one who
must sleep. (See Ch. 18))

16.   And after this [...] "O, my Mind. For I love the
teacher." Poimandres said, "This is the mystery which has been
hid to this day. Nature having had intercourse with Man brought
forth a great marvel. Since Man had in himself the harmony of
the sevenfold powers, which I told you are composed of fire and
spirit, Nature did not delay, but straightway brought forth seven
bi-sexual and marvelous men corresponding to the seven powers."
After this (I said), "O Poimandres, I have great desire to hear
more." Poimandres said, "Be quiet; I have not yet completed the
first explanation." "I am quiet," I said.

17.   "It came to pass," as I said, "that the birth of the
seven took place in the following way. Earth was female, water
the generative element, fire the developer. From the ether she
took the Spirit, and Nature gave birth to bodies in the image of

the Heavenly Man. The Heavenly Man was formed from life and light
into soul and mind, soul from life and mind from light. And so
everything in the sensible world continued until the end period
and the new creatures.

18.   "Hear the rest of the explanation which you want to
hear. When the period was fulfilled, the bond uniting all was
broken by the will of God. All things, which were bi-sexual,
became male and female, man with them, and they became man on
one hand and woman on the other. God spoke by his Holy Word,
'Increase and multiply all creation' (Cf. Gen. 1:28). He who
has a mind, let him know himself as immortal, and know that the
cause of death is love; know that all things exist."

19.   When this was said, Providence, through Fate and the
harmony of the spheres, made living things have intercourse and
established generations, and the races of all things were fulfilled. He who knows himself has come into the good spheres,
but he who loves the body, which comes from the deceit of love,
remains wandering in the darkness, suffering the pangs of death.

20.   "How have they sinned," I asked, "those who do not
know, that they should be banned from immortality?" "You seem
to me rather stupid, after what you have heard. Did I not tell
you to think?" "I know, remember, and give thanks." "If you
understand," he said to me, "tell me why those who are in death
are worthy of death." "Because," I said, "the terrible darkness
produces the wet nature, from which the body is established in
the sensible world, and from which death is nourished."

21.   "You understand correctly. But why is it said, 'he
who knows himself, turns toward himself,' as the Word (*logos*) of
God has it?" I said, "Because the Father of All is light and
life, from which the Man was created." "You speak well. God
the Father is life and light, from which the Man was created.
If, therefore, you learn that He is life and light, and that you
are formed from these, you will turn toward life again." Poimandres said these things. "Still, tell me," I said, "How shall
I turn to life, O my Mind? For God said, 'Let the man who can
understand, understand himself.'"

22.   "Do not all men have intellect?" "Watch your language, friend. I, Mind, dwell with those who are holy and good
and clean and merciful and pious, and my presence is a help.
Indeed, at once they know everything, and they lovingly worship
the Father; they bless, sing hymns in concert, and give thanks
to him with devotion. Before abandoning the body to its own
death, they despise the senses, knowing what their deeds are.
Moreover, I, Mind, do not permit the deeds of the body to be
fulfilled. I am the guard; I lock the entrance of evil things
and shameful works, cutting off their imaginations.
23.   "As for those who are ignorant and evil and sinful
and envious and covetous and killers and impious, I am far away.
I give way to a fearful Devil who brings upon such people the
sharpness of fire, he inflames their senses [?] and he drives
them into worse deeds of lawlessness, in order that they may be
sentenced to harsher punishment later on. Such people do not
cease having their desires as endless appetites, fighting in the
dark, no longer able to satisfy them, and enduring this while
upon him the fire (of desires) increases all the more."
24.   "You have taught me everything well, as I wished, O
Mind, but still tell me concerning the Ascent which takes place."
To this Poimandres said, "First, in the dissolution of the body
of matter, you give this body into change, and the form which
you have disappears and you give to the Devil your way of life
which becomes inactive. And the senses of the body return to
their sources, of which they become a part and again they are
introduced into their works. And anger and desire go into
irrational nature.
25.   "And thus man further ascends upward through harmony,
and in the first zone, he abandons the power of increasing and
decreasing; in the second, the workings of evil, henceforth an
ineffectual deceit; in the third, deceiving lust, now ineffective
in the fourth, the ostentation of arrogance, deprived now of its
effect; in the fifth, unholy boldness and rash temerity; in the
sixth evil appetite of wealth, now ineffective; and in the seventh
zone, false lies that set a trap.

26.   "Then, stripped of the powers that energized him, he
goes into the eighth nature; he has his own power, and he sings
hymns to the Father with those who are there. Those who are
present rejoice at his advent, and, being made like those with
whom he dwells, he hears the sweet sound of certain powers who
praise God; they dwell above the eighth nature. Then, in order,
they move to the Father. They submit themselves to the powers;
they have become powers themselves--they are in God. This is the
good goal of those who have Knowledge--to become God. Why do you
wait? As you have received all things from me, should you not
become a guide to all those worthy, so that through you the human
race may be saved by God?"

27.   Poimandres, having said this to me, mixed with the
powers. I gave thanks and blessed the Father of All. Then I was
sent forth having been given power. I taught the true nature of
the All and the supreme vision. I began to preach to men the
beauty of piety and Knowledge (*gnosis*): "O people, earth-born
men, you who have given yourselves to drunkenness and sleep and
ignorance of God, be sober, cease your debauchery, you who are
enchanted with lawless sleep!"

28.   As they heard this, they gathered around with one
accord. I said: "Earth-born men, why have you given yourselves
to death, when you have power to change to immortality? Repent,
you who wander in error and cohabit with ignorance! Free yourselves from the dark light, change to immortality, put aside
corruption!"

29.   Some stood apart, mocking, giving themselves up to
the way of death. Others heeded the teaching, throwing themselves at my feet. But I raised them up; I became the guide of
the race of men. I taught them the doctrine (*logos*) of how they
should be saved and I sowed among them the doctrines of Wisdom
and they were nourished from the ambrosial water. When it was
evening and the sun's rays began to diminish completely, I called
on them to give thanks to God. When they had completed the
thanks, each turned to his own bed.

30.   I wrote down the good deeds of Poimandres for myself.
I was filled with what I wished and I rejoiced. The sleep of the
body was the wakefulness of the soul, and the closing of the eyes
a true dream, and my silence the gestation of the good, and the
speaking of the Word the generation of good things. This happened
when I received from my Mind, that is, from Poimandres, the Word
of complete authority. Having been divinely inspired by the truth
I came to men. Therefore, I give from my whole soul and strength
this praise to God the Father:

31.   "God is holy, the Father of All.
             God is holy, whose will is fulfilled by his own Powers.
             God is holy, who wishes to be known and is known by
                 his own.
             Holy art Thou, who established all by the Word (Logos)
             Holy art Thou, from whom all Nature was born as an
                 image.
             Holy art Thou, whom Nature did not form.
             Holy art Thou, who art more powerful than all power.
             Holy art Thou, who art mightier than all authority.
             Holy art Thou, who art better than all praise.
             Receive pure, rational (*logikos*) worship from a soul
             and heart held out to Thee, O inexpressible,
             indescribable One, named only in silence!

32.   "I beseech Thee that I never fail in the knowledge
(*gnosis*) fit for our power. Fill me with power, that with this
grace I may enlighten those of mankind who are ignorant, my
brothers, your sons. Therefore, I believe and I witness; I come
into life and light. Blessed be Thou, O Father, and may Thy
Heavenly Man be worshipped with Thee, as Thou hast given to him
all authority" (Cf. John 17:2, 19).

ADDITIONAL SELECTIONS IN PART II

27. Apollonios of Tyana (Philostratus, op. cit., VIII.7.7), see pp. 291-292.

28. Moses (Philo, op. cit., I.148-159), see pp. 316-319.

29. SAYINGS OF PYTHAGORAS

(Iamblichus, *Life of Pythagoras* 82-85; trans. D.R. Cartlidge)

(Introduction: Iamblichus reports on Pythagoras' teachings by saying that Pythagoras' disciples received the master's teachings as if they were "divine dogmas." He then says that there were three types of sayings: 1. those that tell (generally) what a thing is; 2. those that tell more precisely what a thing is; 3. those that tell what to do or what not to do. It is clear that Iamblichus is working from a list of Pythagoras' sayings.)

82.   Those that tell (generally) what a thing is:
        "What are the Islands of the Blest (where the dead
            go)?" "The sun and the moon."
        "What is the oracle of Delphi?" "The Tetraktys".[1]
        "What is harmony?" "What the Sirens (who enchant
            sailors) sing."

        Those that tell (more) precisely what a thing is:
        "What is most just?" "To sacrifice."
        "What is most wise?" "Number. But the next wisest
            is that which gives names to things."
        "What is most beautiful?" "Harmony."
        "What is most powerful?" "Advice."
        "What is most excellent?" "Happiness" (*eudaimonia*).

83.   Those that tell what to do or not to do:
        "It is necessary to beget children, for it is
            necessary to leave behind worshippers of God."
        "It is necessary to put the shoe on the right foot
            first."

---

[1]The perfect Pythagorean conception, or 1 + 2 + 3 + 4 = 10; i.e., "the source and root of everlasting Nature".

"It is not necessary to walk on public paths nor to
bathe in a fountain nor to be washed in public
baths. To all who use these things they are
unnecessary if the users are pure."

84.   Other sayings go like this:
"Do not help someone put down a burden, for it is not
necessary to be the cause of not working; rather,
help him pick it up."
"Do not speak without light."
"Do not wear the sign of a God on your finger (i.e.,
on a ring), lest it be defiled....
"Do not attack your wife; she is one who has asked
for protection."....

85.   "Labors are good, pleasures are bad. As we came
(into the world) for punishment, it is necessary
to be punished."

30. SAYINGS OF THALES, ARISTIPPOS, ARISTOTLE

(Diogenes Laertius, *Lives of Eminent Philosophers* 1.35-37,
2.68-81, 5.17-18; trans. D.R. Cartlidge)

Thales (ca. 636-546 C.E.; philosopher; one of the Seven Sages)

1.35   He said there is no difference between life and death.
Someone said, "Then, why do you not die?" "Because," he said,
"there is no difference." 36. To the question as to which is
prior, night or day, he said, "Night is one day older." Someone
asked him if a man who did evil could escape from the Gods.
"Not even one who thinks evil," he said. To the adulterer who
asked if he should deny that he committed adultery, he said,
"Perjury is no worse than adultery." He was asked what is
difficult to bear? He said, "To know oneself." What is most
easy to bear? "To advise someone else." What is most pleasant?
"To succeed at something." What is divine? "That which has
neither a beginning nor a completion." What was the strangest
thing he had seen? He said, "An old dictator." How can someone best bear troubles? "If he should see his enemies faring
worse." How may we live a most excellent and just life? "If
we do not do what we accuse others of doing." 37. Who is
happy? "The man who has a healthy body, a resourceful soul,
and a well-trained nature." He said to remember friends both
present and absent, not to be pretentious about appearance, but
to be beautiful in the pursuits of life. "Do not gain riches
by evil means," he said, "and do not let a word cause you to
distrust those who have joined with you in trust." "You may
expect from your children the same kindnesses you show to your
parents."

Aristippos (ca. 450-365 B.C.E.; companion of Socrates; profes-
sional rhetorician)

2.68   Diogenes (the Cynic), who was washing his vegetables,
saw him going by and said, "If you learned to stomach these,
you would not have to flatter the courts of tyrants." Aristippo
replied, "If you knew how to get along with people, you would no
be washing vegetables." He was asked what advantage he had
gotten from philosophy; he said, "To be able to get along con-
fidently with everyone." Once he was castigated for his rich
living. "If this is wrong," he said, "luxury would not be found
at the feasts of the Gods" (i.e., with their permission). Once
he was asked what advantage philosophers have; he said, "If all
the laws are repealed, we will live as we do now."

69.   ...Once he was going into the house of a courtesan.
When one of the youths with him blushed, he said, "It is not
entering that is troublemaking, but being unable to come out."
70. Someone showed him a very difficult riddle and said, "Solve
it." "You idiot," he said, "why do you want me to solve it?
It gives us enough trouble as it is." He said, "It is better
to be a beggar than to be uneducated; the beggars must have
money, the others need to be made human.".... 71. Once he sailed
for Corinth. A great storm came up and he was quite fearful.
Someone said to him, "We common people are not afraid, why are
you, a philosopher, so afraid?" "You and I are not frightened
for comparable lives," he said.... 74. He said, to someone who
accused him of living with a whore, "Is there a difference
between living in a house in which many have lived, or in
which no one has lived?" The questioner said, "No." He continued, "What is the difference between sailing in a ship in
which ten thousand have sailed, or in which no one has sailed?"
"No difference." "Then," he said, "there is no difference
between living with a woman many have used or one no one has
used."

81.   A prostitute told him, "I am pregnant by you."   "You
no more know that," he said, "than if after running through the
bushes you knew which one stuck you."   Someone accused him of
casting out his son just as if he were not his own child.   He
said, "Phlegm and lice we know are from our own begetting, but,
because they are useless, we throw them as far away as we can."

Aristotle (384-322 B.C.E.; philosopher and scientist)

5.17   When he was asked what is the gain for those who tell
lies, he said, "When they speak the truth, no one believes
them."   He was once rebuked because he gave money to an evil
man, "It was not his lifestyle, but the man, I pitied."   He
continuously said to his friends and students, whenever and
wherever he lectured, that, as sight takes in the light from
the (air) around it, so does the soul from mathematics.   Many
times and lengthily he said the Athenians discovered both wheat
and laws, but they used the wheat, not the laws.

18.   He said the roots of education are bitter, but the
fruit is sweet.   He was asked what ages very quickly; "Gratitude,"
he said.   Being asked what hope is, he said, "A dream by one who
is awake."   When Diogenes wished to give him some dried figs, he
knew, if he did not take them, Diogenes would have ready a witty
put-down, so he took the figs and said that Diogenes had lost
both the figs and the witticism.   Another time, when some figs
were offered, he took them, held them up as you do with children,
and said, "Diogenes is terrific!" -- and gave them back.   He
said three things are essential for education; natural ability,
study, training.   He heard that he was being slandered by someone.   "He can even whip me," he said, "in my absence."

31. SAYINGS OF ALEXANDER THE GREAT AND OTHERS

(Plutarch, *Morals*, 172B-181F; trans. D.R. Cartlidge)

(Introduction: The Greek biographer and historian, Plutarch, amassed an enormous amount of information about all sorts of famous Greek, Roman, and foreign people. Two of his most famous publications were a multi-volume collection of miscellaneous sayings, observations, and bits of lore, Greek and Roman, called *Morals*. A second, much more ambitious work, was his *Parallel Lives of Greeks and Romans*, containing some fifty matched biographies. In the earlier writing, the *Morals*, Plutarch had several collections of famous sayings: "Sayings of kings," "Sayings of Romans," "Sayings of Spartans," and "Sayings of Spartan Women." Here is a brief excerpt illustrating this kind of literature.)

1. Alexander the Great (*Morals* 179D-181F)

179D   While Alexander was still a child and Philip was accomplishing many things, Alexander was not happy but said to his playmates, "My father will leave nothing for me (to do)." The boys said, "He is getting all this for you." "What good is this," he said, "if I have many things, but do nothing?"

He was quick and fast and his father said that he ought to run in the Olympics. "I would run," he said, "if I were going to have kings as opponents."

179E   A young girl was brought to him in order that she would sleep with him. He asked her, "Why have you come at this (late) hour?" She said, "I had to wait until my husband went to bed." He bitterly reproached his servants, because he had nearly become an adulterer because of them.

Once he was offering incense to the Gods lavishly and picking up handfuls of the frankincense (to throw into the fire), Leonidas, his teacher, who was there, said, "My boy, you may offer incense in this lavish way when you conquer the land which supplies the frankincense." When Alexander conquered the land,

103

he sent a letter to Leonidas, "I have sent you one hundred talents[1] of frankincense and cassia, so that you no longer will be stingy toward the Gods, since you know that we have conquered the land of frankincense."

180B   Once, all was ready for battle and his generals asked him what else they should do. "Nothing," he said, "except to shave the Macedonians' beards." Parmenio was astonished at this strange order. "Do you not know," Alexander said, "that there is nothing better to grab hold of in a battle than a beard?"

180C   Darius (begged for peace and) offered him 10,000 talents and also half of Asia Minor. Parmenio said, "If I were Alexander, I would (not fight any more but) take it." "So would I, by God," he said, "if I were Parmenio."

180E   One of Alexander's (more stingy) friends was entertaining him during a cold winter. The host brought in a small brazier with a tiny fire in it. Thereupon Alexander ordered him to bring either firewood or frankincense.

180F   Once Antipatrides brought a beautiful harp-player to dinner. Alexander fell in love with her at first sight. He asked Antipatrides if he was in love with her, too. He confessed that he was. "You louse," said Alexander, "get her away from the party immediately."

181D   Once (Alexander's forces encountered) a king who held a rock fortress which seemed to be unconquerable, but he nevertheless surrendered himself and his fortress to Alexander. Thereupon Alexander ordered him to continue to rule and actually gave him more land, saying, "The man seems to me to be wise,

---

[1]Approximately $100,000 value.

entrusting himself to a good man rather than to a fortified place."

181E   He sent fifty talents to Xenocrates, the philosopher. The latter would not accept them saying he did not need the money. Alexander asked if Xenocrates did not have a friend (who wanted it). "In my case, all the wealth of Darius was scarcely enough for my friends."

181F   When he was dying, he looked at (all) his companions, "I see that my funeral will be a big one," he observed.

2. Miscellaneous

172B   Artaxerxes, the Persian king, ...considered it as much the attribute of a king and lover of mankind to accept small gifts graciously and eagerly as to give great gifts to others. So, when he was once travelling down a road, a laborer, having nothing else of his own, took water from the river with his two hands and offered it to the king. Artaxerxes accepted it happily and smiled. It is by the eagerness of the giver, not by the usefulness of the gift, that the favor is measured.

173B   Semiramis[1] erected a tomb for herself and inscribed on it, "Any king who has need of money, let him break into this tomb to take whatever he wishes." Darius, therefore, broke into it. He found no money, but he did find another inscription there which said, "If you were not an evil and greedy man, you would not be disturbing the resting place of the dead."

175C   Hiero[2] was reviled by someone because he had bad breath and asked his wife why she had not told him about it. She said, "I thought all men smelled that way."

---

[1]Mythical queen of Assyria, and founder of ancient Babylon.
[2]King of Syracuse, 478-467 B.C.E.

32. TWO STORIES FROM EPICTETUS

(Arrian, *Discourses of Epictetus* 1.2.19-29; trans. D.R. Cartlidge)

(Introduction: Epictetus (see introduction to #25) and his students were discussing one day the curious way different people will accept different degrees of bondage to others. Why is there this difference between people? Why do "different people sell themselves at different prices?" Taking off from this point, Epictetus urges his students -- who were mostly young men about to enter public affairs -- each to discover who he really was and to live his life in a manner appropriate to his own true nature. Likening himself to the purple strip around the border of the toga, which lent grace and beauty to the whole garment and without which it would look quite plain, he told two stories of men who also believed their nature was to stand out against the mass of people.)

Priscus Helvidius indeed saw this (same point), and having seen it, acted upon it. Once Vespasian sent him an order not to come to the Senate, but he answered, "You have the power not to permit me to be a senator, but as long as I am one, I must come to the meeting." "Alright, go, but when you attend, be silent." "Do not call on me during roll call and I will be silent." "But I have to do the roll call." "And I must speak what appears to be right." "But if you speak, I shall kill you." "When, then, did I say to you, 'I am immortal?' You do your job and I will do mine. Yours is to kill, mine to die unafraid. Yours is to banish, mine is to go into exile without grieving."

What did Priscus profit, who was just one man? How does the purple strip help the toga? What except to stick out in it as purple and to the rest to be exposed as a good example? Another man in such circumstances, when Caesar told him not to come to the senate, would have said, "Thank you for excusing me." In fact, Caesar would not have prevented that kind of man from coming, but would have known that either he would sit (silently) like a jug, or, if he spoke, he would say what Caesar wished, and he would pile it on.

107

A certain athlete once behaved in the same way. He
was going to die unless his genitals were amputated. When his
brother came to him (who happened to be a philosopher) and
said, "Well, brother, what are you going to do? Shall we cut
off this part and again go forth (to exercise) in the gymnasium?"
He did not submit, but stood firm and died. Someone asked
(Epictetus), "How did he do this? As an athlete or as a philosopher?"   "As a *man*," Epictetus replied, "a man who had been
proclaimed at the Olympics and competed in them, who had lived
in such places, not simply had a rub-down at Bato's Wrestling
School. Another would have had his neck cut off, if he were
able to live without a neck."

ADDITIONAL SELECTIONS IN PART II

33. Porus (Philostratus, op. cit., II.21), see pp. 271-272.

34. Apollonios of Tyana (Philostratus, op. cit., I.38), see pp. 267-268.

35. Jesus (Coptic Gospel of Thomas), see pp. 177-194.

36. AESOP, *FABLES*

(Trans. and introduction, D.R. Cartlidge)

(Introduction: Everyone knows of Aesop's fables, but no one knows Aesop. There is even some doubt as to the actual existence of Aesop, one of the most widely published authors in western history. According to legend, Aesop was a slave who lived at Athens in the sixth century, B.C.E. The fables of Aesop probably represent a collection which was gradually made down through the centuries. The variety of the contents of the various manuscripts of "Aesop's Fables" demonstrates this. Strictly speaking, a fable is a tale about animals who behave with human attributes. However, the Aesop collection contains other types of story also. Since his animal fables are so familiar, we have included here more of this less familiar material, as well as a couple lesser-known animal fables. The morals were probably added much later. Therefore, we have printed them separately so that our readers may more easily draw their own morals.)

56. The Witch-Woman.

A witch woman promised many charms and appeasements of the wrath of the Gods and she received many orders for her services; from these she made no small living. Because of this, some men accused her of making innovations in the religion; she was dragged to judgment and her accusers succeeded in having her sentenced to death. Someone who saw her as she was led from the courtroom said to her, "Look at you! You promised to appease the wrath of the demons, how is it you cannot persuade men?"

8. Aesop in the Shipyard.

Once, Aesop, the fable-teller, having some time off, went into a shipyard. The workmen teased him until they provoked him to say, "In olden times there was chaos and water, but Zeus wished to make another element of the earth appear. (He ordered that) the earth should gulp down the sea three times. The earth began to do so. The first time (she swallowed)

and the mountains appeared; then the earth gulped more sea and
revealed the plains. If she decides to drink the third time,
your boats will be useless!"

228. Prometheus and Mankind.

Prometheus created men and beasts at Zeus' order.
When Zeus saw that there were many more irrational creatures
(i.e., beasts) than men, he ordered Prometheus to destroy and
to change some of the beasts into men. When Prometheus had
carried out this order, the result was that those men who had
been transformed from beasts had the form of men but the souls
of beasts.

220. The Rich Man and the Tanner.

A wealthy man came to live by a leather-tanner. Since
he could not stand the stink, however, he constantly urged the
tanner to move. The tanner pretended to agree, saying he would
move in a little while. After their debate went on for some
time, the rich man got used to the stench and it no longer
annoyed him.

253. The Money-Lover.

A money-lover turned all his possessions into gold
bars. He then buried the treasure by a wall, and continually
came and checked on it. A certain workman who watched his
arrivals carefully and discerned the truth, when the rich man
left, stole the gold. The money-lover came and found his cache
empty; he cried and wept tearfully. Someone saw him grief-
stricken and learned the cause. He said to the hoarder; "Do
not grieve. Take the stone cover (of the cache) and put it
back in its place and think hard that the gold is still there.
You could not use it better when it was really there."

69. The Enemies.

Two enemies sailed in the same boat. They wished
very much to avoid each other, so the one sat in the bow and
the other in the stern and they stayed there. A great storm
came up and the boat was in grave peril. The man in the stern
asked one of the sailors which part of the boat would sink first.
The sailor said, "The bow." "Now death is no longer a grief
for me, for I will get to see my enemy die first," replied the
man.

7. The Cat and the Birds.

A cat heard that there were some sick birds in a certain roost, so he disguised himself as a physician and, taking
some instruments and medicine, he went there. He stood before
the roost and asked them how they were. "Fine," they replied,
"if you go away."

> (Some tales are attributed to Aesop in a few
> manuscripts, but are probably spurious because they
> are not found in the earliest manuscripts. Here are
> two examples.)

128. The Mule.

There was a certain mule who had grown fat from grain.
It was enjoying running around (the field) and said to itself,
"My father is a fast racehorse, I am in all respects like him."
And then one day it was necessary suddenly for the mule to com-
pete in a race. When the race was ended, it had learned that
its father was only a jackass.

46.   The Man Who Promised the Impossible.

A poor man was sick, in very bad shape. Since he was
a lost cause as far as the physicians were concerned, he turned
to the Gods and promised a costly offering and expensive sacrifices if they would save him. When his wife, who was standing
by him, asked, "Where are you going to get all these things?",
he replied, "Do you think I intend to get well again in order
that the Gods can get all these things from me?"

Morals

56.   This story is for cheaters and those who make big
promises, since they are revealed as to what they are by little
things.

8.   This tale clearly shows that those who scoff at their
betters will get back from them more than they expected.

228.   This tale is applicable to crooked and bestial men.

220.   This tale clearly shows that familiarity soothes
irritations.

253.   This tale clearly shows that to own something is
worthless if you do not use it.

69.   [Several of the fables have slightly different forms.
A great number have many different morals.] Thus, some men,
on account of ill will toward a neighbor, will find some
occasion for their own suffering to see the ill-fortune of the
enemy. Or, this fable shows that many men think nothing of
their own injury, if they only can see their enemy come to harm
before them.

7.   Thus, the evils of men are clear to wise men, even
if the evil-doers make a disguise of being good.

128.   This tale shows clearly that it is necessary, if the
circumstances bring something to mind, not to forget one's
origin; for this life is uncertain.

46.   This tale shows clearly that men make promises easily
which they have no intention of keeping.

37. PLATO, ALLEGORY OF THE CAVE

(Plato, *Republic* 7.1-2 (514-517 A),
intro. and trans., D.R. Cartlidge)

(Introduction: This famous story is in a sort of
dialogue style. The speaker in the first person is Socrates;
his foil is Glaucon. As the story progresses, it becomes clear
to the reader that the tale is an allegory based upon the life
and death of Socrates himself. Plato, the author of the
Republic, who was a pupil of Socrates, has placed the tale in
the master's mouth.)

7.1   "After this," I said, "compare to such an experience
our nature in respect both to education and non-education.
Behold some men who dwell in an underground cave, which has a
long entrance open across the whole width of the cave. The men
have been in the cave from childhood; both their legs and necks
are in bonds, so that they have to stay in one place and can
only see in front of them; they cannot look around because of
the chains. Light shines from a fire above and far behind them.
Between the fire and the prisoners, and higher than they are,
there is a road on which a wall is built, like those screens
put up by puppet masters before the audience, above which they
show the puppets." "I see," he said. "They also see men carrying alongside this wall all types of artifacts which stick up
above the wall, and there are statues of humans and other living
things worked from stone, wood, and all sorts of material. Some
of those carrying the objects are, most likely, speaking; some
are silent." "You speak of an unusual image and unusual prisoners," he said. "They are like us," I said, "for, first of
all, does it seem that these men would have seen anything of
themselves or one another other than the shadows cast on the
wall in front of them by the fire?" "How?", he said, "if they
are forced to hold their heads immobile through life?" "What
of the objects carried by? Is it not the same?" "Of course."

117

"If (the prisoners) could talk to one another, do you not think
that they would consider, when naming what they saw, they were
naming the objects carried by [Greek uncertain here]?" "Necessarily." "If the prison had an echo from in front of them, when
one of those passing by spoke, do you think they would believe
the speaker to be something else than the shadow passing across
the wall?" "By Zeus, I do not," he said. "In every way, then,"
I said, "they would not think true reality was anything other
than the shadows of the objects." "Quite necessarily," he said.
"Think, then," I said, "of their release and healing from these
fetters and their ignorance, what a thing it would be, if by
nature something like this should happen to them. One of them
was let go and was forced to stand suddenly and to turn his
head and to walk and to look up at the light. Doing all this
was painful to him and because of the glare and shining he
could not perceive the objects whose shadows he had once seen.
What do you think he would say, if someone said to him, that
what he had seen before was nonsense, but now he was nearer to
what really is and, being turned toward this reality, now he
sees more correctly? And if someone should make him look at
each of the objects passing by and made him answer what it is,
do you not think he would be at a loss and would think that
(the shadows) he had seen before were more truly real than what
was now shown him?" "Much more real," he said.

7.2   "Therefore, if he were made to look at the light
itself, would it not hurt his eyes and he would run away, turning back to those things which he was able to perceive. And
would he not consider these things, in respect to reality, to
be more clear than what was shown to him?" "Right," he said.
"And if," I said, "someone should drag him forcefully out of
there and up the rugged incline, and should not release him
until he had been dragged into the sunlight, would not he be
in pain and agonize over his being dragged, and when he came
to the light, his eyes would be filled with its glare so that

he could see nothing of the so-called real thing?" "No," he
said, "not right away." "Then, I think, it would be necessary
for him to become accustomed, if he is going to see the higher
things. First, he would most easily perceive the shadows, then
the reflections of men and other things in water, and later, the
things themselves. From this he would more easily at night see
the things in heaven, looking at the light of the stars and the
moon, than the sun and its light by day." "Right." "Finally,
he would be able to look directly at the sun, not reflected in
water or in some foreign context, but he would be able to perceive the sun itself and to see just what it is." "Yes," he
said. "And after this he would realize that the sun is the
provider of the hours and the seasons and that it governs
everything in the visible realm, and that it is somehow the
cause of all these things they had seen." "Clearly," he said,
"that comes next." "If, then, he remembers his first dwelling
place and the knowledge there and his fellow prisoners, do you
not think he would be happy at the change and pity them?" "Yes."
"If there were certain honors and commendations among them,
prizes for those who most cleverly discerned the shadows going
by and were best able to remember which came first and last, and
which came together, and from these things were most able to
divine which shadow was about to come, do you believe he would
be very covetous of them and zealous about these records? Would
he want them anymore? Or, would he believe with Homer and
strongly wish, living on earth, to be another man's serf, poor,
and to suffer anything than to think and live as that way?"
"Yes," he said, "I think he would suffer anything rather than
to live that way." "And think about this," I said, "if such a
man should go down again and take his seat, then would not his
eyes be full of darkness, as he suddenly comes from the sunlight?" "Yes, indeed," he said. "Now if he had to enter the
contest again with these eternal prisoners and judge the shadows, while he is still blind, before his eyes are accustomed
to the dark, and this time for accomodation would not be very

short, would he not be laughed at? Would it not be said about
him that when he went above his eyes were ruined and that to go
above is not even worth the trying? And the one who tried to
free them and lead them up, if it were possible would they not
seize him and kill him?" "They would try their best," he said.

38. PYTHAGORAS' MYSTIC TEACHINGS

(Iamblichus, *Life of Pythagoras* 105; trans. D.R. Cartlidge)

(Introduction: Pythagoras (see introductory note for #7) also taught obscure sayings, according to Iamblichus, which the latter termed "symbols." These were sayings "not written in common language," and Iamblichus lists a few.)

105.   ...If someone should interpret these symbols and not comprehend them by careful interpretation, he will consider them laughable and ridiculous... If, however, (the meaning) should be opened up according to the Pythagoreans' peculiar manner of interpreting these symbols, they will become obvious and clear to the multitude, instead of dark, and they will seem analogous to the prophecies and oracles of the Pythian Apollo,[1] shining forth with an astonishing meaning... It is not improper to mention a few (symbols)... "Do not enter the temple carelessly nor worship willy-nilly, not if you should even be standing at the very doors." "Sacrifice and worship barefoot." "Move away from the common paths; walk the untravelled ones." "Concerning Pythagorean matters, do not speak without light." Such is, typically, the peculiar manner of his teaching through the symbols.

---

[1]The oracle at Delphi, world-famous for its mysterious responses.

39. THE TESTAMENT OF ASHER

(*Testaments of the Twelve Patriarchs*; trans. D.R. Cartlidge)

(Introduction: This is a portion of a larger work called *The Testaments of the Twelve Patriarchs*. It is a pre-Christian, Jewish writing composed (in its earliest form) around 100 B.C.E. Each one of the twelve Jewish Patriarchs leaves a "last will and testament" to his sons full of moral advice. The Testament of Asher is typical of the whole work.)

1.1   This is the Testament of Asher, which he spoke to his sons in the one hundred twenty-fifth year of his life. 2. While he was well, he said to them: Listen to your father, children of Asher, and I will show you everything which is right before God. 3. God gave two ways to the sons of men, and two impulses (*yetzer*), and two practices, and two life styles, and two goals. 4. Because of this everything is in pairs; one is over against the other. 5. For there are two ways, good and evil, in which there are two impulses in our breasts which discern these things. 6. If, therefore, the soul wishes to journey well, it shall do all its practices in righteousness; if it should sin, immediately it shall repent. 7. It considers righteousness, casts away evil, and immediately turns away evil and reproves sin. 8. But if it inclines to the evil impulse (*yetzer ha-ra'*), each of its practices is evil; driving away the good and clinging to the evil: it is ruled by Beliar. If it does good, it turns the good to evil. 9. When it begins to do the good, it drives the result of the deed into evil; because the treasure of the impulse is full of an evil spirit.

2.1   The soul, therefore, although it places good before evil in words, drives the result of action into evil. 2. For example, there is the man who does not have mercy on one who serves evil. This has two sides, but the whole is evil.

3. Then there is the man who loves him who does evil; he would rather die in evil on account of him. In this case it appears that it is two-sided, but on the whole the deed is evil. 4. Even if there is love, still it is evil when he conceals the evil for the sake of a good name. The result of the action is still evil. [The text is uncertain.] 5. Another steals, is unjust, swindles, deceives, and yet shows pity for the poor. This is two-sided, but the whole is nevertheless evil. 6. He who deceives his neighbor angers God; he swears falsely to the Most High and yet shows mercy to the poor. He disobeys and irritates the Lord who gave the Law, and yet gives respite to the poor. 7. He (is like one who) spoils the soul and yet shines up the body; he kills many and shows mercy to a few. This is two-sided, but the whole is evil. 8. Another man commits adultery and fornicates and also abstains from meat. He also does evil while he is fasting [for forgiveness] and he ravages many with the power of his wealth. In spite of the massiveness of his evil, he still abides by (some of) the commandments. This is two-sided, but the whole is evil. 9. Men such as this are (as it says in the Law concerning) rabbits, because they are half-clean, in fact they are totally unclean. 10. For God said thus in the tables of the commandments.

3.1 But you, my children, do not be two-sided as they, good and evil, but cling only to the good, because the Lord God dwells therein and men desire it. 2. Run away from evil, destroy the Devil by your good deeds, because the two-sided are not of God; they are enslaved by their desires, so that they may please Beliar and men like themselves.

(Chs. 4, 5, 6 speak more of the sin of "two-sidedness." Ch. 7 predicts the scattering of Israel and her salvation by a remnant.)

8.1 When he said all this to them, he ordered them, "Bring me into Hebron." He died, while sleeping a good sleep.

2. His sons did what he commanded them. They took him to
Hebron and buried him with his fathers.

40. JESUS, AFTER THE RESURRECTION

(*Pistis Sophia* 1.1, 2.1-8, 4.142-143;
intro., notes and trans., D.R. Cartlidge)

(Introduction: This "gospel" is actually a collection of works, running to some 384 pages in the Coptic edition. The title comes only from a small section of one of the works and was added at a date later than the book's composition. The various parts of the collection should be assigned different dates; the third century C.E. appears to be a period encompassing the whole collection.

The manuscript of the *Pistis Sophia* is long; therefore, we can only present here a few excerpts. The form of the work is a series of discourses and speeches in which Jesus, after his resurrection, reveals sacred and saving knowledge to his disciples. There is a great variety of material, such as the recitation of myth, liturgies, prayers, exegeses of the Old Testament, and more. Therefore, this sampling is not representative of the whole. For more detail, see Hennecke-Schneemelcher, I, pp. 252 ff. There is an English translation of a Latin translation (Schwartze) by G.R.S. Meade, *Pistis Sophia*, London, The Theosophical Publishing Society, 1896.)

1.1   It so happened, however, that after Jesus had risen from the dead, he remained there eleven years, speaking with his disciples, and he taught them only up to the places (*topoi*) of the first laws and up to the places of the first mystery, that within the veil, which is inside the first law, which is the twenty-fourth mystery outside, and below those which are found in the second space of the first mystery, which is before all mysteries -- the Father in the form of a dove.

And Jesus said to his disciples, "I have come here from that first mystery, which is the last mystery, the twenty-fourth." The disciples did not know and understand that mystery, that there was something inside that mystery. Rather they thought that that mystery was the Head of the All and the head of all being. And they thought it was the perfection of all perfections, because Jesus had said to them regarding that

127

mystery, that it surrounds the first law and the five impressions
and the great light, and the five defenders, and the whole
treasure of light."

> (There is more that the disciples do not under-
> stand. The disciples are sitting on the Mount of
> Olives, rejoicing in the knowledge that Jesus has
> given them in the eleven preceding years. As the
> text has indicated, they are only now going to
> receive the most important knowledge.)

2.1   It so happened now that the disciples were sitting
together on the Mount of Olives. They were talking about these
things which were told them, rejoicing with a great joy and
they were very happy and said to one another, "We are blessed,
we beyond all men on earth, because the savior has revealed
these things to us; and we have received the fullness (*plēroma*)
and the whole perfection." They said these things to each
other while Jesus sat a bit away from them.
        2. It happened, then, on the fifteenth of the month of
Tybi, which is the day of the full moon. On that day, as the
sun had risen from its resting place, there came after it a
great light -- power, shining exceedingly bright. There was
no measure to the surrounding light. For this light came from
the light of lights, and it came from the last mystery, which
is the twenty-fourth mystery of the inside and the outside,
which is in the orders of the two spaces of the first mystery.
That light-power came over Jesus and totally surrounded him.
He was seated away from his disciples, and he was shining with
a great light. And there was no measure of the light which was
on him.

> (The disciples can only see the light and they
> are struck with awe and confusion at this epiphany.
> Jesus then ascends, shining, into heaven, leaving
> the disciples to gaze after him.)

3.   ...It happened then, when Jesus had ascended to
heaven, after the third hour, all the (evil) powers of heaven
were in confusion, and they were shaken against each other, they
and all their aeons and their places (*topoi*) and their orders,
and the whole earth shook and all that lived in it.

>   (At this cosmic cataclysm, the whole creation
> is in chaos; the disciples are also frightened. They
> are afraid that the savior will destroy the whole
> world; they weep.)

4.   As they said this and wept together, the heavens
opened at the ninth hour, and they saw Jesus descending.

>   (Jesus is even more shining than when he
> ascended. The disciples cannot stand the light and
> ask Jesus to lessen it. He does so and Jesus begins
> the new and greatest revelation.)

6.   ..."Rejoice and be jubilant from this hour, because
I have gone to the places from which I came.... 7. It came to
pass, as the sun rose in the east, that then through the first
mystery which existed from the beginning, for which the all is
created, out of which I have now come, not in the time before
my crucifixion, but now, it happened that through the order of
this mystery, this garment of light was sent to me...."

>   (Jesus now expounds on the manner of his first
> coming to earth.)

8.   And Jesus went on in the speech, "It happened after
this, I looked down from there out of the order of the first
mystery to the world of mankind, and I found Mary, who is
called my mother in respect to the body made of matter. I spoke
to her in the form of Gabriel. When she had given herself to
me in exaltation, I thrust into her the first power which I had

taken from Barbelo, that is, the body which I had borne into
the heights. Instead of the soul, I thrust into her the power
which I had taken from the great Sabaoth, the good, who is in
the place of the right"...

> (These excerpts are from the beginning of *Pistis
> Sophia*. In the course of the "gospel" Jesus enters
> into conversation with Mary Magdalene and with several
> of the disciples. He explains many mysteries and
> tells the story of the heavenly being, Pistis Sophia,
> who "falls" and then "repents." Much of what ensues
> is exegesis of Old Testament texts, particularly, the
> Psalms.
>
> Our last excerpt is from the fourth section of
> the collection, a separate "gospel." In the climax
> of this "gospel," there are some rituals presented.
> The incantations are not translatable; they are meant
> to be mystic, foreign sounds (such as "abracadabra").
> We have written them phonetically.)

4.142   Jesus said to them, "Bring me fire and vine
branches." They brought them to him. He laid out the offering
and placed on it two wine jugs, one on the right and the other
on the left of the offering. He placed the offering before
them. He placed a goblet of water before the wine jug on the
right, and a goblet of wine before the wine jug on the left.
And he set bread, according to the number of the disciples, in
the middle between the wine goblets and he placed a goblet of
water behind the bread. Jesus stood before the offering; he
placed the disciples behind him, all garbed in linen garments.
In their hands was the number of the names of the father of the
light-treasure. He cried out, saying, "Hear me, Father, father
of all fatherhood, unlimited light. eeaoh, eeaoh, eeaoh, aohee,
oheea, pseenother, thernopseen, nopseether, nephthomaoth,
marachachtha, marmachachtha, ee-ay-ahnah, menaman, amanayee too
ooranoo, eesrahee ohmayn, ahmayn soobaheebahee, apahahp, hahmayn,
hahmayn, derahahrahee hahpahoo, ahmayn, ahmayn, boobiahmeen,
meeahee, hameyn, hamayn, etc...." (The incantations and prayers

continue. Be cautious when repeating these.) Then Jesus spoke to them, "This is the method and this is the mystery which you shall celebrate for men who will believe in you...but hide this mystery and do not give it to all men, only to him who does all things which I have said to you in my commandments. This, therefore, is the true mystery of baptism for those whose sins are forgiven and whose misdeeds are blotted out. This is the baptism of the first offerings, which leads forth to the true place and to the place of light."

143. Then the disciples said to him, "Rabbi, reveal to us the mystery of the light of your Father, since we heard you say, 'There is a fire-baptism, and a baptism of the Holy Spirit of light, and there is a spiritual anointing (*chrism*) which leads the souls to the light-treasure.' Speak to us now of their mystery, so that we may inherit the kingdom of God."

Jesus said to them, "These mysteries about which you ask, there is no mystery higher, which will lead your soul to the light of lights, to the places of truth and the good, to the place of the holy of all holies, to the place in which there is neither female nor male, nor form in that place, but a continuing, indescribable light."

ADDITIONAL SELECTIONS IN PART II

41. Apollonios of Tyana (Philostratus, op. cit., VIII.7), see p. 290.

42. Moses (Philo, op. cit., II.288), see p. 344.

43. THE MARTYRDOM OF ZENO

(Diogenes Laertius, *Lives of Eminent Philosophers* 9.26;
trans. D.R. Cartlidge)

(Introduction: Zeno, the founder of the Stoic school
of Greek philosophy, was an older contemporary of Socrates,
coming to Athens from his native island of Cyprus around the
year 480 B.C.E. There are various conflicting stories of Zeno's
death. One common account relates that he lived to the extra-
ordinary age of 98 and finally strangled himself out of contempt
for his physical frailty. A more popular version, by the time
of Diogenes Laertius, had it that he was executed because of his
attempts to overthrow a (variously identified) local king.)

(Zeno) was a great man, both in respect to philosophy
and as a politician. His books, at any rate, are full of understanding. He was disposed to unseat the tyrant Nearchos --
others say, Diomedon -- and was arrested; thus says Herakleides
in "The Epitome of Satyros." At that time he was questioned
as to the identity of his fellow conspirators and concerning
the weapons which he was taking to Lipara. He named all of
the tyrant's friends, wishing to leave him without supporters.
Then he told the king he had something to whisper in his ear
about certain people. (When the king leaned over) he bit his
ear and did not let go until he was stabbed to death, suffering
the same death as Aristogeiton the killer of the tyrant.

Demetrios says, in "Men of the Same Name", that Zeno
bit off his (the king's) nose. Antisthenes says, in "Successions
of the Philosophers," that after he incriminated the tyrant's
friends he was asked by the tyrant if there were anyone else
(to indict). He answered, "You, the pestilence of the city!"
And to those standing by he said, "I am amazed at your cowardice,
that on account of the very things which I now endure you are
slaves of the tyrant." Finally he bit off his own tongue and
spat it at the tyrant. The citizens were so incited that
immediately they stoned the tyrant to death. The majority (of

135

authors) mainly agree in this. But Hermippos says Zeno was
thrown into a mortar and butchered.

44. THE DEEDS OF THE ALEXANDRIAN MARTYRS

(Introduction and translation, D.R. Cartlidge)

(Introduction: There appears to have been a literary tradition in the Hellenistic world about men who died upholding their principles in opposition to tyrannical rulers. According to numerous scholars, the fragments known as the *Acta Alexandrinorum* (Deeds of the Alexandrian Martyrs) belong to this tradition. There are only a few fragments of papyrus actually extant from this tradition. However, there is considerable evidence that many biographers, historians, and philosophers of the Hellenistic world used these "pagan acts" as source materials for their works. Such men as Diogenes Laertius, Dio Cassius, Epictetus and also many Christians (e.g., Clement, Tertullian) apparently knew this literature.

The *Deeds of the Alexandrian Martyrs* is of interest not only because it is an example of pagan martyr-literature, but also because it represents "the other side" of the running fight that went on between the Jews of Alexandria and the Greek citizens of that city from the first century B.C.E. down to the mid-third century C.E. Readers who, because of their upbringing, may tend to side with the Judaeo-Christian point of view in respect to pagan persecutions, will find these pieces quite revealing. The anti-semitic bias of these accounts is obvious. Recognizing this may help bring the equally biased Jewish and Christian descriptions of the "wicked pagans" into fairer perspective. The date of these stories extends up through the late second century C.E. They do not appear to have been influenced by Christian or Jewish martyrologies.)

1.   Appian

Appian was being led off (to be executed). He saw a corpse and said, "O corpse, when I go into my country I will say to Herakleian, my father...." While he was saying this, he turned and, seeing Heliodoros, he said, "Heliodoros, I am being led away; will you say nothing?" Heliodorus said, "To whom can we speak, we who have no one to hear? Go on, my boy, to die. It is a great honor for you to die for your sweet fatherland. Do not be despairing.".... The emperor called him back. The emperor said, "Now, do you not know to whom you are speaking?"

137

Appian: "I know: Appian speaks to a tyrant."

The emperor: "No. To an emperor."

Appian: "Do not say that. For it was fitting to your divine father Antoninus to be a real emperor. Listen. First, he was a philosopher; second, he despised riches; third, he loved good. To you is given the opposite of these things; you are tyrannical, not a lover of good, and uncouth."

Caesar ordered him to be killed. As Appian was being led away, he said, "Grant me one thing, Lord Caesar."

The emperor: "What?"

Appian: "Order that I be killed in my noble's clothing."

The emperor: "Granted."

Appian took his noble's headband and put it on his head, and he placed his (official boots) on his feet. Then he went out and shouted in the middle of Rome, "Come running, Romans. Behold a once-in-a-lifetime thing -- a city official and elder from Alexandria led to execution!" The guard immediately ran and told the emperor, saying, "Lord, do you sit still for this? The Romans are muttering about this."

The emperor: "About what?"

The consul: "About the execution of the Alexandrian."

The emperor: "Let him be brought back."

When Appian returned, he said, "Who was it who called me back as I was about to greet the grave and those who died before me; Theon and Isidoros and Lampon? Was it the senate or was it you, prince of outlaws?"

The emperor: "Appian, we are accustomed to bring maniacs and senseless men to their senses. You speak only as long as I permit you to speak."

Appian: "By your genius (guardian spirit), I am not crazy nor have I lost my senses; I am advising you of my rank and my privileges."

The emperor: "How?"

Appian: "As a noble and a city official (of Alexandria)."

The emperor: "Are you inferring that *we* are not of noble birth?"

Appian: "That I do not know. I am advising you of my noble rank and privileges."

The emperor: "Now you do not know....(break in the text).

Appian: "If you really do not know, I will show you...(text breaks off. Presumably, after more discourse, Appian is executed.)

2.   (The scene is a confrontation with Caesar (Trajan) about the Jews. The Alexandrians and the Jews set sail for Rome, each group took along its own Gods. The Alexandrians had a bust of Serapion. The text breaks off before we learn what the Jews had which represented their God. As the confrontation unfolds, it is clear that Trajan is sympathetic to the Jews.)

Trajan: "You (Alexandrians) must be anxious to die; you must have a contempt for death. Is that why you answer me so arrogantly?"

Hermaiskos: "But we *should* grieve because your council is filled with filthy Jews."

Caesar: "Behold, I say to you a second time, 'Hermaiskos, are you speaking contemptuously to me because you are confident (in the protection) of your (high) birth?"

Hermaiskos: "What contemptuous answer did I give, greatest ruler? Explain to me."

Caesar: "You made out that my council was (full) of Jews."

Hermaiskos: "So! The name of the Jews *is* noxious to you? You ought, therefore, to help your own people and not be an advocate for these unholy Jews."

After Hermaiskos said this, the bust of Serapis, which the Alexandrian elders had brought, suddenly began to sweat. Trajan was astonished when he saw it, and in a few moments crowds were in Rome making many cries and they were afraid, and fled into the high parts of the hills...(text breaks off.)

(*4 Maccabees*; trans. D.R. Cartlidge)

(Introduction: This little treatise claims to be a philosophical discussion of "pious reason" (1:1). The following selection is one of the author's examples of the way that this "pious reason" has triumphed in Israel's history. It is clear from the story that "pious reason" also means faith, and loyalty to the Jewish way of life. We include it to illustrate the Jewish belief that a righteous man's death could serve as a vicarious sacrifice to atone for the sins of less faithful. The setting is during the Maccabean revolt, 166-162 B.C.E. Antiochus Epiphanes IV, the Seleucid tyrant of Palestine, is portrayed as the villain who is trying to force the Jews to renounce their faith.)

5.1   The tyrant Antiochus, with his court, sat upon a certain high place, and, with his fully armed troops around him,   2. he commanded his personal guards to drag in each one of the Jews, and he ordered the Jews to eat pig's meat and foods offered to idols.   3. If any should refuse to eat the abominable meats, they were to be tortured and killed.
4. After many had been forcibly seized, one of the first of the group, an old man named Eleazar who was a priest and trained in the Law's knowledge, who was also well-known to many in Antiochus' court because of the high esteem in which he was held by his own people, was brought before Antiochus.

(Vss. 5-38. Antiochus asks Eleazar to save his own life by eating the pig's meat because the meat is a gift of Nature, and one should not reject Nature's gifts. Besides, God will forgive such a sin done under duress. Eleazar refuses to eat the profane flesh and challenges Antiochus to do his worst.)

6.1   The guards dragged Eleazar roughly to the torturing place.   2. First, they stripped the old man, so that he was dressed only in the honorable clothes of piety.   3. Then, binding both his arms, they whipped him.   4. "Obey the king's commands!" cried a herald standing by.   5. But the confident

and well-born man, truly an Eleazar,[1] was no more shaken than
if he were being tortured in a dream. 6. He kept his eyes
raised up to Heaven, as his old man's flesh was torn by the
lashes; he was dripping blood, and his sides were gashed.
7. When he fell to the ground because his body could not stand
the pain, he still kept his reason unbowed and upright. 8. One
of the cruel guards kicked him savagely in the side with his
foot to make him get up, 9. but he endured the pain and
despised the force and persevered in spite of the torture.
10. Like a brave athlete, the old man endured the pain.
11. His face was covered with sweat and he was panting; the
nobility of his soul astonished his torturers.

12. Then, partly because of compassion for his old
age, partly out of sympathy because of their former friendship,
13. and partly from astonishment at his courage, some of the
king's men came to him and said, 14. "Why do you irrationally
destroy yourself in this awful way, Eleazar? 15. Let us bring
you the boiled meats, but you only pretend to eat the pig's
meat, and save yourself."

16. Eleazar, as if his tortures were made more painful by their suggestion, cried out, 17. "No! May we children
of Abraham never rationalize so easily, so that with numbed
soul we play a part unfitting to us. 18. For if I should so
reverse myself after I have sought the truth up through my old
age, and have guarded lawfully the honor of such living, I
would be wholly irrational. 19. I would become a symbol of
impiety to the young, so that I would be an example that they
should eat defiled things. 20. It would be shameful if I
should live a little more time, and yet should be mocked by all
men during this little time for cowardice. 21. I would be
considered unmanly by the tyrant and I would not have defended
the divine Law until death. 22. Therefore, O children of
Abraham, die nobly for piety! 23. Guards of the tyrant, why
do you hesitate?"

---

[1]In Hebrew, the name means 'God is my helper'.

24. When they saw his greatness in the face of the tortures and that he was unwavering before their compassion, they dragged him to the fire. 25. There they threw him on it, burning him with torture devices, and they poured evil smelling liquids into his nostrils. 26. When the fire burned to his bones and he was about to faint, he lifted his eyes to God and said, 27. "You know, O God, that I could be saved, but I am dying from fiery tortures for the sake of the Law. 28. Be merciful to your people; may my torture be a satisfaction on their behalf. Make my blood their cleansing,[1] and take my life as a substitute for theirs."[2] When he said this, the noble old man died from the torture, enduring torture unto death for the sake of the Law.

---

[1] From guilt of sin.

[2] His fidelity to the Torah *should* have been rewarded with peace and long life; here he offers his unwarranted death as a substitute to God for the many in Israel who deserved God's wrath for whatever reason.

46. MARTYRDOM OF POLYCARP

(Trans. D.R. Cartlidge)

(Introduction: Polycarp, bishop of Smyrna, was martyred in the first half of the second century A.D. This highly stylized and legendary account is from some time later, and shows clear indications of influence from the Martyrdom of Eleazar, which had become very popular in the Christian church. As in the earlier writing, Polycarp has been arrested and brought before the Roman official. He tries to get Polycarp to swear by the divinity of Caesar and to blaspheme Christ. Polycarp refuses. We pick up the account at this point.)

11.1   The proconsul said, "I have wild animals and I will deliver you to them unless you repent." Polycarp replied, "Call them, for a repentance from that which is better to that which is worse is forbidden us; but to change from evil to righteousness is good." 2. Again he said to him, "Since you are not afraid of the wild animals, I shall have you burned in fire, if you do not repent." But Polycarp said, "You threaten fire which burns for a while and goes out after a short time. For you are ignorant of the fire of the coming judgment and eternal punishment which is for the impious. Why do you wait? Do what you will."

12.1   He said these and many other words and was filled with joy and boldness, and his face was full of grace so that it not only did not fill with anxiety about what was said to him, but the proconsul was astonished, and he sent his herald into the midst of the arena to declare three times, "Polycarp confesses himself to be a Christian." 2. When this was said by the herald, the whole crowd of Gentiles and Jews who lived in Smyrna cried out loudly with uncontrollable anger, "This is the teacher of Asia Minor, the father of the Christians, who destroys our Gods, who teaches many not to sacrifice or to worship." They said this, and cried out, and asked Philip, the governor, to let

a lion attack Polycarp. But he said it was not legal to do
this, since the games were closed. 3. Then they all shouted
out together that Polycarp should be burned alive. For the
vision which had occurred to him earlier, during the night, when
he saw his pillow burning, had to be fulfilled. He turned to
those of the faithful with him and said prophetically, "I must
be burned alive."

13.1   These things happened very fast, quicker than the
telling. A mob quickly formed and from the workrooms and baths
they gathered sticks and firewood. The Jews were especially
eager to help in this, as usual. 2. When the pyre was prepared,
Polycarp removed all his clothes and loosened his belt and tried
to take off his sandals. He did not do this before because the
faithful were always making haste to see who could most quickly
touch his skin. For he had been shown consideration because of
his citizenship (in Heaven) even before his martyrdom. 3. At
once the instruments fitted for the fire were attached to him.
When they were about to nail him he said, "Leave me as I am,
for he who makes me able to endure the fire will give me strength
to remain in the fire without security from the nails."

14.1   They did not, therefore, nail him, but tied him. He
put his hands behind him and was tied, as a noble ram from a
great flock for a sacrifice offering, a whole burnt offering
ready and pleasing to God. He looked up into heaven and said,
"Lord God almighty, father of your beloved and blessed son,
Jesus Christ, through whom we have gained knowledge of thee,
God of angels and powers and all of creation, and of the whole
family of the righteous on earth, who live before you, 2. I
bless thee, because thou hast considered me worthy of this day
and hour, to partake, with the number of the martyrs, of the
cup of thy Christ, for the resurrection of life eternal in
both soul and body, in the immortality of the Holy Spirit.
May I be received in their number today, a living and acceptable

sacrifice to thee, for thou hast prepared and revealed and
fulfilled (this), who art the truthful and true God. 3. Because of this I praise thee for all things, I bless thee, I
glorify thee through the eternal and heavenly high priest,
Jesus Christ, thy beloved child, through whom be glory to thee
with him and the Holy Spirit, now and in the world to come, Amen."

15.1   When he had sent forth his "amen" and completed the
prayer, the men in charge of the fire lit it. A great flame
flared up, and we saw a miracle, we to whom it was given to see.
We have been kept from harm to report to the rest of you what
happened. 2. For the fire seemed to form the shape of a chamber, like the sail of a ship filled with wind, and it surrounded
the body of the martyr in a circle. He was in the middle of it,
not as burning flesh, but as baking bread, or as gold and silver
being refined in a furnace. For indeed, we perceived a sweet
smell, such as the breath of incense or some other rare spice.

16.1   Finally, the lawless men saw that his body could not
be destroyed by the fire, and they ordered the executioner to
go to him and to stab him with a dagger. When he did this, a
dove came out and much blood, so that the fire was extinguished.
The whole crowd marvelled that there was so much difference
between the unbelievers and the elect. 2. And he really was
one of the elect, this most marvelous martyr Polycarp, who in
our time was an apostolic teacher and prophet, the bishop of
the Catholic Church (*katholikēs ekklēsias*) in Smyrna.

47. THE MARTYRDOM OF RABBI AKIBA

(bBerakoth 61b.; trans. D.L. Dungan)

(Introduction: Akiba ben Joseph is one of the most revered names in all of Jewish history, ranking in importance with Moses and Maimonides. It was due to Akiba's leadership in the black days after the destruction of the Second Temple, 70 C.E., that the legal and religious foundations were laid for Israel's long years of Expatriation. On the other hand, Akiba was partly the cause of the Jewish exile as well. For, despite the Roman warning against fomenting insurrection, in 132 he openly proclaimed Simeon ben Cosiba (bar Kokhba) to be the King Messiah, the Liberator of Israel, and thus helped spark a full-fledged rebellion which lasted for three frenzied years. After that, the Romans enacted the hateful decree renaming Jerusalem "Aelia Capitolina," and closing it to Jews forever. Indeed, this historic exclusion was not completely overcome until the recent recapture of the Arab sector of Jerusalem during the six-day war of 1967.

In any case, some time during the fourth or fifth century, long after the tumultuous events of the Bar Kokhba rebellion had subsided, the rabbinic sages in exile in Babylon were examining the meaning of the phrase in Deut. 6:5 "Thou shalt love the Lord thy God with all thy heart, etc." This phrase reminded them of the occasion of R. Akiba's death at the hands of the Romans, for R. Akiba had taught, "'Thou shalt love the Lord thy God...with all thy soul' -- that is, even if He takes away thy soul (=life)." The following excerpt contains the Babylonian sages' memory of how Akiba lived up to his own teaching.)

Our rabbis tell of the time when an evil Kingdom (Rome) forbade Israel to be occupied with Torah. Rabbi Pappos ben Yehudah went and found Rabbi Akiba gathering people (openly) in the streets and instructing them in Torah. He said to him, "Akiba, are you not afraid of the evil kingdom?" He said to him, "I will tell you a parable. To what is it (our situation) similar? It is like a fox who was walking along the bank of the river, watching fishes grouping themselves, first in this spot, then in that. He said to them, "From what are you flee-ing?" They said to him, "From the nets which the sons of man (*benē ādām*) cast upon us." He said to them, "Quick! Come up

149

onto the shore and we will dwell, you and I, in the way my
fathers dwelt with your fathers." They said, "Are you not he
whom they call the smartest of all living things? You are not
smart but stupid! If we are afraid in the place where we can
live, how much more in the place where we would die?"

Not many days later, Rabbi Akiba was arrested and
put in jail. They also arrested Pappos ben Yehudah and
imprisoned him next to him. Akiba said to him, "Pappos, why
are you here?" He said, "Are you not blessed, Rabbi Akiba,
for you were arrested on account of the Torah! Woe to Pappos
who was arrested on account of nothing!"

When the Romans took Rabbi Akiba out to kill him, it
was the time of day appointed to recite the *Shema*.[1] As the
soldiers began to tear the living flesh off his bones with hooks
of iron, he began to recite the Shema. His disciples said to
him, "Master, even here?!" He said to them, "All the days of
my life I have been worried by this verse 'with all thy soul' -
which means, 'even if He takes thy life.' I used to say to
myself, 'When will it be possible for me to fulfill it?' And
now the opportunity has come to me. Shall I not fulfill it?"
Thereupon he lengthened out saying "On-n-n-ne" until he died,
saying "One". A Voice came from Heaven (*bath qōl*) saying,
"Blessed are you, Rabbi Akiba, who died while saying 'One'."
But the angels standing before the Holy One, blessed be He,
said to Him, "Is that how you repay such devotion to Torah?
What about 'Deliver my soul from the wicked....from men, by
thy hand, O Lord'?"[2] He said to them, "'Their (i.e., the
wicked's) portion is (this) life (only).'"[3] A Voice came from
Heaven, saying, "Blessed are you, Rabbi Akiba, for your portion
is life in the Age to Come!"

---

[1] Deut. 6:4, "Hear O Israel. The Lord Thy God, The Lord is One."

[2] Psalm 14:13f.

[3] Psalm 14:13f., i.e., God's answer is a continuation of the
same psalm, only reading the second part with hidden meaning,
brought out in the text by means of the words in the parentheses

ADDITIONAL SELECTION IN PART II

48. Apollonios of Tyana (Philostratus, op. cit., VII),
    see pp. 287-288.

49. ASCENSION OF ROMULUS

(Ovid, *Metamorphoses* 14.805-851; Ovid, *Fasti* 2.481-509;
Livy, Book 1.16; intro. and trans., D.R. Cartlidge)

(Introduction: The ancient story that Romulus, the
legendary co-founder of Rome, was translated to heaven and
became a God was of great importance during the birth of the
Roman empire. Romulus was known, in legend, to have been a
total ruler. To be such also was the desire of the early emperors of Rome; they wanted total power in order to bring peace
to a chaotic political situation. Julius Caesar and Augustus
Caesar consciously sought to project themselves to the public
in such a way as to reflect the image of Romulus. Thus, Julius
was to be the "second founder" of Rome. However, the tyrannical
aspect of Romulus had to be moulded into the image of a Romulus
who was a "strong man" but who was benevolent and who had divine
sanction. Both Ovid and Livy write to that purpose. Ovid is
a poet and Livy a historian, but both were "friends of the
court." It is interesting to see how these two points of view
deal with the same traditions, which are probably from the poet
Ennius. Both exalt the empire, Roman military might, and ex-
pansionism.)

1. Ovid, *Metamorphoses* 14.805-851. (Ovid tells how
    Romulus brought peace to his kinsmen, and then ruled
    them in benevolent fashion until it was time to be
    taken up to be with the Gods.)

Equally to the two peoples (Roman and Sabine), Romulus,
you gave laws. Then, taking off his helmet, Mars spoke to the
father of Gods and men (Jupiter), saying, "The time is here,
father, because the Roman state is strong with a great foundation and does not depend on one man's protection, to give the
gift promised to me and (him) your noble grandson and to take
him from earth to place him in heaven. You once said to me in
the assembled council of the Gods, for I have remembered and
have marked your pious words in my mind, 'one there will be whom
you shall lift up into the blue heaven.' Let now the promise of
your words be made good." The Omnipotent One agreed and he hid
the sky with dark clouds and he terrified the earth with thunder
and lightning. Mars knew these were the ratified signs of the

153

booty promised to him, and, leaning on his spear, boarded his
chariot, the horses straining beneath the bloody yoke, and,
with a blow of the lash, he shattered the air. Gliding down
through the air, he came to rest on the top of the wooded
Palatine hill. There, Romulus was giving his friendly laws to
the citizens, and Mars caught Ilia's son up. His mortal body
became thin, dissolving in the air, as a lead pellet shot by a
broad sling will melt in the sky. Suddenly a beautiful form
more worthy of the high couches (of the Gods), is the form of
Quirinius, who is now wearing a sacred robe.

     (Later,) his wife was mourning him as dead, when
queenly Juno ordered Iris to descend to Hersilia by her arching
way, to speak thus to the widowed queen, "O woman of Latium
and of the people of the Sabines, glorious, most worthy of all
to have been the consort of so great a man, now to (continue to)
be the wife of Quirinius, stop your crying, and, if you wish to
see your husband, follow me to the sacred grove which is on the
hill of Quirinius and which shades the temple of the king of
Rome." Iris obeyed and gliding to the earth through her sacred
(rainbow) arch, she summoned Hersilia in the words commended to
her. Hersilia scarcely raised her eyes and, with a shy look,
said, "O Goddess, for I dare not say who you are, but it is
clear you are a Goddess, lead, O lead, and show me my husband's
face. If the Fates grant me to be able somehow to see it, I
will have gained Heaven." Immediately, she went to Romulus'
hill with the virgin daughter of Thaumas. (When she got) there,
a star from Heaven (*ab aethere*) glided down to earth. With her
hair flaming from the star's light, Hersilia, with the star, goes
up into the sky. The founder of Rome's city receives her with
familiar hands and changes her mortal body and former name.
He calls her Hora, and now as a Goddess, she is united once
more with Quirinius.

2.   Ovid, *Fasti* 2.481-509. (The story is, of course,
            the same, but with some slight difference in the
            emphasis placed upon details. Here, the story of
            Romulus' murder of Remus is briefly mentioned.
            Gradivus (Mars) asks Jupiter to honor his pledge,
            "Although the other is lost, the one who is left will
            be enough for me and for Remus (1. 485-6)." Jupiter
            agrees.)

"With Jupiter's assent, both poles (of the earth)
shook, and Atlas moved the burden of the sky. There is a place,
called by the old ones the marsh of Caprea. By chance, Romulus,
you were there giving laws. The sun disappeared, and rising
clouds obscured the sky, and a heavy rain shower fell. Then it
thundered, the air was torn by flames. The people fled, and
the king (Romulus) flew to the stars on his father's (Mars')
horses. There was grieving, and falsely certain senators were
charged with murder, and that belief might have stuck in the
people's mind. But Proculus Julius was coming from the Alba
Longa; the moon was shining, he was not using a torch. Suddenly
the hedges on the left shook and moved. He shrank back and his
hair stood on end. Beautiful and more than human and clothed
in a sacred robe, Romulus was seen, standing in the middle of
the road. He said, "Stop the (Romans) from their mourning;
do not let them violate my divinity (*numina*) with their tears;
order the pious crowd to bring incense and worship the new
Quirinius, and to cultivate the arts of their fathers, war."
He gave the order and he vanished into the upper world from
before Julius' eyes.

3.   Livy, Book 1.16.

"...when he (Romulus) was holding a maneuver in order
to review the army at the camp near the marsh of Caprea, suddenly
a storm arose, with great lightning and thunder, and it veiled
the king by such a dense cloud that his form was hidden from
the troops; from that time Romulus was not on earth. The

terrified Roman soldiers were finally quieted after the sunlight
came back and restored calm and serenity following that hour of
wild confusion. But, even so, they remained silent and sad for
a long time, as if stricken by the fear of being orphaned, although they readily believed the senators standing nearest him who
said that Romulus had been taken up on high by the storm. Then
at first a few, then all, joyfully declared Romulus, the king
and father of the city of Rome, to be a God, the son of a God.
They asked (him) with prayers for peace; so that he would always
be pleased to wish favor for his children. I believe there
were some even then who argued secretly that the king had been
torn apart by the hands of the senators. Indeed, this rumor
spread also, but very obscurely; the other version was enhanced
by men's admiration for Romulus and their panic. Further, the
strategem of one man is said to have added to the credibility
of the story. For, when the citizens were disturbed by the loss
of the king and were hostile toward the senators, Julius Proculus, as it is told, a man of repute (at least he was the author
of this important thing) addressed the assembly. "Romulus
Quirites," he said, "the father of this city, at the first
light of this day, descended from the sky and clearly showed
himself to me. While I was awed with holy fright, I stood
reverently before him, asking in prayer that I might look at
him without sin. 'Go', he said, 'announce to the Romans that
Heaven wishes that my Rome shall be the capital of the earth;
therefore, they shall cultivate the military; they shall know
and teach their descendants that no human might can resist
Roman arms.' He said this, and went away on high." It is a
great marvel what credence was generated by the man's tale, and
how the loss of Romulus, for which the common people and the
army grieved, was assuaged by the belief in his immortality.

50. THE "TRANSLATION" OF KALLIRROE

(Chariton, *Chaireas and Kallirroe* 3.3;
intro. and trans., D.R. Cartlidge)

(Introduction: This passage is in a book which is
one of the first novels in the western world. The piece is
difficult to date, but is probably as early as the first century B.C.E. The plot of the novel is as complicated as a
soap opera. Kallirroe is not dead. She was kicked by
Chaireas, her jealous husband. She fainted, and everyone
thought she was dead. After she was entombed with pomp,
grave robbers entered the tomb, found her alive, and stole
her away.)

The grave robbers closed the tomb carelessly; they
were careless in the night. Chaireas was guarding and toward
dawn he approached the tomb, supposedly to bring crowns and
jewels, but really he had in mind to kill himself. For he did
not admit that he was unbetrothed from Kallirroe, and he considered death to be the only healer of grief. When he came
close, however, he found the stones moved away and the entrance
open. He looked in and was shocked, seized by a great perplex-
ity at what had happened. Rumor made an immediate report to
the Syracusans about the miracle. All then ran to the tomb;
no one dared to enter until Hermokrates ordered it. One was
sent in and he reported everything accurately. It seemed
incredible -- the dead girl was not there. Then Chaireas
thought *he* ought to see again the dead Kallirroe; but when he
searched the tomb, he was able to find nothing. Many came in
after him, disbelieving. Amazement seized everyone, and some
said as they stood there, "The shroud has been stripped off,
this is the work of grave robbers; but where is the body?"
Many gossips and rumor-mongers were busy in the multitude.
But Chaireas looked up to Heaven and stretched forth his hands,
"Who of the Gods, being my rival, has carried off Kallirroe

157

and now has her with him, not by her will, but rather forcing
her by a destiny more powerful (than human desire)? Perhaps
because of this she died suddenly, so that she should not
know (pain). Thus Dionysos snatched up Theseas' Ariadne and
Zeus, Semele. For I knew that I had a woman who was better
than we (mortals). But it certainly was not necessary so
suddenly and for such a reason to take her from the human
scene. Thetis was a goddess, but she remained with Peles,
and he had a son from her. But I was deserted at the climax
of passion. Why do I suffer? Why am I the unfortunate one?
Shall I kill myself? With whom shall I be buried? For I
have the hope of union with her! If I did not have a common
bedroom with Kallirroe, I shall find a common tomb with her!"

51. THE DREAM OF SCIPIO

(Cicero, *The Republic* 6.9-26; trans. T.B. Curtis)

(Introduction: Few statesmen in the Roman period combined the extraordinarily turbulent, high-level legal and political career and voluminous literary productivity that M. Tullius Cicero achieved. His life (106-43 B.C.) encompassed the final years of Rome's republican form of government, as it collapsed into anarchy, opportunism, and autocracy. Cicero hated the new class of political demagogues, as he considered them, and spent the last decades of his life combatting them, only to fall victim to the forces of Marc Antony. His life-long ideal was the old, aristocratic republicanism, and *The Republic*, his greatest political writing, was devoted to expounding its virtues. Cicero chose as the spokesman for these views in *The Republic* a Roman of the old type, a statesman and general of the previous generation from one of Rome's most illustrious families, Publius Cornelius Scipio Africanus the Younger. He carries the main burden of expounding the various subjects throughout the dialogue: the best form of government, Rome's political history, the ideal statesman (or, as we would say, politician), the nature of civil justice, and so forth. But the actual Scipio, despite his high birth, early military success, and political abilities, was never able to cause the Roman Senate to return to the austere, simple ways of the early Republic, and his efforts to do so earned him many enemies (especially Tiberius Gracchus, whose sister was Scipio's wife). He was finally murdered, and the Senate did not seek overly hard to find the culprits, although there were some obvious candidates. Thus it should be noted that Cicero's choice of principal spokesman would have had a startling poignancy for those among Cicero's circle of friends who agreed with his old-time republicanism. And the final scene of his long, six-book "conversation", namely, this "dream" of Scipio's in which Scipio is apotheosized, or brought up to the level of the Gods, looking first into the future and then into Eternity, this scene would have seemed to the same audience a most moving and sublime conclusion to the whole work. Even today, we can still catch the profound melancholy undertone running throughout, for, despite the eternal bliss promised to honorable men like Scipio, the world of men within which he is told to strive to be honorable is considered a realm of complete futility.)

9.   After arriving in Africa, where, as you know, I was

military tribune of the fourth legion under the consul Manius

Manilius, my first desire was to meet King Masinissa, who for

good reasons was on friendly terms with our family.[1] When I
met him, the old man burst into tears and embraced me. Some-
time after, he looked up to Heaven and said, "To you most
glorious Sun and to you other Inhabitants of Heaven I give
thanks that before I depart this life, I behold within my
kingdom and in these halls Publius Cornelius Scipio, whose
very name gives me new life; so enduring to me is the memory
of that most excellent and invincible man."[2] Then I questioned
him about his kingdom and he in turn asked me about our state,
and thus we spent the entire day in protracted conversation.

10.   Later, after we had been entertained with royal
splendor, we continued our conversation far into the evening;
during this time the old man talked of nothing but Africanus,
recalling not only all his deeds but his every word. When we
departed to rest, a deeper sleep than usual came upon me, as
I was weary from my journey and it was late. I had the following dream, induced, I imagine, by what we had been discussing
earlier; for it often happens that our thoughts and words
produce some such effect in sleep, as Ennius recounts with
respect to Homer, of whom he often used to think and speak
while awake. I dreamed that Africanus was beside me in the
form that I knew from his ancestral bust rather than from his
person. I shuddered when I recognized him, but he said, "Calm
yourself and don't be afraid; commit to memory what I say.

11.   "Do you see that city (from a high vantage point that
was radiant with stars, he was pointing to Carthage) which,

---

[1] P. Cornelius Scipio the Younger had gone in 149 B.C. to
Africa (=Carthage) as a young tribune to take part in the Third
Punic War. There he rejoined an old ally of the Romans, King
Masinissa, who had fought at the side of Scipio's grandfather
and namesake, P. Cornelius Scipio Africanus the Elder, the
Roman general who inflicted the decisive defeat on Carthage to
end the Second Punic War.

[2] I.e., P. Cornelius Scipio the Elder.

though forced by me to submit to the Roman people, is renewing
its former wars and cannot be at peace, to besiege which you
now come, though not yet a full-fledged soldier? Within two
years you shall be consul and shall overthrow Carthage, and you
shall earn by your deeds the surname which you now have as an
inheritance from me. When you have destroyed Carthage and have
conducted a triumph, you shall be made censor; in the capacity
of legate you shall go to Egypt, Syria, Asia and Greece; you
shall be chosen consul a second time in your absence; you shall
successfully conclude a great war; and you shall destroy
Numantia.[1] But when you ride in state to the Capitol you shall
find a republic in turmoil owing to the counsels of my grandson.[2]

12.   "At this time, Africanus, you must show our country
the light of your spirit, your character, and your judgment.
But here I see that the paths of the fates, as it were, are
uncertain. For when your life has accomplished seven times
eight revolutions of the sun, and these two numbers, each of
which for a different reason is regarded as perfect, in Nature's
course have made ready for you the time alloted by the fates,
the whole state will turn to you and your name alone; the senate,
all the optimates, our allies, the Latins all will look to you,
upon you alone the safety of the state will depend, and, in
short, you will be called upon as dictator to restore order to
the republic, provided that you escape the impious hands of
your kinsmen."[3]

---

[1] All these "predictions" Scipio the Younger actually achieved.

[2] I.e., Tiberius Gracchus, the founder of the reform party.

[3] This "prediction" is largely gratuitous, for Cicero is
heightening the pathos of Scipio's untimely death, which was
brought about, perhaps with the aid of his own relatives, before
he reached the pinnacle of his career. This is the reason for
the other's groans--the "prediction" of Scipio's untimely death
evokes sadness from his listeners--much as if someone were to
portray a person predicting to the young John F. Kennedy his
own glorious political future and sudden assassination.

        At this juncture Laelius broke into sobs and the others
groaned deeply, but Scipio said, smiling gently, "Hush, please
don't awaken me; hear me out."

13.   "But, Africanus, bear this in mind, in order that
you may be more zealous in the defense of your country, all who
have preserved, aided or advanced their country have a definite
place in Heaven where the blessed enjoy eternal life. For there
is no earthly happening which is more acceptable to that sovereign God who rules all the universe than the councils and
assemblies of men joined together by law, which are called
states; the rulers and preservers of these go from here and to
here they return."

14.   Though I was at this point thoroughly frightened, not
so much by the fear of death as by the thought of my friends'
plotting, I nevertheless asked whether he himself and my father
Paulus and the others whom we thought of as dead were still
alive. "Those are indeed alive," he said, "who have escaped
from the bondage of the body as from a prison; what you call
life is in reality death. Do you not see your father Paulus
coming toward you?" When I saw him I broke down in tears; he,
however, forbade me to weep, all the time embracing and kissing
me.

15.   When I had stopped my weeping and was able to speak,
I said, "If this is indeed life, my sacred and worthy father,
as Africanus tells me, why do I tarry upon earth? Why do I
not hurry to you here?"
        "It cannot be," said he, "for unless that God whose
realm is all that you survey free you from the prison of the
body, you cannot obtain access to this place. For man has been
created for this purpose, that he might tend that globe called
earth which you see in the middle of this region. And a soul
has been given him from the eternal fires that you call constellations and stars, which being spherical and round masses

animated with divine impulses, accomplish their cycles and
revolutions with amazing speed. Therefore you, Publius, and
all just men, must keep that soul in the care of the body, nor
must you depart life without the order of Him who gave you that
soul, lest you seem to have deserted the post assigned you
as mortal by God.

16.   "But like your father and grandfather, Scipio, cherish
justice and duty, which you assuredly owe your parents and
kinsmen, but most of all your country. Such a life is the path
to Heaven and to the assembly of those who have ceased to live
on earth and who, released from the body, inhabit the place
which you see," (it was the circle that gleamed with the greatest
brilliance among the stars) "which you, after the Greeks, call
the Milky Way."

When I looked about from there, all else seemed
beautiful and wonderful. There were stars which we never saw
from earth and the magnitude of each was such as we never
imagined. The smallest star was that farthest from heaven and
nearest the earth which shone with borrowed light. The globular
masses of the stars, however, far surpassed the size of the
earth. Furthermore, the earth itself seemed to me so small
that I felt contempt for our empire which covered, as it were,
a tiny patch on its surface.

17.   While I was gazing still more closely at the earth,
Africanus said, "How long will you fix your mind upon the
earth? Do you not see what quarters you have entered? The
whole is connected by nine circles, or rather spheres. One of
them which is the outermost is that of Heaven; it encloses all
the rest; it is the supreme God himself, holding and containing
the other spheres; in it are fixed the endless revolving courses
of the stars. Under it there are seven other spheres which
revolve in a direction opposite to that of Heaven. One of these
globes is occupied by that star which men on earth call Saturn.

Next is that dazzling star called Jupiter which is beneficial
and healthful to mankind. Then there is that red star,
terrible to the earth, which you call Mars. The next region
below almost midway between Heaven and earth contains the sun;
he is the leader, chief and director of the other lights, the
mind and regulating power of the universe, of such magnitude
that he illuminates and fills all things with his light. He is
followed by Venus and Mercury, as satellites in their orbits,
and in the lowest sphere revolves the moon set on fire by the
rays of the sun. Beneath the moon there is nothing but what
is mortal and perishable except the souls given to the human
race by the kindness of the Gods. Above the moon all things
are eternal. For the earth which is the ninth and central
sphere is immovable and the lowest, and all bodies by their
natural downward tendency are drawn toward it."

18.   After recovering from my amazement at seeing all
these marvels, I said, "What is that sound so loud and yet so
sweet which fills my ears?" "That melody," said he, "composed
in unequal time which nevertheless is divided into exact harmony is caused by the impulse and motion of the spheres themselves, and by tempering high with low notes it produces varied
harmonic effects; for such great motions cannot be hurried on
in silence and nature declares that one extreme produce a low
tone and the other a high. For this reason that highest sphere
of the starry heaven whose revolving is more rapid, is stirred
with a high and quick sound; while the lowest sphere, that of
the moon, is stirred with the lowest sound; for the earth, the
ninth sphere, remains motionless and in one position, occupying
the center of the universe. The remaining eight spheres, two
of which possess the same velocity, produce seven sounds at
different intervals, which number is the key of almost everything; and learned men by imitating this harmony with stringed
instruments and by singing have discovered for themselves a
way for their return to this place as others have done who,

endued with brilliant intellect, have cultivated divine pursuits
during their mortal lives. Men's ears filled with this sound
have become deaf, for you have no duller sense. Thus the people
who live near the place where the Nile rushes down from the
lofty mountains at the spot called Catalupa have lost their
sense of hearing because of the loudness of the sound. But
this sound produced by the swift revolution of the whole universe is so great that human ears cannot comprehend it, just
as you cannot look directly at the sun because your sense of
sight is overcome by its rays." While gazing at these scenes
in awe, I nevertheless kept turning my eyes back toward the
earth.

19.   Then Africanus said, "I see that even now you are
contemplating the abode and home of men; if it seems small to
you, as it really is, keep your eyes on these celestial things,
and despise the earthly. For what renown can you win from the
speech of men, or what glory that is worth the striving for?
You see that men inhabit only a few, tiny portions of the earth
and that between these spots, as it were, there are vast wilder-
nesses. And those who inhabit the earth are so cut off from
one another that there can be no communication among them, but
some inhabit areas of the earth that are oblique, transverse,
and even opposite you; from such you surely can expect no glory.

20.   "You are to notice that the same earth is encircled
and encompassed, as it were, by certain zones of which the two
that are the farthest from one another, under the poles of the
Heavens, are stiff from the frost, whereas the central and
largest zone is parched by the heat of the sun. Two zones are
habitable, of which the southern (whose inhabitants set their
footprints in a direction opposite to yours) has no connection
with your race. As for the northern zone which you inhabit,
see what a small portion of it is yours. For all the earth
that you inhabit, narrowing at the poles and broadening from
east to west, is but a little island surrounded by that sea

which you on earth call the Atlantic, the Great Sea, or Ocean;
and yet its great name notwithstanding, you see how small it
is. Has your renown or that of any of us been able to leave
these civilized and inhabited lands and cross the Caucasus
Mountains there, which you see, or swim the Ganges? What in-
habitant of the rest of the east or of the distant tracts of
the setting sun or the remote north or south will hear your
name? Moreover, how long will those who speak of us continue
to do so?

21.   "Yet even if future descendants should desire to
transmit to their posterity the achievements of each of us,
which they have heard from their fathers, yet because floods
and conflagrations must occur at appointed times, we are unable
to win lasting glory, much less eternal. And of what consequence
is it if your name is on the lips of those born after you, when
your predecessors never mentioned you?

22.   "They were no less numerous and certainly better men;
especially as none of those who is able to hear our fame can
retain the memory of it for even one year? For men commonly
measure the year by the revolution of the sun, this is, of a
single star; but when all the stars return to the same point
from which they once set out, and bring back after long intervals
the same arrangement of all the heaven, then that truly can be
called a full year. I scarcely dare to say how many generations
of men are contained in such a year. For as once the sun
appeared to men to be eclipsed and extinguished, at the time
when the spirit of Romulus entered these realms, so whenever
the sun shall again be eclipsed in the same place and at the
same time, then you will know that all the constellations and
stars have been recalled to their starting point and that the
year is complete. But be assured that the twentieth part of
such a year has not yet elapsed.

23.   "Accordingly, if you have no hope of returning to this place, where great and preeminent men receive the objects of their aspirations, of what value is your fame among mortals which can scarcely last but a slight part of a single year? Therefore, if you will lift your eyes on high and gaze upon this abode and Heavenly Home, you neither will yield to the gossip of the vulgar nor rest your hopes on human rewards for your deeds; Virtue herself by her own charms should lead you on to true glory. Let others worry about what they may say of you, for talk they will. All such talk, however, is confined to the narrow regions which you see; none concerning any man has endured forever; rather does it die with the man and is erased in the forgetfulness of posterity."

24.   When he had spoken thus, I said, "Africanus, if indeed the path to Heaven lies open to those who have served their country well, though from youth I have followed in the footsteps of my father and yourself, yet now with so great a reward set before me I shall strive with much greater effort." He replied, "Do, indeed, strive and see that it is not you, but your body, that is mortal; for you are not the man that your human form reveals; but the soul of each man is his real self, not the human figure which the eye can see. Know, therefore, that you are a God, if indeed it is a God that has life, sensation, memory, and foresight, and that rules, directs, and moves that body over which it presides just as the sovereign God rules this universe; and just as the eternal God moves the universe which is in part perishable, so an eternal soul moves the frail body.

25.   "For that which is ever in motion, is immortal, but that which transmits motion to another object and is itself moved from another source must of necessity cease to live when the motion ends. Thus only that which moves itself never ceases to move, because it never forsakes itself; rather it is

the source and the cause of motion in other things that are moved. But this cause has no beginning, for all things proceed from a first cause, whereas it cannot be derived from anything else; for that would not be the first cause, if it were derived from another source. And if it never has a beginning, it certainly never has an end. For the first cause, if destroyed, cannot be reborn from any other source nor can it produce anything else itself, because everything must spring from an original source. It follows, therefore, that motion begins with that which is capable of self-motion; this moreover, can neither be born nor die; otherwise all Heaven must tumble down and all nature stop; nor will they have any force from which they can be set in motion again.

26.   "Since, therefore, it is plain that whatever moves itself is eternal, who can deny that this is the natural property of souls? For everything that is set in motion by an external impulse possesses no soul; but whatever has a soul is impelled by an inner motion of its own; for this is the peculiar nature and essence of a soul. Now if a soul alone of all things moves of itself, it assuredly has not been born and is immortal. Employ it in the noblest pursuits. And the noblest concerns are those assumed for the safety of your country; a soul stirred and trained by these pursuits will have a quicker flight to this abode, its own home; and this will be the faster, if even now, while imprisoned in the body, it reaches out and by contemplating what is beyond itself, detaches itself as much as possible from the body. For the souls of those who are devoted to the pleasures of the body and have become slaves to them, as it were, and who under the influence of the desires which are subservient to pleasure have violated the laws of Gods and men, such souls, when they have escaped their bodies, hover round the earth itself, and they do not return to this place until they have been tormented for many ages."

He departed; I awoke from sleep.

52. APOTHEOSIS OF ANTINOUS

(The Pincio Obelisk; Dio Cassius, *Roman History* 69.2;
Pausanius, *Description of Greece* 8.9.7-8; Eusebius,
Ecclesiastical History 4.8.2; Justin Martyr, *Apology*
1.29; Clement of Alexandria, *Protrepticus* 4;
trans. D.R. Cartlidge)

(Introduction: It was widely accepted practice to
worship the Roman Emperors as Gods, for just as in life so also
in the afterlife, they continued to wield great power for good,
among the peoples surrounding the Mediterranean Sea. It came
as something of a surprise, however, when the Emperor Hadrian
in the year 130 A.D. established a cult, not to himself, but
to his favorite slave Antinous, adding scandal to shock since
this slave had not only been the Emperor's pet companion and
lover, but he had died suddenly under very suspicious circumstances by accidental (?) drowning in the Nile. Nor did
Hadrian's immediate proclamation of the divinization of
Antinous, and founding temples for his worship, do much to
stem the wild rumors that began to circulate. Repercussions
of these events were still echoing a century later, when, for
example, the Christian theologian Origen of Alexandria considered outrageous the galling insult of his learned antagonist
Celsus, who said that the superstitious Christians had invented
a new God by divinizing the man Jesus in much the same way that
Hadrian had introduced a new deity by ordering everyone to
worship his dead lover.

The selections pertaining to the apotheosis of
Antinous are of three sorts: Hadrian's own sacred inscriptions
proclaiming Antinous to be Osiris, contemporary pagan comment,
and contemporary Christian comment.)

1.   Hadrian's Memorial to Antinous (the Pincio Obelisk)

(N.B. These inscriptions are very difficult to translate, being composed of extraordinarily confused heiroglyphic
phrases, written by someone who obviously knew little of the
ancient sacred language. But enough can be understood to make
some sense of them. The first of the four carvings is an
inscription dedicated to Hadrian himself; it is followed by
three others which are here given, on the basis of the German
translation by A. Erman.)

Antinous before Thoth

      Antinous the Holy, he grew up to be a beautiful
youth, while he...gladdened (?); his heart...as that of a
strong-armed man; he received the commands of the Gods as...
All the rituals of the priests of Osiris were repeated in
respect to him and all his...as unknown. When his book (?) was
going forth, the whole land was...and...never has anything
similar been done before to earlier persons as (is done) today,
(that is,) his altars, his houses, his titles...He breathes
the air of life. His glory is in the hearts of all men, like
that of the Lords of Hermopolis, the Lords of the hieroglyphs.
His soul grows young again as the...to their season, during
night and day, to each time and each...

      His love is in the hearts of his servants, his fear
(in) all [bellies], his praise is from all men, while they
praise him. He sits in the hall of truth. The excellent
Enlightened Ones in the company of Osiris in Te-zoser...give
him justification. They let his words remain in the whole
land, their heart is made joyful over him.

      He goes to every place where he wants to go. The
door-keepers of the realm of the dead give him every praise (?).
They unlock their locks; they open their doors before him, in
a million of millions of years, daily...his whole life-span,
[im]mortal.

Antinous before Amon

      Osiris Antinous, the Holy, who is in heaven, a...will
be in his place of...made, which names are after his name, for
the brave, who are in this land and the helmsmen and...of the
whole land and likewise all people, who know the place where
Thoth is while they...give, with wreaths on their head...with
all good things. One brings offerings there to his altars,
one lays fragrant divine offerings (?) before him daily, according to the customs (?)...He was extolled by the artists (?) of
Thoth as...his...; he goes in his place...the cities of all

lands, for he hears the pleas of those who call him. He heals
the sick...to him he sends a dream. He accomplishes his work
unto men (?); he does miracles (?)...his heart, because he is
a true offspring of divine seed...in his limbs (?)...body of
his mother (?). He would be...in the house of his birth of....

Antinous before (the carving cannot be deciphered)

     Antinous, who is in heaven, who rests in this place
which lies in the border field of the Goddess of the pleasures
(?) of Rome, he is known as God in the pious places of Egypt.
A temple was built to him; he became honored as a God by the
prophets and priests of Upper and Lower Egypt, by the residents
of Egypt, as many as there are of them. A city was named after
his name, the...soldiers of the Greeks and those who are in the
temples of Egypt, they come to his city...their...acres and
fields are given to them in order to make their life very beautiful. A temple of this God is therein, his name is "Osiris
Antinous the Holy": it (the temple) was built from beautiful
limestone, with sphinxes around it and statues and many columns
like those that in olden times had been made by the ancients
and likewise as had been made by the Greeks. Each God and
each Goddess gives to him the breath of life and he breathes
in a new youthfulness.

2.   Contemporary pagan comments

(Dio Cassius, *Roman History* 69.2)

     While Hadrian was in Egypt he rebuilt the city named
for Antinous. For Antinous was from the city of Bithynium, a
city in Bithynia, which was also called Claudiopolis. Antinous
was his darling boy, and he died in Egypt; he either fell into
the Nile as Hadrian writes or, what seems to be the truth, he
was offered as a sacrifice. As I said, Hadrian was very
interested in the magical arts and used all types of divinations
and incantations. Thus he gave divine honors to Antinous,

either because of his love for him or because he died voluntarily (it apparently was necessary for a life to be freely offered to accomplish what he [Hadrian] wanted). He built a city near the place where he died and he named it after him. He erected statues of him, actually sacred images, almost all over the world. Finally, Hadrian said he had seen a certain star which, it seemed to him, was that of Antinous and he welcomed the mythical stories of his friends; namely, that the star really was created from Antinous' soul and had just then appeared. He was ridiculed on account of these things and also because, when his sister Paulina died, he did not at once pay her any (divine) honors...

(Pausanius, *Description of Greece*, 8.9.7-8)

Antinous also was considered by them[1] to be a God. The temple of Antinous is the newest of the temples in Mantineia. He was a favorite of the Emperor Hadrian. I never saw Antinous personally, but I did see him in statues and pictures. He has sacred honors in other places, and an Egyptian city on the Nile is named after him. He holds the sacred honors in Mantineia for these reasons. Antinous was a native of Bithynia, beyond the Sangarius River. The Bithynians are Arcadians and Mantineians by descent. On account of this, the Emperor founded his worship in Mantineia, and mystic rituals are held for him each year as well as sacred games (in his honor) every fifth year.

There is a building in the gymnasium of Mantineia that has statues of Antinous. The building is marvellous to see because of the jewels with which it is decorated and especially because of its pictures. Most of them are of Antinous who is pictured to look like Dionysus...

---

[1]Pausanius is describing the various deities worshipped in Mantineia, a city of Greece, southwest of Corinth.

3.   Contemporary Christian comments

(Eusebius, *Ecclesiastical History* 4.8.2)[1]

...To such men they made cenotaphs and temples even
up to the present. Among them is also Antinous, a slave of the
Emperor Hadrian. For him the Antinoan games are held, even
though he was our contemporary. And Hadrian created a city
named for Antinous, and ordained prophets (for him).

(Justin Martyr, *Apology* 1.29)

We think it is not improper to mention among these
things also Antinous, our contemporary, whom everyone was
coerced to worship as a God on account of fear, although they
knew who he was and where he came from.

(Clement of Alexandria, *Protrepticus* 4)

In Egypt there is another new God since the Roman King
Hadrian reverently worshipped as divine his lover Antinous, an
exceedingly beautiful boy, to whom he was devoted, after the
Greek fashion, like Zeus was to Ganymede,[2] for lust is not
easily prevented if it has no fear; and now men celebrate the
"Sacred Nights of Antinous", in which those who love shameful
things lawlessly stay awake together. Why do you choose for
me a God who is to be honored by fornication? And why have you
appointed him to be mourned as a son? And why do you go on and
on about his beauty? That shameful beauty is withered by wan-
tonness. Do not become a tyrant, my friend, nor act wantonly
with the beauty of young boys just grown of age; keep it pure,

---

[1] Eusebius is quoting Hegesippus, a Christian writer contemporary with Hadrian. See further for other Christian references, H. Chadwick, *Contra Celsum* (1953) p. 152 n. 1.

[2] Zeus carried away to be his lover the beautiful little
Trojan prince, Ganymede, giving his father in return some
remarkable horses; *Iliad* 5.265.

in order that it may be beautiful....But now there is a grave
for Hadrian's lover, as well as a temple and a city of Antinous,
for graves are held in awe by the Egyptians like shrines; pyra-
mids and mausoleums and labyrinths and other shrines of the
dead--as if they were the graves of their Gods.

ADDITIONAL SELECTIONS IN PART II

PART II

GOSPELS AND BIOGRAPHIES

58. THE COPTIC GOSPEL OF THOMAS

(Trans. D.R. Cartlidge)

(Introduction: This Gospel was found in 1946,
included among dozens of manuscripts from an ancient Coptic
monastic library near the modern town of Nag Hammadi, located
in upper Egypt. The manuscript is not earlier than the 4th
century, although the contents are surely older. It is generally thought by historians that the Gospel of Thomas origi-
nated in Syria and that both Greek version and Coptic version
(from which this translation was made) are translations from
the Syriac. There is a lively controversy at present over the
question whether the Gospel of Thomas is a writing which is
based on a Coptic translation of the Synoptic Gospels, or
whether the Gospel of Thomas is based on a tradition entirely
independent of the Synoptics, in which case some of its sayings
may be more authentic than those now found in our canonical
Gospels. The debate centers particularly around the parables,
as Thomas records them.)

These are the secret words which the living Jesus spoke and
Didymos Judas Thomas wrote them down.

1.   And he said, "He who finds the meaning of these words
will not taste death."

2.   Jesus said, "The one who seeks must not cease seeking
until he finds, and when he finds, he shall be troubled, and if
he is troubled, he will marvel, and he will rule over the All."

3.   Jesus said, "If the ones who lead you say, 'There is
the kingdom, in heaven,' then the birds will go first before
you into heaven (or--the birds of heaven shall go before you).
If they say to you, 'It is in the sea,' then the fish shall go
before you. Rather, the kingdom is within you and outside you.
If you know yourselves, then you will be known, and you will
know that you are sons of the living Father. But if you do not
know yourselves, then you are in poverty and you are poverty."

4.   Jesus said, "The man old in his days will not hesitate
to ask a baby of seven days about the place of life, and he will
live. For many who are first shall be last, and they shall
become a single one."

5.   Jesus said, "Know what is in front of your face, and
what is concealed from you will be revealed to you. For there
is nothing concealed which will not be manifest."

6.   His disciples asked him, "Do you want us to fast, and
how shall we pray, and shall we give alms, and what food regula-
tions shall we keep?" Jesus said, "Do not lie, and do not do
what you hate, because all is revealed before Heaven. For
nothing is hidden that shall not be revealed, and nothing is
covered that shall remain without being revealed."

7.   Jesus said, "Blessed is the lion which the man shall
eat, and the lion will become man; and cursed is the man whom
the lion shall eat, and the lion will become man."

8.   And he said, "The Man is like a wise fisherman who
threw his net into the sea. He drew it up from the sea; it
was full of small fish. The fisherman found among them a large,
good fish. He threw all the small fish back into the sea; he
chose the large fish without regret. He who has ears to hear,
let him hear."

9.   Jesus said, "Behold, the sower went out; he filled
his hand; he threw. Some fell on the road. The birds came;
they gathered them up. Others fell on the rock and did not
send roots into the earth and did not send ears up to heaven.
Others fell among thorns. They choked the seed and the worm
ate them (i.e., the seed). And others fell on good earth, and
it raised up good fruit to heaven. It bore sixty measures and
one hundred-twenty measures."

10.   Jesus said, "I have thrown fire on the world, and
behold, I guard it until it is on fire."

11.   Jesus said, "This heaven will pass away and your
heaven above it will pass away, and the dead do not live, and
the living will not die. In the days when you ate the dead,
you made it alive; when you come into the light, what will you
do? On the day when you were one, you became two. But when
you have become two, what will you do?"

12.   The disciples said to Jesus, "We know that you will
go away from us; who will become great over us?" Jesus said,
"To whatever place you have come, you will go to James the
righteous; heaven and earth came into being for him."

13.   Jesus said to his disciples, "Make a comparison and
tell who I am like." Simon Peter said to him, "You are like a
righteous angel." Matthew said to him, "You are like a wise
man." Thomas said to him, "Master, my mouth will not be able
to say what you are like." Jesus said, "I am not your master
because you drank; you are drunk from the bubbling spring which
I measured." And he took him; he went aside. He spoke to him
three words. When Thomas returned to his companions, they
asked him, "What did Jesus say to you?" Thomas said to them,
"If I tell you one of the words which he said to me, you will
pick up stones; you will throw them at me. And fire will come
from the stones and consume you."

14.   Jesus said to them, "If you fast, you will bring sin
upon yourselves and, if you pray, you will condemn yourselves,
and, if you give alms, you will do evil to your spirits. And
if you enter any land and wander through the regions, if they
receive you, whatever they set before you, eat it. Heal the
sick among them. For that which goes in your mouth will not
defile you, but that which comes out of your mouth is what will
defile you."

15.   Jesus said, "When you see him who was not born of
woman, throw yourself down on your face (and) adore him; that
one is your father."

16.   Jesus said, "Men might think I have come to throw
peace on the world, and they do not know that I have come to
throw dissolution on the earth; fire, sword, war. For there
shall be five in a house: three shall be against two and two
against three, the father against the son and the son against
the father, and they shall stand as solitaries."

17.   Jesus said, "I will give you what no eye has seen and
what no ear has heard and no hand has touched and what has not
come into the heart of man."

18.   The disciples said to Jesus, "Tell us in which way
our end will occur." Jesus said, "Have you found the beginning
that you search for the end? In the place where the beginning
is, there the end will be. Blessed is he who will stand at the
beginning, and he will know the end and he will not taste death."

19.   Jesus said, "Blessed is he who was before he was
created. If you become my disciples (and) you hear my words,
these stones shall serve you. For you have five trees in paradise which do not move in summer or winter and they do not shed
their leaves. Whoever knows them shall not taste death."

20.   The disciples said to Jesus, "Tell us, what the Kingdom of Heaven is like?" He said to them, "It is like a mustard
seed, smaller than all seeds. But when it falls on plowed
ground, it puts forth a large branch and becomes a shelter for
the birds of heaven."

21.   Mary said to Jesus, "Whom are your disciples like?"
He said, "They are like little children; they settle themselves

in a field that is not theirs. When the owners of the field come, they (the owners) say, "Give us our field." They undress before them and release it (the field) to them and give back their field to them. Because of this I say, if the owner of the house knows that the thief is coming, he will watch before he comes and will not let him break into his house of his kingdom and carry away his goods. But you watch especially for the world; gird your loins with great power lest the robbers find a way to come upon you, because the thing you expect, they will find. Let there be a man of understanding among you. When the fruit ripened, he came quickly, his sickle in his hand (and) he reaped it. He who has ears to hear, let him hear."

22.   Jesus saw children being suckled. He said to his disciples, "These children who are being suckled are like those who enter the Kingdom." They said to him, "We are children, shall we enter the Kingdom?" Jesus said to them, "When you make the two one, and when you make the inner as the outer and the outer as the inner and the upper as the lower, so that you will make the male and the female into a single one, so that the male will not be male and the female (not) be female, when you make eyes in the place of an eye, and hand in place of a hand, and a foot in the place of a foot, (and) an image in the place of an image, then you shall enter [the Kingdom]."

23.   Jesus said, "I shall choose you, one from a thousand, and two from ten thousand, and they shall stand; they are a single one."

24.   His disciples said, "Show us the place where you are, for it is necessary for us to seek it." He said to them, "He who has ears to hear let him hear. There is light within a man of light and he (or, it) lights the whole world. When he (or, it) does not shine, there is darkness."

25.   Jesus said, "Love your brother as your soul; keep him as the apple of your eye."

26.   Jesus said, "The chip that is in your brother's eye you see, but the log in your own eye you do not see. When you take the log out of your eye, then you will see to remove the chip from your brother's eye."

27.   "If you do not fast (in respect to) the world, you will not find the Kingdom; if you do not keep the Sabbath a Sabbath, you shall not see the Father."

28.   Jesus said, "I stood in the midst of the world, and I appeared to them in the flesh. I found all of them drunk; I did not find any of them thirsting. And my soul was pained for the sons of men because they are blind in their heart, and they do not see that they came empty into the world; they seek to go out of the world empty. However, they are drunk. When they have shaken off their wine, then they shall repent."

29.   Jesus said, "If the flesh exists because of spirit, it is a miracle, but if spirit (exists) because of the body, it is a miracle of miracles. But I marvel at how this great wealth established itself in this poverty."

30.   Jesus said, "Where there are three Gods, they are Gods; where there are two or one, I am with him."

31.   Jesus said, "A prophet is not acceptable in his own village; a physician does not heal those who know him."

32.   Jesus said, "A city they build and fortify upon a high mountain cannot fall, nor can it be hidden."

33.   Jesus said, "What you hear in your ear, preach in [others'] ear[s from] your housetops. For no one kindles

a lamp and puts it under a basket, nor does he put it in a hidden place, but he sets it on a lampstand so everyone who comes in and goes out will see its light."

34.   Jesus said, "If a blind man leads a blind man, the two of them fall into a pit."

35.   Jesus said, "It is impossible for one to enter the house of the strong man and rob it violently, unless he bind his hands; then he shall pillage his house."

36.   Jesus said, "Do not be anxious from morning to evening and from evening to morning about what you will put on yourselves."

37.   His disciples said, "On what day will you be revealed to us and on what day will we see you?" Jesus said, "When you undress without being ashamed, and you take your clothes and put them under your feet as little children and tramp on them, then you will see the Son of the Living (One) and you will not fear."

38.   Jesus said, "Many times you desired to hear these words which I say to you and you have no one else from whom to hear them. There will be days when you will seek me, and you will not find me."

39.   Jesus said, "The Pharisees and the Scribes took the keys of knowledge; they hid them. They did not enter, and they did not allow to enter those who wanted to enter. But you be wise as serpents and as innocent as doves."

40.   Jesus said, "A vine was planted without the Father and it has not strengthened; it will be pulled up by its roots (and) it will rot."

41.   Jesus said, "He who has in his hand, it shall be given to him; and he who does not have, even the little he has shall be taken away from him."

42.   Jesus said, "Be wanderers."

43.   His disciples said to him, "Who are you that you say these things to us?" "By what I say to you, you do not know who I am, but you have become as the Jews. They love the tree, they hate its fruit; they love the fruit, they hate the tree."

44.   Jesus said, "One who blasphemes the Father, it will be forgiven him, and one who blasphemes the Son, it will be forgiven him, but one who blasphemes the Holy Spirit, it will not be forgiven him, either on earth or in Heaven."

45.   Jesus said, "They do not pick grapes from among thorns, nor do they gather figs from among camel's thistles; they do not give fruit. F[or a go]od man brings forth good fr[om] his treasure; a b[ad] man brings forth evil from his evil treasure in his heart, and he speaks evil. For out of the abundance of his heart, he brings forth evil."

46.   Jesus said, "From Adam to John the Baptist, among those born of women, no one is greater than John the Baptist, so that his eyes...[here the text is uncertain]. But I said that whoever among you shall become as a child shall know the Kingdom, and he shall become higher than John."

47.   Jesus said, "A man cannot mount two horses; he cannot stretch two bows. A servant cannot serve two masters; either he will honor the one and the other he will scorn.... No man drinks old wine and right away wants to drink new wine; and they do not put new wine into old wineskins lest they tear, and they do not put old wine into new wineskins lest it spoil it.

They do not sew an old patch on a new garment, because there
will be a tear."

48.   Jesus said, "If two make peace between themselves in
the same house, they shall say to the mountain, 'Move away,'
and it will be moved."

49.   Jesus said, "Blessed are the solitary and the chosen,
because you will find the Kingdom; because you come from it,
you will again go there."

50.   Jesus said, "If they say to you, 'Where did you come
from?' say to them, 'We come from the light, where the light
came through itself. It stands [...] and reveals itself in
their image.' If they say to you, '(who) are you?' say to
them, 'We are his sons and we are the chosen of the living
Father.' If they ask you, 'What is the sign of your Father who
is in you?' say to them, 'It is a movement and a rest."

51.   His disciples said to him, "When will be the rest
of the dead and when will the new world come?" He said to
them, "What you look for has come, but you do not know it."

52.   His disciples said to him, "Twenty-four prophets
spoke in Israel and all of them spoke about you." He said to
them, "You have left the Living One who is before you and you
have spoken about the dead."

53.   His disciples said to him, "Is circumcision profitable or not?" He said to them, "If it were profitable, their
father would beget them circumcized from their mother. But
the true circumcision in the Spirit has found complete usefulness."

54.   Jesus said, "Blessed are the poor, for yours is the
Kingdom of Heaven."

55.   Jesus said, "He who does not hate his father and his mother cannot be my disciple and (he who) does not hate his brothers and his sisters and (does not) carry his cross in my way will not be worthy of me."

56.   Jesus said, "He who has known the world has found a corpse, and he who has found a corpse, the world is not worthy of him."

57.   Jesus said, "The Kingdom of the Father is like a man who had (good) seed. His enemy came by night, he sowed a weed among the good seed. The man did not let them pull up the weed. He said to them, 'Lest you go and pull up the weed and you pull up the wheat with it.' For on the day of the harvest the weeds will appear; they will pull them up and burn them."

58.   Jesus said, "Blessed is the man who has suffered; he has found the Life."

59.   Jesus said, "Look upon the Living One as long as you live, lest you die and seek to see him and you cannot see."

60.   (They saw) a Samaritan carrying a lamb; he was going to Judea. He said to his disciples, "Why does he carry the lamb?" They said to him, "That he may kill it and eat it." He said to them, "As long as it is alive he will not eat it, but (only) if he has killed it and it has become a corpse." They said, "Otherwise he cannot do it." He said to them, "You yourselves seek a place for yourselves in rest, lest you become a corpse and be eaten."

61.   Jesus said, "Two will be resting on a couch; the one will die, the one will live." Salome said, "Who are you, man? As if from the One (?) you sat on my couch and you ate from my table." Jesus said to her, "I am He Who Is, from Him Who is the Same. The things from my Father have been given to me."

(Salome said,) "I am your disciple." (Jesus said to her,) "Therefore, I say, if anyone should be the same (lit., deserted) he will be filled with light, but if he is divided, he will be filled with darkness."

62.   Jesus said, "I tell my mysteries to those who are worthy of my mysteries. What your right (hand) will do, do not let your left (hand) know what it does."

63.   Jesus said, "There was a rich man who had many goods. He said, 'I will use my goods so that I will sow and reap and plant and fill my warehouses with fruit so that I will not be in need of anything.' He said this in his heart. And in that night he died. He who has ears, let him hear."

64.   Jesus said, "A man had guests and when he had pre-pared the banquet, he sent his servant to invite the guests. He went to the first; he said to him, 'My master invites you.' He said, 'Money is owed me by some merchants. They will come to me in the evening; I will go and I will give them orders. Please excuse me from the dinner.' He went to another; he said to him, 'My master invited you.' He said to him, 'I bought a house and they ask me (to come out) for a day (to close the deal). I will not have time.' He went to another, he said to him, 'My master invites you.' He said to him, 'My friend is going to marry and I will prepare a dinner; I will not be able to come. Please excuse me from the dinner.' He went to another; he said to him, 'My master invites you.' He said to him, 'I have bought a town, I go to collect the rent. I will not be able to come. Please excuse me from the dinner.' The servant returned; he said to his master, 'Those whom you invited asked to be excused from the dinner.' The master said to his servant, 'Go outside to the streets, bring those whom you find so that they may feast.' Buyers and merchants will not enter the places of my Father."

65.   He said, "A good man had a vineyard. He gave it to
some farmers so that they would work it and he would receive its
profits from them. He sent his servant so that the farmers
would give him the profits of the vineyard. They seized his
servant, they beat him and almost killed him. The servant went
back; he told his master. His master said, 'Perhaps he did not
know them.' He sent another servant. The farmers beat the
other one. Then the master sent his son. He said, 'Perhaps
they will respect my son.' Those farmers seized him, they
killed him, since they knew he was the heir of the vineyard.
He who has ears, let him hear."

66.   Jesus said, "Show me the stone which those who built
rejected. It is the cornerstone."

67.   Jesus said, "He who knows the All, but lacks (i.e.,
does not know) himself, lacks everything."

68.   Jesus said, "Blessed are you when they hate you and
persecute you, and no place will be found where you have [not]
been persecuted."

69a.   Jesus said, "Blessed are those whom they persecuted
in their heart; these are they who knew the Father in truth."

69b.   "Blessed are those who are hungry, so that the belly
of him who hungers will be filled."

70.   Jesus said, "When you beget what is in you, him whom
you have, he will save you. If you do not have him in you, he
whom you do not have in you will kill you."

71.   Jesus said, "I shall destroy [this] house and no one
will be able to build it [again]."

72.   [A man] s[aid] to him, "Speak to my brothers so that they shall divide my father's possessions with me." He said to him, "O man, who made me one who divides?" He turned to his disciples, he said to them, "I am not one who divides, am I?"

73.   Jesus said, "The harvest is great, but the workers are few; but beseech the Lord to send workers to the harvest."

74.   He said, "Lord, there are many standing around the cistern, but no one in the cistern."

75.   Jesus said, "Many are standing at the door, but the solitary will enter the bridal chamber."

76.   Jesus said, "The Kingdom of the Father is like a merchant who had goods; he found a pearl. This was a prudent merchant. He gave up (i.e., sold) the goods, he bought the one pearl for himself. You also must seek for the treasure which does not perish, which abides where no moth comes near to eat, nor worm destroys."

77.   Jesus said, "I am the light which is above all of them, I am the All; the All came forth from me and the All reached me. Split wood, I am there; lift the stone up, you will find me there."

78.   Jesus said, "Why did you come to the field? To see a reed shaken by the wind? And to see a [man clo]thed in soft clothes? [Behold, your] kings and your great ones are clothed in soft (clothes) and they [shall] not be able to know the truth."

79.   A woman in the crowd said to him, "Blessed is the womb which bore you and the breasts which fed you." He said to (her), "Blessed are those who have heard the Word of the Father (and) have kept it in truth. For there will be days when you will

say: 'Blessed is the womb which has not conceived and the
breasts that have not suckled.'"

80.   Jesus said, "He who has known the world has found
the body, but he who has found the body, the world is not
worthy of him."

81.   Jesus said, "He who has become rich, let him become
king, and he who has power, let him renounce it."

82.   Jesus said, "He who is near me is near the fire, and
he who is far from me is far from the Kingdom."

83.   Jesus said, "The images are manifest to the man, and
the light in them is hidden in the image of the light of the
Father. He will reveal himself and his image is hidden by his
light."

84.   Jesus said, "When you see your likeness, you rejoice.
But when you see your images which came into being before you,
(which) do not die nor are manifest, how much you will bear!"

85.   Jesus said, "Adam came into existence from a great
power and a great wealth, and he was not worthy of you. For,
if he had been worthy, he [would] not [have tasted] death."

86.   Jesus said, "[The foxes have] h[oles] and the birds
have [their] nests, but the Son of Man does not have any place
to lay his head and to rest."

87.   Jesus said, "The body is wretched which depends on a
body, and the soul is wretched which depends on these two."

88.   Jesus said, "The angels and the prophets have come to
you and they will give you that which is yours and you give to

them what is in your hands, (and) say to yourselves, 'On which
day will they come and receive what is theirs?'"

89.   Jesus said, "Why do you wash the outside of the cup?
Do you not know that he who made the inside is also he who made
the outside?"

90.   Jesus said, "Come to me because my yoke is easy and
my mastery is gentle and you will find your rest."

91.   They said to him, "Tell us who you are so that we
can believe in you." He said to them, "You examine the face of
the heavens and the earth, and (yet) you have not known him who
is in front of your face, nor do you know how to examine this
time."

92.   Jesus said, "Search and you will find, but those
things which you asked me in those days, I did not tell you
then; now I want to speak them, and you do not ask about them."

93.   "Do not give what is holy to the dogs, because they
will throw it on the dung heap. Do not throw the pearls to
the pigs, lest they become...[text uncertain]."

94.   Jesus [said], "He who searches, will find...it will
open to him."

95.   Jesus [said], "If you have money, do not lend it at
interest, but give [to those] from whom you will not receive
it (back again)."

96.   Jesus [said], "The Kingdom of the Father is like a
woman, she took a bit of leaven, she hid it in dough, she made
big loaves. He who has ears let him hear."

97.   Jesus said, "The Kingdom of the [Father] is like a
woman who was carrying a jar which was full of meal. While
she was walking on a distant road, the handle of the jar broke;
the meal spilled out behind her onto the road. She did not
know; she was not aware of the accident. After she came to
her house, she put the jar down; she found it empty."

98.   Jesus said, "The Kingdom of the Father is like a man
who wanted to kill a powerful man. He drew the sword in his
house, he thrust it into the wall so that he would know if his
hand would stick it through. Then he killed the powerful one."

99.   The disciples said to him, "Your brothers and your
mother are standing outside." He said to them, "Those here who
do the will of my Father, they are my brothers and mother; they
will enter the Kingdom of my Father."

100.   They showed Jesus a gold (coin) and they said to him,
"Caesar's men demand taxes from us." He said to them, "Give
Caesar's things to Caesar; give God's things to God, and what
is mine give to me."

101.   "He who does not hate his [father] and his mother in
my way will not be able to be my [disciple] and he who does
[not] love his father and his mother in my way, will not be
able to be my [disciple], for my mother [according to the
flesh gave me death (conjecture: Quispel)], but [my] true
[mother] gave me life."

102.   Jesus said, "Woe to them, the Pharisees, for they
are like a dog lying in the food-trough of oxen, for he does
not eat, nor let the oxen eat."

103.   Jesus said, "Blessed is the man who knows in which
part (of the night) the robbers will come, so that he will rise
and gather his [...] and gird up his loins before they come in..

104.   They said [to him], "Come, let us pray today and let us fast." Jesus said, "Why? What sin have I committed, or by what (transgression) have I been conquered? But after the bridegroom has left the bridechamber, then let them fast and pray."

105.   Jesus said, "He who acknowledges his father and mother, will be called the son of a harlot."

106.   Jesus said, "When you make the two one, you shall be Sons of Man and when you say, 'Mountain, move away,' it will move."

107.   Jesus said, "The Kingdom is like a man, a shepherd, who had a hundred sheep. One of them, which was the largest, wandered off. He left the ninety-nine; he searched for the one until he found it. After he tired himself, he said to the sheep, 'I love you more than the ninety-nine.'"

108.   Jesus said, "He who drinks from my mouth will be as I am, and I will be he, and the things that are hidden will be revealed to him."

109.   Jesus said, "The Kingdom is like a man who had a treasure [hidden] in his field, and he did not know it. And [after] he died, he left it to his son. His son did not know, he received the field, he sold [it] and he who bought it, he went, while he was plowing, [he found] the treasure. He began to lend money at interest to [whom] he wished."

110.   Jesus said, "He who has found the world and becomes rich, let him deny the world."

111.   Jesus said, "The heavens and the earth will roll back in your presence, and he who lives by the Living One will not

see death nor...." because Jesus said, "He who finds himself,
the world is not worthy of him."

112.   Jesus said, "Woe to the flesh which depends on the
soul; woe to the soul which depends on the flesh."

113.   His disciples said to him, "On what day will the
Kingdom come?" (He said,) "It will not come by expectation.
They will not say, 'Look here,' or, 'Look there,' but the
Kingdom of the Father is spread out on the earth and men do
not see it."

114.   Simon Peter said to them, "Let Mary leave us, because
women are not worthy of the Life." Jesus said, "Look, I shall
guide her so that I will make her male, in order that she also
may become a living spirit, being like you males. For every
woman who makes herself male will enter the Kingdom of Heaven."

                The Gospel according to Thomas

59. THE GOSPEL OF PHILIP

(Trans. D.R. Cartlidge; intro. and notes, E.H. Pagels)

(Introduction: The Gospel of Philip, virtually
unknown until 1946, was discovered in the same collection as
the Gospel of Thomas. Certain gnostic Christians in Egypt and
Syria considered these two gospels, along with the Secret Sayings of the Savior, recorded by Matthias, to be three especially
sacred writings, containing nothing less than the secret wisdom
that Jesus entrusted to Philip, Thomas, and Matthias, as one
gnostic source relates:

> When Jesus had finished speaking these words, Philip
> arose quickly, letting fall to earth the book he was
> holding, for it was he who wrote down all that Jesus
> said and all that he did. Philip stepped forward
> and said, "My Lord, is it to me alone that you have
> entrusted the care of this word, so that I am to
> write all that we shall say and all that we shall
> do?"....Jesus answered, "Listen, blessed Philip, so
> that I may tell you. It is to you, as well as to
> Thomas and to Matthias that I, by the authority of
> the First Mystery, have entrusted the writing of all
> that I shall say and that I shall do, as well as all
> that you shall see... (*Pistis Sophia*, 42).

The Gospel of Philip contains allusions to the gospels
and letters of the New Testament. This indicates that these
gnostic Christians knew and used these writings, although they
considered them to be only the ordinary, common tradition
accessible to all Christians, including those who were only
"infants" in terms of their spiritual development. But the
gnostics valued the Gospels of Philip, Thomas, and Matthias
as the gospels of an *esoteric* tradition, which could be communicated only to those who were spiritually "mature". For to be
"mature" meant to be "initiated" into gnostic tradition (the
same Greek word, *teleios*, can be translated either way).

The Gospel of Philip is neither a narrative gospel,
like those included in the NT, nor a collection of sayings,
like the Gospel of Thomas. Instead it contains a series of
short meditations on mystical subjects. The present form of
this manuscript comes from a fourth century Coptic text,
although apparently it is related to a second century Greek
"Gospel of Philip," from which only a fragment remains
(Epiphanius, *Pan.* 26.13.2-3). Commentators disagree on the
question of whether the present manuscript preserves the
original form of that earlier gospel; it may have been abridged
or amplified.

195

In one sense, it is paradoxical that the gnostics wrote gospels at all. The Valentinian gnostics, from whom the Gospel of Philip comes, claimed that truth could not be communicated in writing, but only in "living speech" to those who were ready to receive it (Iren. *Against Heresies*, 3.1-3). This may explain why this gospel is written in strange, symbolic language: it was meant to be read only by initiates, and to remain unintelligible to the casual, "uninitiated" reader.

The theme of this "gospel" is the relation between the "immature"--the "uninitiated" Christians--and the "mature," or "initiated," *gnostic* Christians. The opening section (1-6) characterizes these two distinct groups: the "immature" are represented as Hebrews, slaves, the dead, by contrast with the "mature" who are Gentiles, sons, the living.

Paradoxically, these two groups, as different as light and darkness, life and death, right and left, are actually "brothers to one another" (10). What has separated them (so that they now seem like opposites) is that the "immature" have been misled and deceived by the words and the names used in Christian teaching. For example, a person may hear the name "God" without knowing the reality the name expresses: to him, the name conveys only an image of God (11). One cannot learn truth without using names (12), but such names (i.e. Father, Son, Holy Spirit) often have been used to deceive people into worshipping those that are not gods (13, 14, 50). Saying 85 describes this situation with irony: "God created man, and man created God. So it is in the world. Men make gods and they worship their creation. It would be appropriate for the gods to worship them!"

Immature Christians, deceived by mere words, speak "in error" about two basic Christian doctrines--the virgin birth and the resurrection. They say of the virgin birth that "Mary conceived by the Holy Spirit" (17). They say of the resurrection that "the Lord died first and then rose" (21). But such persons "do not know what they are saying" (17).

Gnostic Christians interpret each of these doctrines symbolically (67). They say of the virgin birth that Mary symbolizes Wisdom (Sophia), the true Mother from whom Christ comes; and his father is the "Father in Heaven" (17). This is a "mystery: the Father of All united with the Virgin who came down" (82). The writer goes on to explain that the resurrection does not mean that dead bodies are to revive: rather, to receive the *logos* and *spirit* of Christ is to be "resurrected" (63), i.e., "raised from the deadness of (worldly) existence." He adds that in one way it is valid to speak of rising "in the flesh"--in the sense that all we are and all we do is done "in the flesh" (23).

The reason that there are two such different views of Jesus is explained in saying 25: "Jesus did not reveal himself as he really was, but he revealed himself as people would be able to see him." To the great he appeared as great; to the small as small. To some he appeared as *Christ*, to others only as *Jesus* (19, 20). In every case he adapted his revelation to the capacity of his audience.

There are, then, basically two types of Christians. Some only see Jesus in the same way that they see the sun, or anything else, as something outside themselves (44). But those who are "mature" *become what they see*: "you saw the Spirit, and you became Spirit; you saw the Christ and became Christ; you saw the Father, and you shall become the Father" (44). They are no longer simply "believers" like the rest; they themselves are being transformed, and becoming divine!

Furthermore, these two types of Christian understand baptism in different ways. To the "immature," baptism means that they receive the *names* of the Father, Son, and Spirit (67). From that time on, "they call themselves Christians" (59). Yet so far they have only the *name*, but not the reality (59). The "mature" actually receive the Father, Son, and Spirit: not their names only, but their actual indwelling *presence*. Such a person is "no longer (merely) a Christian but a *Christ*!" (67, 95).

The eucharist (Lord's Supper), too, has a different meaning for each. The "immature" see it only in terms of an animal sacrifice (14, 50); they offer the bread and wine as the "body and blood" of Jesus, sacrificed as a lamb slain for "the sins of the world" (27, cf. Jn. 1:29; Mt. 26:28). From a gnostic point of view, this conception is utterly repulsive; it turns God into "a man-eater" (50)--and those who participate in the meal, by inference, are cannibals! The gnostics, however, receive the bread and wine as symbols of the *logos* and *spirit* of Christ (23, 100). They recognize that to receive it in this way is to receive *and to become* the "wholly perfect man" (100, 106, 108). For them, the eucharist signifies not an animal sacrifice, but a *royal wedding feast* (cf. Mt. 22:11) which celebrates their union with the Spirit (27).

Yet the symbol of marriage has another dimension: it also signifies the final reunion of the *immature* Christians with the *gnostics*! Although for the present they form two separate groups, in the future they shall be rejoined into one. According to sayings 73 and 78, this is the secret symbolic meaning of the story of Adam and Eve. As Eve was separated from Adam, so the naïve believers have been separated from the gnostics; yet these two shall be rejoined as a man and woman are joined in marriage. This is the "mystery of marriage" which is celebrated in the sacrament that the gnostics call the "bride-chamber" (82, 103).

Is the "bridechamber" a secret gnostic sacrament
unknown to other Christians? Some scholars think that it is a
gnostic version of the "sacred marriage" enacted in ancient
fertility religions as well as in certain of the mystery cults
contemporary with early Christianity. Did the gnostics enact
ritual intercourse in their "bridechamber?" Some ancient
sources suggest that they did, although one phrase in the Gospel
of Philip suggests that the gnostic sacrament culminated with a
kiss, symbolizing spiritual conception (31, 55).

Yet the conclusion of the Gospel of Philip suggests
another interpretation: that the "mystery of marriage" is the
gnostic term for the *secret meaning of the eucharist* that all
Christians celebrate in common. For this "mystery," according
to saying 125f, is "hidden" but not "in darkness": it is
"hidden in a clear and perfect day." In one sense, it is perfectly open, being celebrated daily in the church, in plain
view of all Christians; but it is hidden in the sense that only
initiates recognize it as a *marriage feast* and perceive its
true meaning. It symbolizes not only the union that "mature"
gnostics enjoy with the divine; but it also signifies that the
"immature" will eventually also attain *gnosis*, and be joined in
union ("in marriage") with the "mature." This means that
eventually *all* shall be joined with the divine, and become
divine!

For this purpose the gnostics, although they are
"free", must be willing to serve and to help the "slaves" (87,
110, 114). They do this out of love (110), being careful not
to hurt or offend anyone (118). The gnostic teacher must learn
to recognize what each person needs, and offer to each the
appropriate "nourishment" (119).

The immature, the slaves, will finally become free
(125). But the one already initiated into gnosis already has
"received the light" (127). For such a person, "the world has
become the *aion*"--that is, his present existence already has
been transformed into the fulness of the divine presence (127).

For the author of the Gospel of Philip there are, then
two Christian traditions: one is the public, *exoteric* tradition
(which includes the gospels and letters of the NT); the other is
this secret, *esoteric* tradition that was originally given by
Jesus only to a few of the disciples and is now communicated
only in private to those who are "spiritually mature." The
gnostics' claim to have access to secret, esoteric Christian
tradition proved intolerable to many Christians in the second
century: it came to be branded as "heresy" and "false teaching." Its teachers, accused of being Satanically inspired,
were given the choice of either repudiating their claims or
leaving the church (see, for example, Irenaeus *Against Heresies*,
5.26).

This introduction and the notes offered below are of
the most elementary sort: the serious student is referred to
the commentaries of R.M. Wilson and J.E. Ménard, as well as to
articles mentioned in the notes.)

1.   A Hebrew man makes a Hebrew and they call him thus:
a proselyte. But a proselyte does not make a proselyte...they
are thus...and they make others...it is enough for them that
(or, "in order that") they shall be.

2.   The slave seeks only to be free. However, he does
not seek after his lord's possession. The son, however, is not
only a son but writes himself into the inheritance of the father.

3.   Those who inherit dead things, they are dead and
inherit dead things. Those who inherit living things, they
live, and they inherit living things and the dead things.
Those who are dead inherit nothing. For how will the one who
is dead inherit? If the dead one inherits the living he will
not die, but the dead one will live more.

4.   A Gentile man does not die, for he has not lived so
he cannot die. He lives who has believed the truth; and he is
in danger that he will die, for he lives after the day Christ
came.

5.   The world is created, the cities are bedecked, the
dead are carried out.

6.   When we were Hebrews, we were orphans. We had only
our mother. But when we became Christians, we gained a father
and mother.

7.   Those who sow in winter reap in summer. The winter
is the world; the summer is the other aion. Let us sow in the
world so that we may reap in the summer. On account of this it

is seemly for us not to pray in the winter. That which comes
out of the winter is the summer. But if someone reaps in the
winter, he will not reap, but he will tear out.

8.   Like this one, he will not produce fruit...not only
if he comes out...but on the Sabbath [his field?] is unfruitful.

9.   Christ came to ransom some, but others he saved,
others he redeemed. Those who were strangers he ransomed and
made them his and he [saved them?]. These he made as securities
in his will. Not only when he appeared did he lay aside his
soul as we wished, but since the foundation of the world, he
laid aside his soul. He came to take it when he wished, because
it had been set aside as a pledge. It was under the control of
robbers and it had been held prisoner. But he saved it, and
those good ones who were in the world, he ransomed, and the
evil ones.

> (The last lines of vs. 9 refer to the conception
> that those who are "from above" have been captured
> by "the robbers," the powers (archons) that rule this
> lower world (see Paul's phrase in Rom 8:38; also Eph
> 6:12; Jn 12:31). According to saying 13, these
> "rulers" wanted to deceive man, who had an affinity
> with the "truly good ones"--the divine powers--in
> order to enslave him to themselves. Compare the
> conception in *Poimandres*, which describes how a
> portion of the higher realm of Light became mixed in
> the lower realm of Darkness, Evil, and Matter.)

10.   The light and the darkness, the life and the death,
the right and the left are each other's brothers. They cannot
separate from one another. Therefore, the good are not good
nor are the evil evil, nor is life life, nor death death. On
account of this, each one will dissolve into its beginning
origin (*archē*). But those that are exalted above the world
cannot dissolve, they are eternal.

11.   The names which are given to the worldly things contair

a great error. For they turn aside their meaning from the
things which are the real meaning to things which are not the
real meaning. For whoever hears (the word) "God," does not
know the real meaning, but he knows the unreal meaning. It
is the same way with (such words as) "the Father" and "the Son"
and "the Holy Spirit" and "the life" and "the light" and "the
resurrection" and "the Church" and all the other names. They
do not know the real meaning, rather, they know the unreal
meaning...they have come to know the real meaning...they are
in the world...in the aeon they would not name a day in the
world, nor would they list them under worldly things. They
have an end in the aeon.

12.   There is only one name which one does not speak out
in the world, the name which the Father gave to the Son. It
is above everything. It is the name of the Father. For the
Son would not become the Father, if he had not put on the name
of the Father. Those who have this name truly know it, but
they do not speak of him. Those who do not have it do not know
it. But the truth engendered names in the world for us, because
it is impossible to know it (the Truth) apart from names. The
Truth is a single thing and is many things. It is this way
for us, to teach us this in love through its many-ness.

13.   The archons wanted to deceive man because they saw
that he was kindred to the truly good ones. They took the name
of the good ones, and gave it to those that are not good, so
that by names they could deceive him and bind them to the ones
that are not good. If they do them a favor, they are taken
away from those who are not good, and become set in those that
are good. They know them. For they (the archons) wish to take
the free man and enslave him forever.

14.   There are powers which...man; they give...do not
wish....Therefore, they will become....For, if the man...

sacrifices become...and they offered up animals to the powers...
these are the ones to whom they make offerings. They offered
them up, to be sure, still living. When, however, they were
offered, they died. The Man was offered up dead to God, and
he lived.

15.   Before the Christ came there was no bread in the
world. Thus, in paradise, the place where Adam was, there
were many trees as food for the animals. There was no wheat
for food for man. Man ate as the animals. But, when the
Christ, the perfect man came, he brought bread from heaven so
that man could eat in a human way.

16.   The archons believed that they could do what they
did by their own power and will. However, the Holy Spirit
worked all in secret through them as he willed. The truth is
sown in every place; she (the Truth) was from the beginning,
and many see her as she is sown. But there are only a few who
see her who reap her.

          (This passage sets forth an idea fundamental
          in gnostic thought: that the cosmic rulers (archons),
          although they think they are free to act on their
          own, are actually being used as the instruments of
          the higher powers: See Against Heresies, 1.5.1-6.)

17.   Some say Mary was impregnated by the Holy Spirit.
They err. They do not know what they say. When did a woman
become pregnant by a woman? Mary is the virgin whom no Power
corrupted. She is a great puzzle (?) to the Hebrews, who are
the apostles and apostolic men. This Virgin, whom no Power
defiled...the powers defiled them (or, themselves) and the Lord
did not (or, would not) say: "My Father, who is in Heaven,"
if he had not had another Father. But he simply said...[text
missing].

          (In later Jewish tradition, the spirit was
          understood to be female, as the Hebrew word (ru'ah)

for spirit is feminine. Here this is used to argue
against the popular Christian view of the virgin
birth.)

18.   The Lord said to the disciples..."Come into the
Father's house, but do not take anything from the Father's
house, nor remove anything."

19.   Jesus is a secret name; Christ is a revealed name.
For this reason, "Jesus" does not exist in any other language,
but his name is "Jesus", as they call him. But Christ is his
name; in the Syriac, it is Messiah, but, in the Greek, it is
Christ. Actually, everyone has it according to his own language. "The Nazarene" is the revealed name among the secret
things.

20.   The Christ has everything in himself, man, angel,
or mystery, and the Father.

21.   They are in error who say, "The Lord first died and
then he arose." For first he arose and then he died. If someone first achieves the resurrection, he will not die. So truly
as God lives, that one would...[text uncertain].

22.   No one will hide a great, valuable thing in an equally
great thing. However, people often put things worth countless
thousands into a thing worth a penny: It is this way with the
soul. It is a precious thing which came into a worthless body.

23.   Some fear that they will arise naked. Therefore,
they wish to arise in the flesh and they do not know that those
who carry the flesh, (they) are naked.

        (In this passage one can see an ancient dispute
        concerning the resurrection. The question was: in
        what form does a person rise from the dead? Some
        gnostics argued that both the body and the soul are
        "taken off" like garments and left behind while the

> spirit rises to divine life. This author cites
> Paul's discussion in I Cor 15:50 and Jesus' saying
> in Jn 6:53 to show that whoever "leaves off" his
> own "flesh and blood" is not "naked," because he is
> "clothed" with the "flesh and blood" of Christ,
> which symbolize the *logos* and *spirit*. For discussion,
> see A.H.C. Van Eijk, "The Gospel of Philip," *Vig. Chr.*
> 25 (1971), 94f.)

They who...who disrobe themselves, (they are) not naked. Flesh
(and blood can) not inherit the kingdom (of God). What is this
which will not inherit? That which is ours. But what is this
which will inherit? That which is Jesus' (flesh?) and his
blood. Therefore he said: "The one who does not eat my flesh
and drink my blood does not have Life in him." What is it?
His flesh is the Logos and his blood is the Holy Spirit. Whoever has received these has food and drink and clothing. I
blame those who say it will not rise. Then they are both to
blame. You say: "The flesh will not rise," but tell me, what
will rise, so that we may praise you? You say: "The spirit in
the flesh, and this light is in the flesh." This is also a
Logos which is in the flesh. Whatever you say, you do not say
anything outside the flesh. It is necessary to rise in this
flesh; everything is in it.

24.   In this world those who put on clothes are worth more
than clothes. In the Kingdom of Heaven the clothes are worth
more than those who have put them on through water and fire,
which purify the whole place.

25.   Those who are revealed are so through those who are
made manifest, those who are secret are so through those who
are secret. Some are hidden through those who are made manifest.
There is water in water, there is fire in an annointing (*chrism*).

26.   Jesus stole everything. For he showed himself not to
be as he really was, but he appeared in a way that they could
see him. To those...he appeared. He appeared to the great as

great. He appeared to the small as small. He appeared to the
angels as an angel, and to men as a man. Because of this, his
Logos hid from everyone. Some, to be sure, saw him and they
thought that they saw themselves. But, as he appeared in glory
to the disciples on the mountain, he was not small. He became
great; however, he made the disciples great, so that they were
able to see him as he was, i.e., great. He said on that day
in the thanksgiving (eucharist): "You who have united with the
Perfect, the Light, the Holy Spirit, have united the angels
also with us, with the images."

27.   Do not scorn the Lamb. For without it one cannot see
the King. No one, if he is naked, is able to find his way to
the King.

28.   The Heavenly Man has many more children than the
earthly man. If the children of Adam are more numerous, and
still die, how much more the children of the Perfect One who
do not die.

> (These phrases "man of heaven" and "man of
> earth" are taken from Paul's discussion of resurrec-
> tion, I Cor. 15:47f. But a very peculiar twist is
> added at the end and the text turns toward the sub-
> ject of "begetting sons." Although the text is
> partly destroyed, it is clear that "spiritual con-
> ception" is being described, and that it somehow
> parallels the original conception of the Logos,
> the Word (=Christ), which came forth out of the
> mouth of God.)

29.   The father makes a child, and the child cannot make
a son. For he who is begotten cannot beget; the child begets
brothers, not children.

30.   Everyone who is born in the world is born through
nature, and the others through [the Spirit.] [Those] born
through him...to the man...from the promise...above.

31.   ...from the mouth...(if) the Logos came from there,
he would [word uncertain: Till & Wilson transl. "nourish"]...
from the mouth and become perfect. The perfect become pregnant
through a kiss and give birth. Because of this we also kiss
each other and are made pregnant by the grace among us.

> (Is this "holy kiss" the sacramental act of
> the "bridechamber"? Irenaeus, a contemporary
> opponent of the gnostics, says that the same gnostics
> acted out repeated sexual unions in the "bride-
> chamber": see his account, *Against Heresies* 1.13
> and 1.21.3 (*ANF* 1.334f, 345f). For discussion, see
> R.M. Grant, "The Mystery of Marriage in the Gospel
> of Philip," in: *After the NT* (Phila, 1967), 183-94;
> E. Segelberg, "The Coptic-Gnostic Gospel according
> to Philip," *Numen* 7 (1960) 189-200.)

32.   There were three who always walked with the Lord:
Mary, his mother, and her sister, and Magdalene whom they call
his lover. For Mary is his sister and his mother and his lover.

> (Just as Christ came to remove the separation
> of female from male, which was the cause of death
> [see vs. 71], so also he was at all times "united"
> with his female alter-ego in the successive states
> of his activity: as Christ with the Holy Spirit in
> Heaven, then as Savior with Sophia, then (somehow)
> with Mary his mother -- in conception, and as Jesus
> with Mary Magdalene; see Irenaeus *adv. haer.*1.1.7;
> 1.3.1 *ANF* 1.319, 325.)

33.   "The Father" and "the Son" are single names. The
Holy Spirit is a double name. For they are everywhere: they
are above, they are below; they are in secret, they are in the
revealed. The Holy Spirit is in the revelation, it is below,
it is in secret, it is above.

34.   The saints are ministered to by the evil powers for
the powers are blind because of the Holy Spirit. Therefore,
they will believe that they serve a man when they work for the
saints. Because of this, one day a disciple sought from the
Lord something from the world. He said to him: "Ask your

mother, and she will give you from strange [things]."

35.   The apostles said to the disciples, "Let our whole offering engender salt." They named..., "salt." Without it no offering is acceptable.

36.   But Sophia is barren [without] child. Because of this, they call her...salt. The place where they...in their manner, the Holy Spirit...her children are numerous.

37.   What the Father has belongs to the Son also, and as long as the Son is little he is not entrusted with what is his. When he becomes a man his Father gives to him everything that he has.

38.   Those who have gone astray, whom the Spirit engenders, they go astray also through it. Because of this, through the same breath (pneuma) the fire burns and is extinguished.

39.   Echamoth is one thing and Echmoth is another. Echamoth is simply Sophia (=Wisdom). Echmoth, however, is the Sophia of death, which is the Sophia of death [dittography], which is she who knows death, whom one calls "the little Sophia."

40.   There are animals which are tamed by man such as the calf and the donkey and others such as these. There are others not tamed; they live to themselves in the desert. The man plows the field with the animals which are domesticated. Thus from the field he feeds himself and the animals, whether they are tamed or not tamed. It is this way with the perfect Man. Through powers which are tamed, he plows and readies everything to come into being. For on account of this the whole place (i.e., this world) stands, the good as well as the evil, the right and the left. The Holy Spirit shepherds everything and

reigns over all powers which are subordinate and those not
subordinate, i.e. those who are to themselves.... [text is
mutilated here].

41.   ...moulded him...you would find his sons high born
creations. But if he was not moulded, but was begotten, you
would find that his seed was well begotten. But he was moulded
and begotten. What a lofty birth that is.

42.   First came adultery and, afterwards, murder. And he
was begotten in adultery, for he was the child of the serpent.
Therefore he became a man-killer like his father, and he killed
his brother. But every intercourse between those different
from one another is adultery.

43.   God is a dyer. As the good dyes, which are called
"true", perish with the things which are dyed in them, thus it
is with that which God has dyed. Since his dyes are unfading,
they are immortal through his herbs. But God baptizes whom he
baptizes in water.

44.   To no one is it possible to see anything of those
who are established unless he becomes as they. It is not thus
with the man who is in the world. He sees the sun and is not
a sun, and he sees the heaven and the earth and all other
things, and he is not these -- it is this way with the truth.
But you saw something of that place and you became these: you
saw the Spirit and became Spirit; you saw the Christ and became
Christ; you saw the Father, you shall become Father. On
account of this...you surely see everything and...not yourself.
But you see yourself [in that place]. What you see you shall
[become]...

45.   Faith receives, love gives...without faith. No one
can give without love. Because of this, so that we indeed can

receive, we have faith. But, so that we can give truly, [Till
conjectures: "we must love"] since if someone gives without
love, he gains nothing from what he has given.

46.   He who has not received the Lord is still a Hebrew.

47.   The apostles who were before us named (him) thus,
"Jesus the Nazoraian, the Messiah," which is to say, "Jesus,
the Nazoraian, the Christ." The last name is "Christ"; the
first is "Jesus." The one in the middle is "Nazoraian."
"Messiah" has two meanings: "Christ" and also "the measured"
(ed. note: The Coptic *shēu* is punned with "Messiah"). "Jesus"
means in Hebrew "the Salvation." "Nazara" means "the Truth."
"The Nazarene" means "the Truth" also. "Christ" is measured.
The Nazarene and Jesus are they who have been measured.

48.   When the pearl is thrown down in the muck it does not
become more despised, nor, if it is anointed with balsam will
it become more valuable. But it always has its value to its
owner. It is the same way with the children of God. Wherever
they may be, they still have value to the Father.

49.   If you say, "I am a Jew," no one will be moved. If
you say, "I am a Roman," no one will be troubled. If you say,
"I am a Greek, a barbarian, a slave, a freeman," no one will
be bothered. If you [say], "I am a Christian"...will tremble.
May it be...this way....The one...cannot endure...name.

50.   (Some think) God is a man-eater. On account of this
[...they kill] the Man for him. Before they killed the Man,
they killed animals. For those were not Gods for whom they
killed (victims).

51.   Glass and pottery vessels are both made with fire.
But if glass vessels are broken, they are made again, for they

are created with a breath (*pneuma*). But pottery vessels, if
they are broken, they are destroyed, for they are created without a breath.

52.   An ass which turned a millstone in a circle went 100
miles. When he was turned loose he found he was still at the
same place. There are men who make many trips and get nowhere.
When evening came for them, they saw no city nor town nor
creation nor nature nor power nor angel. The poor fellows
labored in vain.

53.   The Eucharist is Jesus. For they call him in the
Syrian "*pharisatha*," which is, "the one who is spread out."
For Jesus came and he crucified the world.

54.   The Lord went into the dye-shop of Levi. He took
seventy-two colors: he threw them into the kettle. He took
them all out white and he said: "Thus the Son of Man came, a
dyer."

            (It was popularly believed that there were
        seventy-two nations in the inhabited lands of the
        earth. This same idea lies behind the story of
        Jesus sending out seventy-two more disciples, after
        he had already sent out the Twelve, in Luke 10:1-20.)

55.   Wisdom (*Sophia*), whom they call barren, is the mother
of the angels, and the consort of Christ is Mary Magdalene.
The [Lord loved Mary] more than all the disciples, and he
kissed her on the mouth many times. The other [women?] [saw]...
him.

            (This is another reference to the male/female
        union of Jesus-Christ and Sophia-Mary. Note the
        'holy kiss' performed by them as an example to
        Christians.)

They said to him: "Why do you [love her] more than all of us?"
The Savior answered and said to them: "Why do not I love you
as her?"

56.   A blind man and one who can see, if they are in the
dark there is no difference between them. When the light comes,
then the one who sees will see the light, and the one who is
blind will stay in the darkness.

57.   The Lord said: "Blessed is the one who exists before
he comes into being. For he who exists, he was and will be."

        (The Elect are in actuality splinters of the
        Light which became trapped in the realm of Darkness;
        the individual soul, once "awakened", finally "knows
        itself," i.e., whence it came and whither it is
        going; cp. Gospel of Thomas 49,50; Acts of Thomas 15.)

58.   The greatness of man is not revealed but it is hidden.
Because of this he is lord of the animals which are stronger
than he, which are great according to that which is revealed
as well as hidden. And this (i.e., man's lordship) gives to
them their stability. But if a man leaves them alone, they
kill one another (and) bite one another and eat one another
because they can find no food. But they have now found food,
because man has worked the ground.

59.   If anyone goes down to the water and comes up having
received nothing and says: "I am a Christian," he has taken
the name by extortion. But if he receives the Holy Spirit, he
has the gift of the name. He who has received a gift, it is
not taken from him. But he who has taken something by extortion,
it is demanded back from him.

60.   It is this way...if anyone is in a mystery. The
mystery of marriage is great. For...the world...for the con-
stitution (*sustasis*) of the world is the man but the constitu-
tion [of the man] is marriage. Understand [the union?] for it
has [great?] power. Its image is in [a defilement of the body].

61.   Among the unclean spirits there are male and female.
The male (spirits) cohabit with the souls which dwell in a
female form. But the female are those which are mixed with
the ones in a male form, through one who is unpersuaded. And
no one can escape them if they detain him, if he does not
receive a male power or a female, which is the bridegroom and
the bride. But one receives (these?) from the imaged (*eikonikos*)
bride chamber. When the ignorant women see a male who is alone,
they leap on him and deride him and defile him. It is the same
way with ignorant men. If they see a beautiful woman, living
alone, they persuade her, they force her, wishing to defile her.
If, however, they see a man with his wife living beside one
another, the woman cannot go in to the man, nor can the man go
in to the woman. Thus it is, if the image and the angel are
joined with one another, neither can any dare to go in to the
man or the woman. He who comes out of the world, they cannot
hold him any more, because he was in the world. It is clear
that he is raised above desire...of fear. He is lord over...
he is more precious than envy. If...comes they seize him (and)
strangle...and how will this one be able to escape...how will
he be able...often some...we are faithful...demons. For if
they had the Holy Spirit, the unclean spirit could not cling to
them.

> (This passage suggests that an actual husband/
> wife union may have been a prerequisite for partici-
> pation in the "bridechamber" sacrament. Alternatively
> the passage may have a symbolic meaning: the "man"
> symbolizes the "mature," gnostic Christian, and the
> "woman" the "immature" believer (compare Gospel of
> Thomas, 113). Read this way, the passage shows that
> although each must struggle with temptations induced
> by demonic forces when alone, the two become invul-
> nerable and strong when they are joined together.)

62.   Do not be afraid of the flesh, nor love it. If you
fear it, then it will be your master. If you love it, it will
swallow and strangle you.

63.   Either one is in this world, or in the resurrection,
or in the places in the middle. God forbid that I be found in
them. In this world there is good and evil. Its good is not
good, and its evil is not evil. But there is evil after this
world, true evil, which they call "the middle". It is death.
As we are in this world, it is fitting to us to acquire the
resurrection so that, when we peel off the flesh, we will be
found in the Rest, not making our way in "the middle". For
many wander astray off the path. For it is good to come out
of the world before man sins.

> (Gnostic writers often describe this world as
> "the middle place"--midway between lifeless matter
> and the divine spirit. Ordinary existence in this
> world is "death", compared to spiritual awareness.
> Whoever is raised from ordinary existence into
> spiritual awareness is "raised from death to life":
> to experience this is to be "resurrected"!)

64.   A few neither want nor are able, but others if they
want have no profit since they do not do...for wanting made
them sin. As for the unwillingness, however, righteousness
will be hidden from them both. And the wanting...not to do.

65.   An apostolic man...Asia, saw some who...their house
on fire. They...air (?) in...fire, they lay...the fire...it is
water in...and they said to them...able to save...their will.
They received [death?] as punishment, which they call...dark-
ness. [The enemy comes] out of water and fire.

66.   The s[oul] and the Spirit were created out of water
and fire and light (which?) the son of the Bridechamber(?).
The fire is the chrism, the light is the fire. I do not speak
of the fire which is formless, but of the other whose form is
white, which is light and beautiful and gives beauty.

67.   The truth did not come naked into the world, but
came in the types and the images. The world will not receive

the truth in any other way. There is a being-born-again, and
an image of being-born-again. It is truly fitting that they
become born again through the image. What else is the resurrection? And the image-through-the-image, it is fitting that
it arise. The Bridechamber and the image-through-the-image, it
is fitting that they enter into the truth, which is the recapit-
ulation (*apokatastasis*). It is fitting not only for those who
receive the name of the Father and the Son and the Holy Spirit,
but for those who have taken them into themselves. If someone
does not take them (into) himself, the name also will be taken
away from him. But one receives them in the anointing (*chrism*).
The One who came (?) in the power of cross (?)...the apostles
call it "the right" and "the left". For this reason, one is
no longer a Christian, but a Christ.

68.   The Lord [did?] all in a Mystery, a Baptism, an Anoint
ing, and a Eucharist, and a Salvation, and a Bridechamber...

>   (This verse is significant, for it lists what
>   seem to be six sacraments, perhaps in ascending
>   order of importance for salvation. See also below
>   vs. 76. For further discussion, see the articles
>   cited in note to vs. 13.)

69.   [Text is mutilated for 9 lines]...which is called
"the one below", and he who has the hidden is over him. For
it is right that they should say "the inside" and "the outside"
what is outside the outside. Because of this the Lord called
destruction the outer darkness; there is nothing outside it.
He said, "My Father, who is in secret." He said, "Go into
your chamber, close the door, (and) pray to your Father who is
in secret," which is he who is inside them all. He who is
inside them all is the Pleroma. After him there is none inside
of him. He is the One, of whom they say "what is over them."

70.   Before Christ, some came forth; where they came from
they can no longer enter and they enter where they can no

longer come out. But Christ came. Those who went in he brought
out; those who came out, he brought in.

71.   When Eve was in Adam, there was no death. When she
separated from him, there was death. If she goes in again,
and he takes her, there will be no death.

> (This verse refers to a specific interpretation
> of Genesis 1:27 "God created man (Adam) in his own
> image, in the image of God he created him; male and
> female he created them." This was understood to
> mean: male-female he created *each one*, i.e., that
> Adam was originally androgynous [explaining how God
> could take Eve out of Adam's side], and furthermore
> that God himself was male/female, since he made
> Adam a male-female in *his own image*. Redemption,
> i.e. the defeat of death, will occur when the whole
> process is reversed. See below vs. 78.)

72.   "My God, my God, why, Lord, did you forsake me?" He
said these words on the cross, for he separated the place...
which was begotten by [the Holy Spirit?] through God...[text
broken and undecipherable].

73.   No Bridechamber is for animals, nor is it for slaves,
nor for women who are defiled, but it is for free men and virgins.

74.   We are born through the Holy Spirit, but we are born
again through Christ. In both we are anointed through the
Spirit. When we were born we were united.

75.   No one can see himself in water or in a mirror without light. Nor again will you be able to see in light without
water or a mirror. On account of this it is fitting to baptize
in both the light and the water. But the light is the anointing (*chrism*).

76.   There were three houses for offering-places in Jerusalem. The one was open to the west; they called it "the holy".
Another was open to the south; they called it "the holy of the
holy". The third was open to the east; they called it "the
holy of the holies". It was the place into which the high
priest came alone. Baptism is the holy house...(*chrism*?) the
holy of the holy. The holy of the holies is the Bridechamber.
Baptism has the resurrection [and the] salvation in order to
hasten into the Bridechamber. But the Bridechamber is in that
which is greater than...you will not find...those who pray...
Jerusalem...Jerusalem...Jerusalem, those who wait...which one
calls...[h]oly of the holy ones...veil...bride chamber if not
the image...above...its veil was torn from the top to the
bottom. For it was right for some from below to go up.

        (An allegory of their sacraments based on the
    temple in Jerusalem. Unfortunately the text breaks
    off at this point, but it does reveal the superior
    importance and rank of the sacrament of "the Bride-
    chamber.")

77.   The powers cannot see those who put on the perfect
light, and they cannot hold them. But one will put on the
light in the mystery, in the joining.

        (Referring to the powers, scil. in the Midst,
    who try to restrain the souls of men and women
    ascending towards the heavens after death. The
    "light" put on in the Bridechamber is of course the
    "light" toward which they shall rise. See above
    vs. 63.)

78.   If the woman had not separated from the man, she
would not die with the man. His separation became the beginning (*archē*) of death. Christ came, so that he would remove
the separation, which was from the first. Again he joined the
two and to those who died in the separation he gave life and
joined them.

79.   But the woman joins with her husband in the Bridechamber. Those who have joined in the Bridechamber will no
longer be separated. On account of this Eve separated from
Adam, because she was not joined with him in the Bridechamber.

80.   The soul of Adam came from a breath. Its joining
is...which was given to him in his mother [and in] his soul
they gave him a...her place, when he...words higher than the
powers. They bewitched him....

          (The text becomes too broken to translate
          further. The "separation" here is the division of
          Adam-Eve into two different physical bodies, with
          differing sexes. These people took Gen. 1-3 very
          seriously, and could read quite clearly that the
          separation into Adam and Eve preceded lust, which
          preceded banishment and death. So they proposed
          to reverse the whole process, or, better, they
          gratefully accepted the reversal brought by Christ.)

81.   ...Again he was begotten. Again he was begotten as
a child (son). Again he was anointed. Again he was redeemed.
Again he redeemed.

82.   If it is fitting, I will speak a mystery: the Father
of All joined himself with the Virgin who came down, and a light
surrounded him that day. He revealed the great Bridechamber.
Therefore, his body came into being that day. He came out of
the Bridechamber as one who came into being from the bridegroom
and the bride. Thus, Jesus established the All through these.
And it is fitting for each of his disciples to enter his Rest.

83.   Adam came into being from two virgins: from the Spirit
and from the virgin Earth. Therefore, the Christ was born from
a Virgin so that he could bring order to the stumbling which
was in the beginning.

84.   There are two trees in paradise. The one engenders

a[nimals]; the other engenders men. Adam [ate] from the tree
which brought forth animals; [he be]came a beast and he begat
a beast. Because of this they worship...Adam. The tree...
fruit is...engenders men...the man...God created the m[an...
ma]n created God.

85.   It is like this in the world. Men create gods and
they worship those whom they have created. It would be better
if the gods worshipped men.

86.   As the truth is the work of man, they are created
by his power. Because of this they call them powers. His
works are his children, they are created from a Rest. Therefore, his power dwells in his works, but the Rest is revealed
in the children. And you will find this piercing to the image.
And this is the image-man, who does his works from his power,
but producing his children from Rest.

87.   In this world the slaves serve the free. In the
Kingdom of Heaven, those who are free will serve the slaves.
The children of the Bridechamber will serve the children of
the marriage. The children of the Bridechamber have a name...
the Rest...them. They do not need...[text broken].

88.   [text indecipherable]

89.   [text indecipherable]

90.   Those who say 'They will die first and rise again'
are in error. If they do not first receive the resurrection
while they live, when they die they will receive nothing.

           (In typical Gnostic fashion, the Resurrection
        is considered to be a present event, happening now;
        cp. Gospel of Thomas 51, Gospel of John 5:24, II Tim.
        2:18. See note on vs. 63.)

So also they speak about Baptism, saying that Baptism is a great thing, because if people receive it they will live.

91.   The apostle Philip said: "Joseph, the carpenter, planted a garden because he needed the wood for his craft. He made the cross from the trees which he planted.   And his seed hung on what he had planted.   His seed was Jesus, but the planting was the cross."

> (The idea that Joseph made the cross for his own son is a typical late legendary addition to the "biographical" details of Jesus' life.   In the section which follows, there is more discussion of the two trees, one which killed Adam ["the law", i.e. tree of knowledge of good and evil] and one which gives life ["tree of knowledge" *gnosis*].   Compare the Gospel of Truth, 18.23f.)

92.   But the tree of life is in the middle of paradise and the olive tree from which the Chrism is made by him for the resurrection.

93.   This world is an eater of corpses.   One hates everything one eats in it.   The truth is an eater of life.   B[ecause of th]is no one who is nurtured by [the truth] will die.   Jesus came out from that place and brought foods out from there and he gave [life] to those who wished, [so that] they do not die.

94.   ...para]dise, the ma[n...para]dise...[text broken]... This is the place where I will eat all things, since the tree of knowledge (*gnosis*) is there.   That one killed Adam, but the tree of knowledge made man live.   The law was the tree.   It has the power to give the knowledge of good and evil; neither did it make him cease evil, nor did it let him do good, but it created death for those who ate.   For, when he said, "eat this; do not eat this," he created the beginning of death.

95.   The Anointing (*chrism*) is greater than Baptism. For
by the Anointing we are called "Christians," not because of
Baptism. And they call Christ (so) because of his Anointing.
For the Father anointed the Son, and the Son anointed the
apostles, and the apostles anointed us. He who has been
anointed has the All; he has the resurrection, the light, the
cross, the Holy Spirit. The Father gave him these things in
the Bridechamber; he received (through faith).

96.   The Father was in the [Son], and the Son in the Father.

97.   The Lord spoke well when he said, "some went into the
kingdom of heaven laughing and came out...." [text broken].

98.   So it is also with the bread and the cup and the oil,
even if there is something higher than these.

99.   The world came into being through a sin. For he who
created it wished to create it imperishable and immortal. He
failed and did not attain his hope. For the imperishability
of the world did not come about, and neither did the imperishability of him who created the world. For there is no imperishability of things, but of sons. And no thing can attain
imperishability if it does not become a son. But whoever cannot receive, how much more can he not give?

> (A very important passage indicating the Gnostic
> belief that *creation as such* was evil. The creator-
> being here referred to is clearly a rebellious, mal-
> evolent, demonic power. It apparently means the
> Creator-God of the Jews, i.e., the God of Genesis
> 1-3, who created the world in the vain attempt to
> create it "imperishable." But since he could only
> create "things," and had no power to generate "sons,"
> his creation remained perishable.)

100.   The Cup of Prayer holds wine, it holds water. It
serves as a type of the blood by which they give thanks. And

it is full of the Holy Spirit and it belongs to the completely
perfect Man. When we drink this, we will take to ourselves
the perfect Man.

101.   The living water is a body. It is fitting that we
clothe ourselves with the living Man. Therefore, when he comes
to go down to the water, he disrobes in order that he may put
this one on.

102.   A horse begets a horse; a man begets a man; a God
begets a God. It is thus with the bridegroom and the bride.
They...[?]...out of the...[text broken].

>   (Significant discussion of the three main
>   sacraments; the Eucharist, a Greek word meaning
>   "thanks-giving", as the text says, Baptism and the
>   Bridechamber. "Living" water simply means running
>   water. All lead in concurrent ways toward the
>   creation of a Divine Being; immortal, clothed in
>   light.)

103.   These are the places where the children of the Bridechamber are. The union in this world is man and woman, the
place of the power and the weakness. In the aeon the form of
the union is different. But we name them by these names (104)
that are named and they are higher than the strong. For in the
place of violence there are those more worthy than the violence.
It is not the one, it is the other. However, both are one.
This is the one who cannot rise above the understanding of the
flesh.

105.   All who have the All, it is not right that they all
know themselves. Indeed, some, if they do not know themselves,
will not enjoy what they have. However, those who have learned
themselves, will enjoy them.

106.   They will not only be unable to comprehend the perfect
Man, they will not be able to see him. For if they see him they

will comprehend him. In no other way will anyone be able to
create for himself this grace, if he does not put on the perfect light...he will go...this is the perfect....

107.   [It is fitting] that we become...before we [come out
of the world]. He who has achieved the All...these places will
not be able to be...that place, but he will [go] in the middle
as imperfect. Jesus alone knows the end (telos) of these.

108.   The holy man is all holy, including his body. For,
if he holds the bread, he will make it holy, or the cup, or
anything else which he holds, he will make it pure. And how
is it he will not make the body pure?

109.   As Jesus made perfect the water of baptism, in this
way he poured out death.

> (The gnostics said that the baptism administered
> in the Christian church was only the "baptism of John
> the Baptist" that cleanses mankind from sin and death
> (Against Heresies, 1.21.1). But they claimed to have
> received also the "Anointing" (95) which conveys the
> Holy Spirit. Those who receive it become gnostics
> (95); indeed, they become "Christ"; see vs. 67.)

110.   He who has the knowledge (gnosis) of the truth is
free. But the free man does not sin. For he who sins is the
slave of sin. The Mother is the truth. The knowledge is the
Father. To whomever it is given not to sin, the knowledge of
the truth lifts up the heart, that is, it makes them free and
raises them over the whole place (the earth). Love (agapē),
however, builds up. And he who has become free through the
knowledge is a slave on account of love to those who cannot yet
take the freedom of knowledge. But knowledge makes them fit to
become free. Love [takes] nothing, how will it [take]...it
does not [say]...this is mine...it is yours.

111.   Love...it is wine and perfume. All those who shall be anointed with it are pleasured. Those who stand outside while the anointed are standing there are also pleasured. Those who are anointed with ointment, if they cease anointing themselves (?) and go, those not anointed but only standing outside them, if they go (?), they continue still in their stink. The Samaritan gave nothing to the wounded man except wine and oil. Love is nothing other than the oil. And it healed the wounds. For love covers a great many sins.

112.   The man whom the woman loves, those she will give birth to are like him. If he is her husband, they are like her husband. If he is an adulterer, they are like the adulterer.

113.   Man mixes with man; horse mixes with horse; ass mixes with ass. The kinds mix with the same kinds. Therefore the Spirit also mixes with the Spirit and the Logos has union with the Logos [and the light] has union [with the light. If you] become Man [the Man will] love you. If you become [Spirit], it is the Spirit who will unite with you. If you become Logos, the Logos will mix with you. If [you] become light the light will have union with you. If you become one of those above, those above will rest in you. If you become horse or ass or calf or dog or sheep or any other animal, those outside and below will not be able to love you, neither the Man nor the Spirit nor the Logos nor the light nor those of above nor those inside. They will not be able to find rest in you and you will have no part in them.

114.   He who is an unwilling slave will be able to be free. He who has become a freeman by the grace of his lord, and has sold himself into slavery, will no more be able to be a freeman.

115.   The farming of the world is (done) through four elements. They gather them into the barn through water and earth

and wind and light. The farming of God is also through four,
through faith (*pistis*) and hope (*elpis*) and love (*agapē*) and
knowledge (*gnōsis*). Our earth is faith, in it we take root.
The water is hope, through it....The wind is love, through it
we grow. The light, however is knowledge, through it we....

116.   The grace is...[text broken]...their souls. This is
Jesus the Christ. He tricked the whole place and did not burden anyone. This is why this kind of person is so blessed; he
is the Perfect Man. For this is the Logos.

117.   (Let) us ask about it, as it is difficult to set
someone straight again. How can we accomplish this great deed?
How are we to (118) give rest to anyone? First of all, it is
not right to grieve anyone, either someone great or small,
unbeliever or believer. Then (one must?) give rest (only) to
those who rest in what is good. There are some for whom it is
profitable to give rest to him who lives well. He who does
good cannot give rest to them, for he does not come willingly.
But he does not grieve them (either); for he does not oppress
them. Yet he who does well grieves them often, only not because of him, but their own wickedness causes them to be grieved
He who has the nature gives joy to the good. Some however griev
badly through this.

119.   A master of a house gained for himself all things:
children, slaves, cattle, dogs, pigs, corn, barley, chaff,
grass, ...flesh, acorns. He was wise and he knew the nourishment for each. He set bread and...before the children. To
the slaves he gave castor [oil and] meal. To the cattle...and
chaff and grass...dogs he threw bones...he threw acorns and...
bread. It is like this with the disciple of God. If he is
wise he understands the discipleship. The bodily forms will
not deceive him, but he will look to the condition of the soul
of each one and speak to him. There are many animals in the
world who have the form of man. If he recognizes them, he will

give acorns to the pigs, but he will give barley and chaff
and grass to the cattle. He will give bones to the dogs. He
will give first (?) to the slaves; he will give the full (?) to
the sons. [Till conjectures: the first element of teaching to
the slaves; the full teaching to the sons].

120.   There is a Son of Man and a son of the Son of Man.
The Lord is the Son of Man, and the son of the Son of Man is
he who is created through the Son of Man. The Son of Man
received from God the power to create. He is able to beget.

121.   He who has received the ability to create is a
creature. He who has received begetting is an offspring. He
who creates cannot beget. He who begets can create. But they
say, "He who creates, begets." But his offspring is a creature.
Therefore the offspring are not his children but...he who creates
works in...and he is...he who begets...and...image. He who
cre[ates]...in the open. He who begets...a child in secret.

122.   No [one can] know which d[ay the man] and the woman
(will) couple with one another except they alone. For worldly
marriage is a mystery for those who have taken a wife. If the
marriage of pollution is hidden, how much more is the unpolluted
marriage a true mystery. It is not fleshly, but it is pure.
It does not belong to lust, but to the will. It does not belong
to the darkness or the night but belongs to the day and the
light. If a marriage is laid bare it has become fornication.
And the bride becomes a whore not only when she receives the
seed of another man but indeed if she leaves her bed chamber
(and) is seen. She may be revealed only to her father and
mother and the friend of the bridegroom and the children of
the bridegroom. To these it is given to go into the bridechamber each day. The others must desire only to hear her
voice (and) to enjoy the ointment; let them be fed with what
falls from the table, like the dogs. Bridegrooms and brides

belong to the bridechamber. No one can see the bridegroom or
the bride unless he become these.

123.   When Abraham...he should see what he was going to
see, [he circumciz]ed the flesh of uncircumcision. He taught
us that it is right to destroy the flesh...this world so long
as their...and they live...they die according to...of the
revealed man...the guts of the man are hidden, he is living,
the man. If the guts come out of him and are exposed, the man
will die. It is the same with a tree. As long as its root is
hidden it sprouts. If its root is exposed, the tree withers.
It is thus with every birth in the world, not only with the
revealed but with the hidden. As long as the root of evil is
hidden, it is strong. If however it is recognized, it is
destroyed. If it is revealed, it perishes. Therefore the Logos
says: "The axe is already laid at the root of the tree." It
will not cut it off. What one cuts off sprouts again. But
the axe digs down to the bottom until it digs up the root.
Jesus pulled out the root of the whole place, but others only
partially. Let each of us, however, dig down to the root of
evil in him and pull it out of his heart to the root. It will
be pulled out if we recognize it. But if we do not know it,
it makes its root fast in us and brings forth its spirit in
our hearts. It is our lord and we are its slaves. It captures
us so that we do what we do [not wish] and what we wish, we do
[not] do. It is powerful, because we have not recognized it.
As long as it is (like this), it works. The...is mother of
the...ignorance...they will be perfect when the whole truth is
revealed. For the truth is like (?) ignorance: when it is
hidden it rests in itself; when it is revealed and recognized
it is praised, because it is stronger than ignorance and error.
It gives freedom.

124.   We now have the revealed things of creation. We say:
"They are the worthwhile, strong things. But the hidden things
are worthless and weak." Thus it is with the revealed things

of the truth; they are weak and worthless. But the hidden
things are strong and worthwhile. However, the mysteries of
the truth are revealed as types and images. But the Bridechamber is hidden. It is the holy one in the holy one.

125.   The veil at first covered how God administered the
creation. But when the veil is torn, and the things within
are revealed, it will leave this house as a desert; rather,
it will be [destroyed?]. But the whole divinity will not flee
out of these places back into the holies of holies. For it
cannot mix with the [unmixed light] and the faultless fullness
(*plērōma*), but it will [be] under the wings of the Cross [and
under] its arms. This ark will [be for them] escape when the
deluge of water overpowers them. If some are in the tribe of
the priesthood, they will be able to enter behind the veil with
the high priest. Because of this the veil was not torn only
on top, because it would be open only for those above. Nor
was it torn only at the bottom, since it would be revealed only
to those below. Rather, it was torn from the top to the bottom.
Those of above opened to us of below; therefore, we will go into
the secret of truth. This truly is the worthwhile which is
strong. But we will go in there through worthless types and
weaknesses. They are really worthless in respect to the perfect glory. There is a glory which is greater than glory.
There is a power greater than power. Therefore, this has
opened the perfect to us, and the secret of the truth. And
the holy ones of the holy ones are revealed, and the Bridechamber urged us in. As long as it is hidden, wickedness is
really brought to nothing, but it is not removed from the midst
of the seed of the Holy Spirit. They are slaves of evil. When
it is revealed, then the perfect light will pour over all and
all in it will receive the [Anointings]. Then the slaves will
become free and the prisoners will be redeemed. (126) [Every]
plant my Father in heaven does not plant [will be] rooted out.
Those who are alienated will be united. Everyone who [will go

in] to the Bridechamber will [beget the light?]. For [they do
not beget] as the marriage which...are in the night. The
fire...in the night; it is extinguished. But the mysteries
of marriage are fulfilled in the day and light. That day and
its light does not set.

127.   If anyone becomes a child of the Bridechamber, he
will receive light. If anyone does not receive it while he is
in these places (i.e., "this world"), he will not be able to
receive it in the other place. The one who has received light
cannot be seen nor can he be held, and no one can torment him,
even if he lives in the world. And also, if he should go out
of the world, already he has received the truth in images. The
world became the (Eternal) Aion, for the Aion is become for him
the fullness (*plerōma*), and it is thus: it is revealed only to
him. It is not hidden in the darkness and the night, but it is
hidden in a perfect day and a holy light.

            The Gospel according to Philip

60. THE GOSPEL OF PETER

(Trans. D.R. Cartlidge)

(Introduction: This Gospel is known to have been in circulation around A.D. 175 in Syria, and could be based on traditions going back into the first century. The translation here given is based on the only extant Greek fragment still preserved, which was discovered in 1886 in the grave of a Christian monk near Akhmim, in Upper Egypt. It is clearly a part of a larger document, perhaps originally resembling one of the canonical Gospels, from which it seems to have drawn many phrases and scenes, inter-mixing new (or older) material with what has been taken over. Besides the remarkable resurrection scene, which is unique in presently known Gospel literature, this Gospel is significant in the way it reflects the rising tide of militant antisemitism in the second century Church, as evidenced by the way in which the Gospel writer systematically altered his narrative (assuming he relied on the canonical Gospels) to intensify the Jewish elders' fierce desire to exterminate Jesus, while at the same time altering Pilate's role to one of innocent helplessness. It may also be that the author of the Gospel of Peter had traditions independent of the canonical gospels which underlie the work as we have it. The uniqueness of the resurrection scene would be evidence for this supposition. The tendency for increasing antisemitism in the Church is nonetheless present here. The same trend can be seen in another second-century Christian writing dealing with Jesus' death, the Acts of Pilate.)

1.   1.   ...None of the Jews washed his hands, neither did Herod nor any of his judges. As they did not wish to wash, Pilate got up. 2. And then Herod the King ordered the Lord to be taken away. He said to them, "That which I ordered you to do to him, do it."

2.   3.   Joseph, who was a friend of Pilate and of the Lord, stood there and, seeing that they were about to crucify him, came to Pilate and requested the body of the Lord for burial. 4. Pilate sent to Herod and requested his body.
5. Herod said, "Brother Pilate, if someone had not asked for him, we would have buried him, since the Sabbath dawns. For it is written in the law: the sun is not to set on one who has

been killed." And he delivered him to the people on the day
before Adzumos (Unleavened Bread), their feast.

3.   6. They took the Lord and they ran and roughed him
up and said, "Let us drag the Son of God (to judgment); we have
him in our power." 7. They garbed him in purple and seated
him upon the judgment seat and said, "Judge justly, king of
Israel!" 8. And one of them brought a crown of thorns and
put it on the Lord's head. 9. Others standing there spit in
his face; others slapped his cheeks; some stuck him with a
reed, and whipped him, saying, "By this honor, we honor the
Son of God!"

4.   10. And they brought two criminals, and they crucified the Lord between them. He was silent as if he had no pain.
11. When they had set up the cross, they inscribed on it,
"This is the King of Israel." 12. And when they had taken
away his clothes, in front of him they divided them and cast
lots for them. 13. But one of the criminals reviled them and
said, "We suffer thus because of the evil we did; this man is
the savior of men, what wrong did he do you?" 14. So they
were angry with the thief and gave orders that the criminal's
legs should not be broken; thus, he died in torment.

5.   15. It was noon, and darkness gripped all Judea.
(The Jews) were worried and anguished lest the sun had already
set, since he (Jesus) still lived. It is written for them that
the sun is not to set on one who has been killed. 16. One of
them said, "Give him gall mixed with vinegar to drink." They
mixed it and gave it to him to drink. 17. Indeed, they fulfilled everything, and they brought their sins to full fruition
on their own heads. 18. Many went around with lamps; they
thought it was night. They fell...[Greek uncertain.] 19. And
the Lord cried out, "My power, (my) power, you have left me!"
He said this and was taken up. 20. That same hour (the ninth)

the veil of the Jerusalem temple was split in two.

6.   21. Then they pulled the spikes out of the Lord's hands, and they placed him on the ground. There was an earthquake which shook the whole earth, and there was great fear. 22. Then the sun shone again and they realized it was the ninth hour. 23. The Jews rejoiced, and they gave his body to Joseph in order that he should bury it because he had seen what good things he (Jesus) did. 24. He took the Lord, washed him, wrapped him in linen, and placed him in his own tomb, called the Garden of Joseph. 25. Then the Jews, the elders, and the priests, knowing what evil they did to themselves, began to beat their breasts and say, "Woe, on account of our sins; the judgment and the end of Jerusalem are at hand." 26. I with my companions was greatly grieved. We trembled and were wounded to the heart; we were hiding, for we were sought by them as criminals, as if we wished to burn down the temple. 27. Because of all these things, we fasted and sat mourning and crying night and day until the Sabbath.

7.   28. The scribes, Pharisees, and elders gathered together and, hearing that all the people murmured and beat their breasts, said, "If such great miracles have happened at his death, behold how righteous he is!" 29. The elders were afraid and they came begging to Pilate and said, "Give us soldiers, in order that they may guard his tomb for three days, so that his disciples will not come and steal him, and then the people assume that he is risen from the dead, and they should harm us." 31. Pilate gave them Petronius, the centurion, along with soldiers to guard the tomb; and the elders and scribes came with them to the tomb. 32. They, with the centurion and the soldiers--since they were all there together-- rolled a huge stone and placed it over the door of the tomb. 33. They sealed it with seven seals, erected a tent there, and stood guard. 34. The morning of the Sabbath dawned; a

crowd came from Jerusalem and its surroundings in order that
they might see the tomb sealed up.

8.   35.   In the night before the dawn of the Lord's day,
while the soldiers guarded two by two, there was a great noise
in heaven,   36.   and they saw the heavens open and two men,
having great splendor, come down from there and draw near the
tomb.   37.   The stone which had been placed at the door rolled
away by itself and moved to the side.   The tomb was opened and
both youths went in.   38.   When the soldiers saw this, they
awakened the centurion and the elders, for they were there on
guard.   39.   As they recounted what they had seen, again they
saw three men coming out of the tomb; two supported one of them
and a cross followed them.   40.   The heads of the two reached
to heaven, but the one whom they bore with their hands reached
beyond the heavens.   41.   And they heard a voice speaking from
the heavens, "Have you preached to those who are sleeping?"
42.   And, obediently, (a voice) was heard from the cross,
"Yes."   42.   Therefore, they decided among themselves to go and
reveal these things to Pilate.   44.   While they were deciding,
again the heavens were seen to open, and a certain man descended
and went into the tomb.

9.   45.   When they saw these things, those with the centurion went quickly by night to Pilate, abandoning the tomb
they guarded; they explained everything which they had seen;
they were greatly upset and said, "Truly he was a Son of God."
46.   Pilate answered, "I am pure in regard to the blood of the
Son of God; this was your decision."   47.   Then they all
approached and begged him to order the centurion and the
soldiers to say nothing of what they had seen.   48.   "For it
would be better for us," they said, "to bear the guilt of a
great sin before God than to fall into the hands of the Jewish
people and to be stoned."   49.   Pilate, therefore, ordered the
centurion and the soldiers to say nothing.

10.   50.   At the dawn of the Lord's day, Mary Magdalene,
a disciple of the Lord, afraid because of the Jews, since they
were inflamed by wrath, had not done at the tomb what custom
demanded women should do for those who had died and whom they
loved.   51.   (Thus she) brought with her some friends and came
to the tomb where he was buried.   52.   They were afraid lest
the Jews should see them, and they said, "Because we were not
able to weep and beat our breasts on the day he was crucified,
let us now do these things at his tomb.   53.   But who will roll
away for us the stone placed before the door of the tomb, so
that, when we go in, we can sit beside him and do what ought
to be done?   54.   For the stone is huge and we are afraid lest
someone should see us.   Even if we are not able to enter, at
least we can place beside the door that which we bring in his
memory; let us weep and beat our breasts until we return to our
house."   55.   They came and found the tomb opened, and, approach-
ing near, they bent down to look in.   There they saw a youth
seated in the middle of the tomb; he was handsome and wore a
shining robe.   He said to them,   56.   "Why did you come?   Whom
do you seek?   Not him who was crucified?   He is risen and has
gone.   If you do not believe, bend over and see the place where
he was laid, because he is not there.   For he is risen and has
gone to the place from which he was sent."   57.   Then the women
were frightened and fled.

11.   58.   It was the last day of Adzumos and many returned
to their homes; the feast was over.   59.   We, the twelve disciples of the Lord, wept and were grief-stricken.   Each, grieving at what had happened, returned to his own house.   60.   But
I, Simon Peter, and Andrew, my brother, took our nets and went
to the sea (of Galilee); and with us was Levi, the son of
Alphaeus, whom the Lord...[text breaks off at this point].

61. THE ACTS OF THE HOLY APOSTLE THOMAS

(Resumé and trans., D.R. Cartlidge)

(Introduction: The identity of the chief figure in this writing, Didymos Judas Thomas, is largely unfamiliar to those of us nurtured in Western Christianity. His real name is simply Judas (in Hebrew, Judah,) and both Didymos and Thomas mean 'twin'. Thus this is Judah the Twin - of Jesus! His fame was widespread from Egypt to Syria and on over to India, where he was reputedly the first apostle to bring Christianity, and his memory is still revered there to this day.

This account of his missionary adventures was most likely written in the first half of the third century A.D. The document is made up, however, of traditions which go back much earlier. The place of origin of the Acts of Thomas is considered by most historians to have been eastern Syria, probably Edessa. The original language of the document was Syriac. However, the extant Syriac text has been highly "catholicized", i.e., it has been altered to be made more orthodox and acceptable to the Western Church. Thus, the Greek version, in most cases, appears to reflect a better Syriac text than the one now preserved in Syriac manuscripts. The most important exception to this is in chs. 108-113, "The Hymn of the Pearl."

The Acts of Thomas has been influenced in its style and form by various Gospels, the canonical book of the Acts of the Apostles, and the Hellenistic novel. Its theology is certainly influenced by gnostic Christianity. It is quite possible that the Acts of Thomas is part of a Thomas tradition which includes among its literature, the Coptic Gospel of Thomas, and the Book of Thomas the Athlete. The Infancy Gospel of Thomas might also belong to this same tradition.

As we have stated, the Greek version is generally more authentic than the Syriac. This translation is based on the Greek, mainly the "longer" Greek tradition. Where the Syriac differs from the Greek and appears to have the better reading, we have relied upon the translation of G. Bornkamm, in Edgar Hennecke, *New Testament Apocrypha*, Vol II. The Arabic numbers in parenthesis are the chapter divisions of Lipsius-Bonnet.)

First Act.

(1)   The apostles are all gathered in Jerusalem:
Simon Peter, Andrew, James the Son of Zebedee, John his brother,
Philip, Bartholomew, Thomas, Matthew, James the son of Alphaeus,
Simon the Cananaean, and Judas the brother of James. They
apportion the earth for their missionary activities, each to
be an apostle to a separate region. Thomas "who is called
Didymos" is assigned to India. He objects because "a weakness
of the flesh" prohibits his travel, and, as a Hebrew he cannot
preach the gospel to Indians. The Savior appears to him at
night and assures Thomas, "my grace is with you." Thomas says,
"Send me to some other place you wish for I am not going to
the Indians." (2)   Jesus appears to an Indian merchant named
Abban and, knowing that Abban has been sent to buy a carpenter
slave, sells Thomas to Abban. When Jesus leads Thomas to Abban,
the merchant asks, "Is this your master?" Thomas says, "Yes,
this is my Lord." "I have bought you from him," said Abban.
And the Apostle was silent. (3)   Thomas, the next morning,
goes off with Abban. They sail, with a favorable wind, and
arrive at Andrapolis. (4)   As they leave the ship, they hear
the sound of a festival. It is the wedding of the King's
daughter. Abban and Thomas go to the wedding. (5) The apostle,
to everyone's astonishment, puts on a show of very bad manners
by not eating or drinking anything at the banquet. At the
guests' questions about his abstinence, he says, "I have come
here for something greater than food or drink." The guests at
the wedding anoint Thomas with oil. A flute girl, being a
Hebrew, recognizes something divine in Thomas and stands near
him. (6) One of the cup-bearers slaps Thomas. Thomas curses
the cup-bearer, then sings this hymn:

>   "The maiden is the daughter of light,
>   the royal aura of kings rests and stands upon her,
>   looking upon her is delight,
>   she is aglow with shining beauty.

Her clothes are like spring flowers,
from them is diffused a scent of sweet fragrance.
The King is established in the crown of her head,
he feeds those who are established under him with
    his ambrosia.
Truth sits upon her head,
she reveals joy by (the motion) of her feet.
Her mouth is open, it is pleasing,
[Syr. with it she sings loud songs of praise.]
Thirty-two sing to her hymns of praise.
Her tongue is like the curtain of the door,
which is flung open to those who are entering.
[Syr. Like steps her neck mounts up,]
which the first artisan created.
Her two hands make signs and trace out, proclaiming
the dance of the blessed aeons,
her fingers [Syr. open] the gates of the city.
Her bedchamber is light,
wafting the fragrance of balsam and all sweet aromatics;
giving out the sweet smell of myrrh and (fragrant)
    leaves.
Inside are scattered myrtle and all sorts of sweet
    smelling blossoms,
the doorways are decorated with reeds.

(7) Her groomsmen surround her, their number is seven,
she has chosen them.
Her bridesmaids are seven,
they dance before her.
There are twelve in number who serve before her,
they are her subjects.
They gaze and look to the bridegroom,
so that they may be enlightened by looking at him,
and they shall be with him forever in eternal joy,
and they shall be at that marriage at which the
    princes gather,
and linger over the banquet

of which those who are eternal are worthy.
They shall dress in royal clothes
and shall be garbed in magnificent garments,
and both shall be in joy and exultation,
and they shall glorify the Father of the All,
whose haughty light they received;
they were enlightened by the vision of their Lord,
they received his ambrosial food
which has nothing lacking,
and they drank from his wine
which gives them neither thirst nor desire.
They glorified and praised, with the Living Spirit,
the Father of Truth and the Mother of Wisdom."

(8) Only the flute girl understands the hymn because it is in
Hebrew. She adores Thomas; she plays her flute for the guests
but keeps looking over at Thomas. The cup-bearer, who slapped
Thomas, goes to the well. There he is killed by a lion and a
black dog brings his hand back to the feast (which fulfills
Thomas' curse). (9) This amazes the guests. The King invites
Thomas to pray for the bride. The apostle demurs, but is persuaded. (10) Thomas then is led to the bridal chamber and he
prays over the couple.

(11) "The King ordered the groomsmen to leave the
bridal chamber. When all had gone and the doors were closed,
the groom lifted the veil of the bridechamber, so that he
should bring the bride to himself. He saw the Lord Jesus, in
the likeness of Judas Thomas the apostle, speaking to the
bride. But he (Thomas) had just blessed them and left them.
He (the groom) said: 'Did you not leave in front of everyone?
How did you get here?' The Lord said to him: 'I am not Judas
Thomas, I am his brother.' And the Lord sat down on the bed
and ordered them to sit on chairs and he began to speak to them."

(12) Jesus begins to preach a sermon to the young
couple. He adjures them to refrain from "filthy sexual intercourse" so that they will not beget children, who will only

force the parents to become thieves in order to support their
wants. Furthermore, says Jesus, most children are worthless
or demon-possessed, or become lunatics, sick and so on. Even
if they stay healthy, they will commit innumerable sins. "But
if you obey and guard your souls pure to God, you will produce
living children, whom hurts do not touch, and you will be care-
free, living a life without grief and care...waiting to receive
that marriage which is incorruptible and true, and you shall be
its groomsmen entering that bridechamber which is full of immortality and light." (13) At this, the couple refuses to have
sex with each other, they give themselves instead to the Lord,
and "abstained from filthy lust." When the King comes in to
them in the morning he is surprised to find the couple not shy
with each other, but, as the Queen (who has also come in) says
to her daughter, "Why are you sitting there that way, child?
You are not ashamed but are acting as if you have lived with
your husband for a long time!"[1] (14) "The bride answered,
'Truly, father, I am in much love and I pray to my Lord that
the love which I have known this night will remain with me,
and I seek for the husband whom I knew today. [Syr. - The
reason I do not veil myself] is because the mirror [Syr. - veil]
of shame has been removed from me. I am no longer ashamed or
bashful, for the deed of shame and bashfulness has been taken
far from me. And I am not frightened, because the fear did not
remain with me. I am in joy and delight because the day of
delight was not disturbed, and because I have set aside this
man and this marriage which passes away from before my eyes,
for I am joined in another marriage. And [I rejoice] because
I did not have intercourse with the temporary man whose end is
regret and bitterness of soul, but I am yoked with the True
Man.'"

(15) The groom also makes a speech: "'I thank you,
Lord, who was preached through the stranger and was found in us;

---

[1]Compare the opposite case, Gen. 3:1-7.

who has put me far from corruption and sown life in me; Who
has delivered me from this chronic disease which is hard to
cure and heal and has placed me into eternity and wise health;
who has shown yourself to me and has revealed to me everything
about me which I am; who has redeemed me from the fall and has
led me to the better; who has redeemed me from temporary things
and made me worthy of immortal and eternal things; who has
humbled yourself to me and my insignificance, so that placing
me beside greatness you should unite me with myself; who did
not hold back your own mercy from me who was perishing, but
you showed me how to seek myself and to know who I was and who
and how I am now, so that I should become again what I was;[1]
whom I did not know, but you yourself hunted me out; whom I
did not comprehend, but you received me; whom I have experienced
and now cannot speak of you; whose love ferments in me, and I
am not able to speak as I ought, but what I am able to say about
Him is short and very little, and does not come close to His
glory. He does not blame me as I am bold to speak to Him and
say what I do not know; I say this because of love for Him.'"
(16) The King is very unhappy at this. He sends out orders to
arrest Thomas. But Thomas has set sail, leaving the flute girl
weeping because he did not take her along.

Second Act.

        (17) Thomas and Abban arrive in India and report to
King Gundaphorus. The King asks Thomas if he will build a
palace for him. Thomas says, "Yes...because for this I came
to build and to work as a carpenter." (18) The King and Thomas
discuss plans for the palace. Thomas will build the palace
during the winter, which is not the usual practice. Thomas
draws master plans in the dust, with a reed. (19) The money

---

[1]This statement is a very close parallel to a classic gnostic
creed found in Clement of Alexandria, *Excerpts from Theodotos*,
78.2. It means that salvation is for man to become as Adam was
before his Fall, i.e., non-sexual, or bi-sexual. Cp. the Gospel
of Philip and Coptic Gospel of Thomas.

which the King gives Thomas to build the palace is distributed
to the poor. The King asks if the palace is built. Thomas
says it is, except for the roof. "...Let it be roofed," says
the King. (20) The King finally finds out how his money has
been spent and that the palace has not been built. He calls
Thomas for a reckoning. (21) The King asks if the palace is
built. Thomas says it is. The King asks to see the palace and
is told that he cannot see it in this life, "but when you leave
this life you will see it." Thereupon the King orders Thomas
thrown into prison and contemplates how best to torture him to
death. Meanwhile, the King's brother, Gad, falls ill. Gad
blames his illness on Thomas and asks that the apostle be
swiftly killed. (22) Gad dies and, in heaven, sees the palace
Thomas built for his brother. (23) Gad is released from heaven
to tell his brother of the wonderful palace. He does so,
(24) and the King sends for Thomas, asking him for instruction
in the Gospel. (25) The apostle prays joyfully, (26) Gad and
Gundaphorus will not let him alone. They finally ask for "the
seal"[1] which will make them Christians. (27) The apostle
"seals" them. They hear the Lord's voice. The apostle takes
oil and pours it on their heads and gives a prayer:

> "Come, holy name of Christ which is above every name.
> Come, power of the Most High and perfect compassion.
> Come, highest gift.
> Come, compassionate Mother.
> Come, fellowship of the male.
> Come, you who reveal the concealed mysteries.
> Come, Mother of the seven houses in order that your
> rest may be in the eighth house.
> Come, Elder of the five members: understanding,
> thought, wisdom, compassion, reasoning.
> Have union with these youths.

---

[1]Or baptism, with the gift of the Holy Spirit. Anointing
with oil was a common substitute for water.

Come, Holy Spirit, and cleanse their testicles,
and especially seal them in the name of the Father,
Son, and Holy Spirit.

When dawn comes they all celebrate a eucharist (Lord's
Supper). (28) The apostle preaches an ascetic sermon, (29) he
blesses all present, and he fasts. The Lord appears and sends
Thomas "two miles down...the road." He has a task for the
apostle.

Third Act.

(30) The apostle finds the corpse of a beautiful boy
beside the road and discerns evil at work. (31) A great serpent comes out of a hole and admits that he killed the boy
because there was a beautiful woman with whom the serpent fell
in love. The snake found the young man kissing her and having
intercourse with her, and killed him. The apostle asks the
snake to identify himself. (32) Among other evil deeds, the
snake is the one who tempted Eve; he caused Cain to kill Abel;
he is the Satan. (33) The apostle commands the snake ("in the
name of Jesus") "to...suck out your poison which you put into
this man, and draw it out and receive it from him." The snake
is unwilling, but Thomas compels him to do it. The young man
becomes healed; the snake swells up, explodes, and dies.
(34) The young man expresses his freedom from Satan. (35) Thomas
warns him not to take his attraction to Jesus lightly. (36-37)
A sermon, by Thomas, based upon the miracle.

Act Four.

(39) "While the apostle was yet standing in the road
and talking with the crowd, a donkey's colt came up and stood
in front of him. (The colt) opened his mouth and said: 'Twin
Brother (*didymos*) of Christ, apostle of the Most High and
brother-initiate of the hidden word of Christ, who received

his secret sayings,[1] co-worker of the Son of God, who though
free became a slave and was sold and led many into freedom;
member of a great race which condemned the enemy and redeemed
its own; who brings life to many in the country of the Indians -
for you came to men who have gone astray, and through your mani-
festation and your divine words now they are turning toward the
One who sent you, the God of truth - climb up and sit on me and
rest until you enter the city.'" (40) The apostle asks the colt
who he is. The colt says that he is a descendant of Balaam's
donkey; Jesus rode one of the colt's ancestors into Jerusalem.
Thomas is awed at this and refuses to ride. The colt persuades
Thomas (41) and, after the ride up to the city, when Thomas
dismounts, the colt falls dead. The crowd asks Thomas to raise
the colt. Thomas says he could raise the colt "in the name of
Jesus" but it is not useful and helpful to do so.

Act Five.

(42) The apostle is confronted by a "very lovely
woman" who says that she has been tormented by "the Adversary"
for five years. (43) One day as she was coming from her bath,
she relates, a troubled man, weak with love for her, accosted
her. He wanted to have sexual intercourse with her. She refused; she never had sexual intercourse even with her betrothed.
She asked her maid if she had seen the youth; the maid replied
that she had seen an old man. In the night, the demon-youth
raped her. This violation has been going on for five years.
She asks Thomas to exorcise the demon. (44) Thomas, by means
of a prayer-incantation calls the demon to him. (45) The demon
appears and tries to put a counter spell on Thomas, "What have
we to do with you, apostle of the Most High?"[2] (46) The demon
is unsuccessful and leaves, weeping for love of the woman. He

---

[1]Possibly a reference to the preface of the Coptic Gospel of
Thomas.

[2]The whole scene is based on Mark 5:7ff.

vanishes in smoke and fire. (47-48) Thomas raises a prayer of
confession, thanks, and supplication.[1] (49) He blesses the
crowd. The woman asks for "the seal" and the eucharist.

(50)   And he began to say,
            [Syr. - "Come, gift of the Most High.]
            Come, perfect mercy.
            Come, fellowship of the male.
            [Syr. - Come, Holy Spirit.]
            Come, she who understands the mysteries of the elect.
            Come, she who has companionship in all the contests
            of the noble athlete.
            [Syr. - Come treasure of glory.
            Come, dearest compassion of the Most High.]
            Come, silence that reveals the great acts of the whole
            greatness.
            Come, she who reveals secret things, and makes the
            forbidden manifest.
            Holy Dove, who begets twin young,
            Come, hidden Mother.
            Come, she who is revealed in her deeds and who present
            joy and rest to those who are united with her.
            Come, and unite with us in this eucharist which we
            celebrate in your name, and in the love-feast (agapē)
            to which we are gathered at your call."

Act Six.

        (51) There is a young man who had committed a sinful
act. He comes and takes the eucharist in his mouth; his two
hands wither so that he is unable to put them to his mouth.

---

[1]There is a reference to the Gospel of Thomas, saying 13.
Thomas' prayer begins: "O Jesus, who art the hidden Mystery revealed to us, You are He who manifested all mysteries to us,
who set me apart by myself from all my companions, also speaking three words in my ears consuming me, nor am I able to say
them to others..."

The witnesses to this event inform Thomas and he asks the youth what crime he had committed. The youth replies, "A woman who lives outside the town loved me and I loved her. When I heard your sermon I came forward to receive the seal with the others. But you said, 'Whoever shall unite in foul intercourse, especially in adultery, shall not receive life from the God whom I preach.' Since I was very much in love, I asked her, trying to persuade her, that she would become my consort in chastity and pure conduct, which you spoke about. She refused. Because she would not agree, I took a sword and killed her, for I could not stand it if she committed adultery with another." (52) The apostle responds by condemning "insane sexual intercourse." He asks that a bowl of water be brought. He prays over the bowl and tells the young man to wash his hands; the youth does so and is healed. (53) The apostle and the young man go to the inn and find the beautiful girl lying there, dead. (54) Thomas said to the young man, "Go and hold her hand and say to her, 'I, by my hands, killed you with iron and with my hands, by the faith in Jesus, raise you.'" The youth does so, and the woman is restored to life. (55-57) She tells the apostle that a man in black led her to hell and showed her horrible visions, terrible tortures happening to people who had sexual intercourse and bore children. (58) Thomas assures her of the forgiveness of her sin. (59) All the witnesses to this believe. (60-61) A prayer by Thomas.

Act Seven.

(62-64) A captain of a certain King Misdaeus comes to Thomas and tells him that his (the captain's) wife and daughter are possessed by demons who are sexually assaulting their women. (65) The captain is told he must believe in Jesus, and then his women will be healed. The captain confesses his faith and says, "Help my little faith."[1] Thomas gathers the

---

[1]Based on Mark 9:24.

crowd around him.   (66) A sermon about Jesus' constant care
for his own is preached.   (67) The apostle blesses all who are
gathered there.

Act Eight.

            (68) Thomas travels on with the captain and wagon
driver.   (69) It is very hot and the animals pulling their
wagon become tired.   A herd of wild donkeys is nearby and
Thomas tells the wagon driver that if he believes in Jesus he
should go to the wild donkeys and ask for four of them to pull
the wagon.   (70) The captain does so, in spite of his fear.
The donkeys obey him, all of them, not just four.   Thomas
rebukes them, asking again for only four.   Again all the donkeys
want to pull the wagon for the apostle.   Thomas rebukes them,
and finally the excess number of donkeys moves off.   (71) They
come to the city where the captain and the driver tell everyone
of the miracle and a great crowd gathers.   (72) The apostle
prays   (73) and commands one of the wild donkeys to go to the
court of the King to summon all the demons there.   (74) The
donkey goes, accompanied by a great crowd.   He summons the
demons.   (75) The captain's wife and daughter come forth.   The
apostle commands the demons to be exorcised "in the name of
Jesus."   The women fall down as if dead.   The demons rebuke
Thomas   (76) and one asks to be set free.   (77) The apostle
banishes the demons.   The women are still lying as if dead.
(78) The wild donkey exhorts the apostle to heal the women and
(79) the crowd to believe in Jesus.   (80) The apostle replies
in a prayer to Jesus, and then   (81) restores the women.   The
wild donkeys go back to their grazing grounds.   Thomas watches
over them that they are not harmed.

Act Nine.

            (82) We are introduced to Mygdonia, wife of Charisius
a close relative of the King.   She comes, from curiosity, to see
this wonder-worker, Thomas.   Mygdonia arrives in a sedan chair,

borne by her slaves, but the crowds are so great around Thomas
that she must send for more servants to beat aside the throng
so that she can see Thomas. Thereupon, the apostle rebukes
them. (83) He promises the slaves that their burden is heavy
now, but God never lays upon man yokes too heavy to bear.
(84) To bear their burdens they must refrain from adultery,
murder, theft, and other vices, especially "from horrid intercourse and the couch of uncleanness." (85-86) Thomas continues
his speech, an exhortation to "holiness." (87) The crowd is
very excited over his sermon. Mygdonia throws herself at the
apostle's feet and begs that she "may become (God's) dwelling
place, and rejoice in the prayer and the hope and his faith,
and that (she) too may receive the seal, and become a holy
temple and he should dwell in (her)." (88) The apostle adjures
Mygdonia to give up her wealth, fame, pomp of adornment, and to
renounce sex, "the fellowship of child-bearing." He bids her
to "go in peace." She is afraid she will not see Thomas again,
but he assures her that Jesus will be with her. She goes home.
(89) Charisius, her husband, comes to the dinner table and sees
that his wife is not present. At his inquiry, the servants tell
him that Mygdonia is ill in her bedchamber. He hurries to her
and asks what is wrong. She says she is ill. (90) Charisius
brings dinner to the room, but she still refuses to eat; he dines
alone. She also refuses to sleep with him. (91) When Charisius
wakes, he describes a strange dream to her. He says that he and
his friend the King were at table and an eagle came and bore off
two partridges to his nest. The eagle came back and took a dove
and a pigeon. The King shot an arrow at the eagle, but it passed harmlessly through the bird. Mygdonia says, "your dream is
good, for you eat partridges daily, but the eagle has not
tasted partridge till now." (92) Charisius gets up, and acci-
dentally puts his left sandal on his right foot. He takes this
for another bad omen.

(93) Mygdonia hurries to Thomas. (94) She confesses
to the apostle that she has accepted Thomas' words. Thomas
delivers a sermon urging her to an ascetic life.

(95) Charisius comes to breakfast and misses his wife
She has, he is told, gone to the "stranger" who is a doctor of
souls. She returns and goes to bed alone. She again will not
come to dinner. (96) Charisius remonstrates with her, warning
her that Thomas is a magician. (97) Mygdonia is silent; when
Charisius leaves she prays for strength to overcome her husband's "shamelessness." (98) Her husband returns to her after
dinner and wants to have sexual intercourse. She rejects him
for "My Lord Jesus, who is with me and rests in me, is greater
than you." She runs naked away from him, and goes to sleep
with her nurse. (99) Charisius is upset. He expresses his woe
in a long speech in which he bemoans the loss of his wife.
(100) Charisius continues his complaint. He has lived with his
wife less than a year and an "evil eye" has snatched her away.
Charisius vows vengeance upon Thomas. He asks King Misdaeus
to give him "the stranger's head." He also wants satisfaction
in the matter of Siphor, the captain, who brought Thomas to the
city and who is sheltering the apostle. Charisius describes
Thomas as one who "teaches a new teaching, saying this, that
no one is able to live unless he gives away all his goods and
becomes a renouncer like he is; and he works fast to make many
companions to himself." (101) Day dawns and Charisius goes to
King Misdaeus and reports what has happened. (102) Misdaeus
promises action. He sends messengers to Thomas (Mygdonia is
again there, listening to the apostle's sermon) and they rebuke
Thomas through the captain, Siphor. The apostle tells Siphor
not to worry. (103) Thomas asks Mygdonia what caused this uproar. She tells him it is because she will not sleep with her
husband. Thomas encourages her to continue her good works.
(104) Meanwhile, the captain reports back to the King and tells
him how Thomas has helped him by healing his wife and daughter.
(105) The King sends men to bring Thomas to him, but the crowds
frighten them and they return without Thomas. Charisius vows
he will fetch Thomas himself. (106) He accosts Thomas, arrests
him, and brings him to King Misdaeus. To the King's questions,
the apostle stands mute. They give Thomas one hundred

twenty-eight lashes and lock him up. The king and Charisius
consider, meanwhile, how they will kill him. (107) The apostle
goes to prison rejoicing that he can suffer for his Lord.
(108) Thomas, in prison, sings the famous Hymn of the Pearl.[1]

(108)   When I was a small child,
         in the realms of my father I
         lived in wealth and among delicacies.
         My parents provisioned me and
         sent me from the East, our home;
         from the riches of the treasury
         they made up a load, both great and yet
         light, so that I was able to bear it alone.
         [Gold from Beth 'Ellaye and silver from great Gazak]
         and chalcedony stones from India [and opals from
            Kushan.]
         They girdled me with steel, [which crushes iron.
         And they took off me the splendid robe
         which in their love they had wrought for me,
         and the purple toga,
         which was woven to the measure of my stature,]
         and they made an agreement with me,
         engraving it in my heart, so I would not forget.
         They said to me, "If you go down into Egypt
         and carry off from there the one pearl
         [which is in the midst of the sea,
         in the abode of the loud-breathing serpent,
         you shall put on again your splendid robe
         and your toga, which lies over it,]
         and with your brother you shall become
         herald (heir) in our kingdom."
(109)   I left the East upon the difficult and
         dangerous way, with two couriers,
         for I was very inexperienced to do this.

---

[1]Syriac text is in brackets.

I went over the borders of Mesene,
the gathering-place of the East's merchants;
I came to the country of Babylon
[and entered within the walls of Sarbug.]
When I came into Egypt, the couriers with me left me.
I went immediately to the serpent
and [nearby his abode I stayed,
until he should slumber and sleep],
so that I could take my pearl away from him.
As I was alone, [I was a stranger
to my hosts who were my companions.]
But there I saw one of my fellow countrymen from
the East, a free man, a youth gracious and favored,
a son of the mighty.
He came and joined me, and I made him
my bosom companion, my friend, to whom I communicated
I warned him to watch the Egyptians and their unclean
    companionship[1]
But I put on clothes like theirs
[that they might not suspect] that I had
come from without to take the pearl,
and the Egyptians would wake the serpent against me.
But for some reason I do not know, they learned
that I was not their countryman.
They treated me with guile and I ate their food.
I forgot that I was the son of a king,
And I served their king.
[and I forgot the pearl
for which my parents had sent me.]
And from the heaviness of their food,
I fell into a deep sleep.
(110)   While I suffered all this,
my parents were aware of it and suffered for me.

---

[1]The text seems incorrect. It probably should read, "He
warned me, etc."

A proclamation was announced in our kingdom
that all should come to our gate.
And then the kings of Parthia and those
in office and the rulers of the East
[made a resolve] concerning me [that I
should not be left] in Egypt. [They wrote
to me a letter, and every noble set his name to it.
(When it arrived)
I awoke and stood up from my sleep],
I took it and I kissed it and read it.
It had been written concerning what was
engraved in my heart.
I remembered immediately that I am
the son of kings, and [my noble birth asserted itself.]
I remembered the pearl for which I was sent into Egypt.
I began to cast a spell on the fearful serpent.
I subdued him by naming my father's name.
[And the name of our next in rank,
and of my mother, the Queen of the East.]
And I snatched the pearl
and I turned to go to my father's house.
I stripped off their dirty robe
and left it in their country.
I directed myself to the way to
the light of my homeland, the East.
[And my letter, my awakener,
I found before me on the way.]
It, as by voice it had awakened me as
I was sleeping, led me to the light.
[Written on Chinese tissue with red ochre,
gleaming before me with its aspect
and with its voice and its guidance
encouraging me to haste,]
"From your father, King of Kings, and
your mother, the Queen of the East,
and your brother [our other son],

to our son in Egypt, peace.
Arise and wake from sleep,
and hear the words of [our letter],
and remember you are a son of kings.
Become sane again concerning your yoke of slavery!
Remember your robe with the golden hem!
Remember the pearl for which you were sent to Egypt!
[Remember your splendid robe,
and think of your glorious toga,
that you may put them on and deck yourself therewith],
that your name may be called in the book
of life [of heroes],
[and you with your brother, our crown prince,
be heir in our kingdom.]"

(111)   [And the letter was a letter]
which the king sealed [with his right hand]
against the evil servants of Babylon
and the tyrant demons of Labyrinthos.
[It flew in the form of an eagle,
the king of all birds,
it flew and alighted beside me
and became all speech.
At its voice and the sound of its rustling
and drawing me with its love,]
I went forward to Sarbug,
I left Babylon on my left hand
and came to Mesene by the great seashore.
[And my splendid robe which I had taken off,
and my toga with which it was wrapped about,
from the heights of Hyrcania
my parents sent thither
by the hand of their treasurers,
who for their faithfulness were trusted therewith.]

(112)   I did not remember my splendor [its dignity,
for I had left it in my childhood in my father's house.
Suddenly I saw my garment, it became like

me as in a reflection,
and I saw all myself upon it,
and I knew and I saw myself through it,
because we were divided apart,
and then, again, we were one form.
It was not otherwise
concerning the treasurers who brought
me the garment, I saw them as two, but both
a single form, there was one symbol of the
king impressed on both.
They had treasure and riches in their hands,
they gave me honor,
and my splendid robe
was decorated in gold and gleaming colors
[with gold and beryls,
chalcedonies and opals,
and sardonyxes of varied color.
This also was made ready in its grandeur,
and with stones of adamant
were all its seams fastened.]
And the image of the King of Kings
was all over it.
And sapphire stones in its
magnificence were sewn to it with harmony.
(113)   And I saw that throughout it were
moving the motions of knowledge.
And it was ready to become speech.
I heard its homily,
[which it whispered at its descent],
"I am his, the most manly of all men,
on account of whom [they reared me
before my father,]
and I perceived myself his manhood.
And all the kingly motions
rested on me, its motions increasing."
It hurried forward from the hands of [its

bringers, that I might take it],
and my desire quickened me to hasten
to greet and receive it.
Reaching out I (took it);
I was decorated with (its) colors,
and I put on my royal toga completely.
I put it on and went
into [the gate of greeting and homage].
I bowed my head and worshipped
the glory of the father who had sent it to me,
because I had done his commandments
and he also had done what he promised.
I joined [at the gate of his satraps...
with his great ones.]
He rejoiced over me and he received me
with him in the kingdoms.
All his subjects hymned with beautiful voices.
He promised me that I indeed would
go with him into the gate of kings,
in order that with my gifts and
my pearl we would appear before the king."[1]

(114) We again join Charisius who goes home thinking
that he has solved his problem. He finds Mygdonia in mourning.
He rebukes her, reminding her of his conjugal rights. (115)
Mygdonia does not listen. Charisius renews his attack. (116)
He reminds Mygdonia of how much he loves her. (117) She replie
"The one whom I love is better than you and your wealth...Your
beauty will vanish....Jesus alone abides eternally. Jesus him-
self will liberate me from the shameful things I did with you."
Charisius offers to free Thomas if his wife will love him again
(118) He falls asleep, and Mygdonia sneaks out to meet Thomas.

---

[1]This hymn is taken by many scholars to be a classic example
of the "redeemed redeemer" of gnostic theology. For more on
this hymn see H. Jonas, *The Gnostic Religion*, Boston, 1963,
pp. 112-129.

Act Ten

(119) Thomas reassures Mygdonia that Jesus will not desert her. (Thomas has miraculously escaped from prison.) (120) Mygdonia asks for "the seal" of Jesus. They go and wake Mygdonia's nurse and she fetches water and bread for a eucharist. (121) Oil is poured out and Mygdonia is baptized in a nearby spring. (122) Thomas returns to prison (again with a miracle). (123) Charisius goes into his wife, finds her praying and again begs her to return to him. (124) He continues, "Recall the day on which you first met me. Tell me straight, was I more beautiful to you then, or Jesus at this time?" Mygdonia responds with a sermon which is much like the bride's speech in chap. 12. (125) Charisius goes and tells the king all that happened. The king wants to kill Thomas, but Charisius wants to frighten the apostle so that Thomas will tell Mygdonia to return to her husband. Thomas is brought before the king. (126) They argue about what he is preaching and the effects it is having. (127) Misdaeus sets Thomas free and tells him to repair Charisius' marriage. Thomas refuses. (128) Charisius pleads with the apostle to give Mygdonia back to him. Thomas again refuses. (129) They return to Charisius' house where Mygdonia expresses her new happiness. (130) Thomas tests Mygdonia by telling her to go to Charisius. She passes the test by refusing. Charisius threatens to tie up his wife to keep her from Thomas. (131) Thomas leaves and goes to captain Siphor's house. (132-133) A baptism and eucharist at Siphor's house.

Act Eleven

(134-138) In this act, Tertia, the wife of Misdaeus, the king, becomes a member of Thomas' group. She, of course, begins to withhold her favors from her husband. Misdaeus says that Thomas has "bewitched" Tertia and in a rage has Thomas seized.

Act Twelve

      (139-149) Vazan, the son of Misdaeus, is converted.

Act Thirteen

      (150-158) Vazan receives baptism. His wife is mira-culously healed. There is a eucharist.[1] In chap. 153, the apostle utters this striking prayer: "Glory be to thee, O multiform Jesus; to thee be glory who hast revealed thyself according to our mode, humanity."

The Martyrdom of the Holy Apostle Thomas

      (159) Thomas goes to prison. Tertia, Mygdonia, and Marcia go with him to be imprisoned. Thomas tells them he will "no longer speak to them while still in his body." He is to be taken up to Jesus. (160) The apostle states that he is not Christ, but is his servant. He tells the women to wait in Christ and to stand fast in the faith. (161) He enters the house and prays that the doors be as they were. The doors shut and seal themselves. The women are left grieving. (162) Thomas finds the guards upset because the apostle goes out and comes into the prison at will. They go to Misdaeus and entreat him to let Thomas, "that magician," go or move him to another prison. They shut the doors, go to sleep, and, when they awaken, the doors are open. The king goes to inspect the seals on the door; the seals are intact. The king accuses the guards of lying, but they protest that they are telling the truth. (163) Thomas is brought before the king. In the dialogue which follows Misdaeus asks: "Who is your master? And what is his name? And of what country?" Thomas said, "My Lord is my master and yours, the Lord of heaven and earth." Misdaeus said "What is his name?" And Judas said, "You are not able to hear his true name at this time. But I say to you the name given to

---

[1] Remember, the eagle took two partridges, a pigeon and a dove

him for a time is Jesus the Christ." Misdaeus points out that
he has not been precipitous in ordering Judas to be killed, but
that this is the last straw. (164) The king considers how to
kill the apostle, for Misdaeus is afraid of the crowds. The
king and some soldiers decide to take Judas outside the city.
Misdaeus commands four soldiers to kill Judas, and he returns
to the city. (165) The crowd wants to rescue Thomas, but he
is led away. Thomas comments, in prayer, that as he was made
from four elements he will be killed by four soldiers. (166)
Thomas preaches to the soldiers. (167) He asks Vazan to persuade the soldiers to let him go aside and pray. Vazan does
so. Thomas confesses that his work is done. He was a slave;
now he is to be set free. "I say these things not as a doubter,
but that those who need to hear may hear." (168) Thomas tells
the soldiers to fulfill their instructions, and they proceed
to kill him with their spears. All the brethren grieve. They
wrap Thomas in fine cloths and put him in an ancient royal tomb.
(169) Siphor and Vazan are reluctant to go home. During their
vigil, Thomas appears to them and tells them that he has gone
to heaven. Meanwhile, Misdaeus and Charisius attempt to lead
their wives astray but with no success. Thomas appears to
Tertia and Mygdonia and gives them encouragement. The two
husbands give up. All the brethren assemble under the new
leadership of Siphor and Vazan, whom Judas had appointed as
elder and deacon. (170) One of Misdaeus' sons becomes demon-
possessed. The king decides that he will go to the apostle's
tomb, get one of Thomas' bones and use it to heal his son.
Thomas appears to the king and says, "If you did not have faith
in the living, will you, indeed, believe in the dead? But do
not be afraid. Jesus, the Christ, acts humanely toward you
because of his great goodness." But Misdaeus did not find the
bones, for one of the brethren had taken them away, and carried
them to the West. So he took dust from the place where the
bones of the apostle had lain; he attached it to his son and
said, "Jesus, I believe in you, now that he (i.e., Satan) who
always confuses men so that they cannot look to your rational

light, has left me." And when his son became healthy by this
deed, Misdaeus joined the rest of the brethren, submitting
himself to Siphor (now an Elder in the new congregation). And
Misdaeus asked all the brethren to pray for him so that he
should have mercy from our Lord Jesus Christ. (171) "The acts
of Judas Thomas the apostle are hereby completed, which he did
in the land of the Indians, fulfilling the command of the One
who sent him; to Whom be glory for ever. Amen."

62. FLAVIUS PHILOSTRATUS: THE LIFE OF APOLLONIOS OF TYANA

(Trans. and notes, D.L. Dungan)

(Introduction: Apollonios of Tyana was almost a contemporary of Jesus of Nazareth, being born around 20 C.E. He lived near Tarsus during his youth, and then spent the majority of his adult life touring all over the Mediterranean region, reforming various cities' religious rites and lecturing to one and all on topics of personal morality. He seems also to have been a healer and diviner of the future. In any case, after his death a number of followers and several shrines preserved his memory, and gradually he came into imperial favor. By the end of the second century, the wife of the emperor Septimus Severus (193-211) was interested enough to ask one of the more accomplished writers in her literary circle to compose a fitting account of Apollonios' life and teachings. Not much later, another emperor, Severus Alexander (222-245) had in his private palace shrine, not statues of the Roman Gods, but busts of other Gods: Alexander the Great, Orpheus, Abraham, Jesus Christ -- and Apollonios of Tyana!

Apollonios had practiced an ascetic or frugal way of life modelled on the example set down centuries before by the Greek mathematician and philosopher, Pythagoras. Thus, Philostratus begins his account by briefly describing Pythagoras' habit of abstaining from eating meat, or wearing clothing made of skin or hair, or participating in bloody sacrifices. Then Philostratus takes up the story of Apollonios. It is important to note that Philostratus gives, as his main reason for writing, the fact that Apollonios had gotten the rather low reputation of having been some sort of wizard, i.e., a dangerous sort of person who dabbled in devilish arts. Thus this whole writing is an attempt to defend Apollonios' integrity.)

I.2   People always say he did these things (for which he became famous) by magic tricks. Therefore, I feel compelled to do something about the widespread ignorance of Apollonios' true character. (To this end I shall) accurately relate the times when he said or did something, and (set the record straight concerning) the manner of wisdom by means of which he succeeded in being considered both divine and Godlike. I have collected some of my source material from cities where he was revered, others from temples, whose rituals at that time being

in a state of idleness were reformed by him, others from things
others said about him, and the rest from his own letters, for
he corresponded with kings, sophists, philosophers, the citizens
of Elis and Delphi, with Indians, and Egyptians, concerning the
Gods, customs, morals, laws; whichever way someone might be
sinning he straightened him out. But the more accurate source
material I collected in the following way.

I.3   There was a man named Damis, not unwise, who once
lived in the ancient city of Nineveh. Having departed with
Apollonios in order to learn philosophy, he kept a record of
the things in which he participated, and the things Apollonios
himself said, his opinions and arguments and whatever he said
in the nature of prophecy. And some relative of Damis brought
the tablets of these as yet unknown memoirs to the knowledge of
the Empress Julia. I happen to be a member of the circle around
her -- for she indeed welcomes and approves of all the rhetorical
exercises -- and she commanded me to rewrite these essays and to
be careful in the narrative of them, for it was narrated by the
Ninevite clearly enough but not with much attention to style.
I also read the book of Maximus of Aigai which contained all
the doings of Apollonios at Aigai, and also a Testament
(*diathēkē*) written by Apollonios. From these sources it is
possible to learn how divinely inspired his philosophy was,
but do not pay any attention to Moiragenes, who wrote a four-
part book (attacking) Apollonios, since he was ignorant of many
things concerning the man. As I said, therefore, I have gathered
these scattered sources and taken some care in combining them
together, but let the work be to the honor of the man about whom
it is written, and for the benefit of those who love learning,
for indeed they might learn something here that they do not yet
know.

I.4   The home of Apollonios, then, was Tyana, a Greek city
in the land of the Kappadokians. His father had the same name,
and he came from an old family of the original settlers, richer

than others there, although it is a wealthy country. While his
mother was pregnant with him, the shadowy figure of an Egyptian
God appeared to her, namely Proteus, who can change his form at
will according to Homer. She, not frightened at all, asked him
to whom she would give birth. "Me," he said. "But who are you?"
she asked. "Proteus," he said, "the Egyptian God." Need I
describe to those of you who are familiar with the writings of
the poets how wise Proteus was, how changeful and always different he was, mightier than death, both knowing and, it seems,
foreknowing all things? Keep this thought of Proteus in your
mind, then, especially when, as the story progresses, it shows
Apollonios foreknowing even more than Proteus, and superior to
the many perilous straits and hardships he encountered, especially in the very moment they occurred.

I.5   It is said that Apollonios was born in a meadow nearby
the temple recently dedicated to him there. And the manner in
which he was born should not be left unknown, for when the hour
of birth had drawn nigh to his mother, a vision came telling her
to go to this meadow and pick some flowers. Well, she had no
sooner arrived when she was mysteriously put to sleep, lying in
the grass, while her maidservants were scattered out over the
meadow picking flowers. Then some swans which lived in the
meadow came and formed a ring around her while she slept and,
as is their custom, they suddenly flapped their wings and honked
all at once (and indeed there was also a breeze blowing across
the meadow).[1] She jumped up because of the sound and gave birth
--for any sudden panic will cause birth to take place, even before its time. The inhabitants of that area say that at the
same time she was giving birth a bolt of lightening seemed to
strike the earth and then bounce back upward into the air where
it vanished. By this sign, the Gods, I believe, revealed and
foretold that Apollonios would become superior to all things

---

[1]Lit. "...something of a Zephyr was in the meadow." What
this detail means is unclear.

earthly, even drawing near to the Gods, and soon.

> (Then after a brief mention of another story of
> Apollonios' divine ancestry, ch. 6, Philostratus
> describes the precocious brilliance of the young
> Apollonios.)

I.7   When he grew up enough to begin learning his letters,
he was already demonstrating a good memory and power of concen-
tration, and he could speak pure Attic Greek for he was not
influenced by the barbarian speech of the Kappadokians. All
eyes were constantly turned toward him, in fact, and he was
admired by the hour. When he was fourteen years old, his
father took him to Tarsus, to Euthydemos the Phoenician. This
Euthydemos was a good rhetorician and began to teach him.
Apollonios liked his teacher well enough, but he began to find
the character of the city disgusting and not helpful for philosophical interests. For, more than anywhere else, the people
of Tarsus crave luxurious living, and joke about everything and
constantly shout insults at each other. They are as worried
about fancy clothes as the Athenians were about wisdom. The
River Kydnus runs through their city, and they sit along its
banks like a lot of chattering waterbirds, which is why
Apollonios wrote to them in a letter, "Stop getting drunk on
water." And so, having asked his father, Apollonios moved
his teacher to Aigai, a town nearby, where it was peaceful, as
befits the study of philosophy, and where he found a more high-
minded atmosphere. There was even a temple to the divine healer
Asklepios, where Asklepios himself would appear to men.
          Philosophizing together with him there were Platonists,
Chrysippists, and Aristotelians. He also attended to the arguments of Epicurus, for not even them did he overlook. But
those of Pythagoras he understood with a certain indescribable
wisdom. His teacher in the Pythagorean doctrines was not very
good, however, nor did he live philosophically, but instead
constantly gave in to his gluttony as well as to the sexual
urge, forming his life according to Epicurus. He was Euxenos

from Herakleia in Pontos, and he knew the doctrines of Pythagoras the way birds learn things from men, for birds can say,
"Hello!" and "Good luck!" and "God bless you!" and such like,
not understanding what they are saying nor with any feeling of
concern for men, but simply because of their trained tongues.
Apollonios, however, just as young eagles fly beside their
parents while their feathers are soft and are cared for by
them in flight, later on are able to mount up, flying above
their parents, especially if they notice them greedily skimming
along at ground-level on the scent of a victim, so also
Apollonios remained by Euxenos while he was a child and was led
by him through the steps of argument, but when he had advanced
to the age of sixteen, he eagerly rushed onward toward a life
like Pythagoras', being "feathered" for it by Something Greater.
Not that he ceased loving Euxenos, but he requested from his
father a place outside the town where there were delicate
gardens and fountains. "You live there in your way," he said
to Euxenos, "but I will live according to the way of Pythagoras."

I.8   Euxenos realized that Apollonios was set on a lofty
ambition and he asked him how he was going to start out to
attain it.   "The way doctors do," Apollonios replied; "by
cleaning out the intestines they enable some not to get sick
and they heal others." Having said this, he stopped eating
food made from animals, arguing that meat was dirty and coarsened
your mind. Instead, he used to eat dried fruits and fresh
vegetables, arguing that whatever the earth herself gives is
clean. And he said that although wine is a clean drink, coming
to men from so cultivated a plant, nevertheless we should not
drink it since it causes the mind to riot, darkening the divine
element of the soul, namely reason. When he had finished
cleaning out his intestines in this fashion, he took to going
barefoot as his "high fashion" and also put on linen clothing,
abstaining from clothing made out of the hair or skin of animals.
Moreover he let his hair grow long and began living in the temple
of Asklepios. Those who lived near the temple were astonished

at all this and even the God Asklepios once told the priest how
happy he was that Apollonios was a witness of his miraculous
healing of the sick at the temple. People from all over Kilikia
and elsewhere gathered at Aigai upon hearing stories of him,
and the Kilikian saying, "Where are you running to? To see the
boy?" began to circulate, even becoming known as a proverb.

> (Philostratus then gives several fragmentary anecdotes
> from this period, the healing of a young man with
> swollen limbs, the rejection of some expensive sacri-
> fices from a rich but wicked nobleman trying to buy
> a healing from Asklepios, the shocked refusal of the
> lecherous advances of the debauched governor of the
> province, and so on. The following is an excerpt of
> his "wisdom" during this period.)

I.11   He used to philosophize as follows about not exceeding
moderation in the matter of sacrifice and temple gifts. Once
when many were gathered at the temple not long after the rejec-
tion of the wicked Kilikian nobleman he began asking the priest
this:

> "Well, then," he said, "are the Gods just?"
> "Indeed, by all means most just," answered the priest.
> "Really? And intelligent?"
> "Who is more intelligent than the Gods?" the latter

replied.

> "And do they know the affairs of mankind, or are they

ingorant of them?" continued Apollonios.

> "But that is especially where the Gods have the advan-

tage over men," the priest answered, "for men because of weakness
do not even know their own affairs while the Gods are granted
knowledge both of ours and their own."

> "All excellently said, O Priest, and most true.

Since, therefore, they know all things, it seems to me one who
comes before God with a good conscience about his life should
pray the following prayer: 'O Gods! Give to me what you owe
me!' For good things are owed to holy people, are they not,
O Priest, but to those who are wicked the opposite. And the

Gods do well when they find someone healthy and abstaining
from wickedness to send him on, crowned not with crowns of
gold, to be sure, but all good things. But if they see people
spotted with sin and ruined, they will abandon them to Justice,
so much do they detest them, particularly since they dare to
invade temples in an impure state."

> (This imitation of a Platonic dialogue seems mediocre
> in its intellectual content, if it is taken to be an
> authentic example of the thought of the original
> Apollonios. On the other hand, there is reason to
> doubt that this piece of conventional wisdom actually
> stems from Apollonios, since this kind of pretentious
> praise of virtue was just the sort of glib moralism
> a popular writer like Philostratus easily produced.
>
> Next, Philostratus relates the death of Apollonios'
> father, the subsequent settling of family affairs
> [carefully pointing out how Apollonios always put
> virtue before money] and Apollonios' decision to
> undertake the Pythagorean vow of five years of total
> silence -- one of that sect's more notorious exercises.
> When it was completed, Apollonios began his trek east-
> ward toward the sages of faraway India. He stopped
> temporarily at "the great city of Antioch." At this
> point Philostratus takes the opportunity to describe,
> in an obviously idealized way, a typical day in the
> life of Apollonios.)

I.16   At the rising of the sun, he would perform certain
rites by himself which he explained only to those who had
trained in silence for four years. Then after these things,
at a suitable time, if the city were Greek and the sacred
ritual familiar, calling the priests together, he would philosophize concerning the Gods and set them straight, if somehow
they had deviated from the accepted (ritual) ordinances. But if
the customs were barbarian and strange, known only in that
place, then Apollonios would investigate those who had established them and on what occasions they had been established,
and, upon ascertaining these things, he would seek to find ways
in which he might improve them or suggest something wiser than
the current practices. Then he would hunt up his associates
and command them to ask about anything they wanted to, for he

said that philosophers needed thus, at earliest sunrise, first
to commune directly with the Gods, later to talk about the Gods,
and after this to pass the time examining human affairs. After
he had spoken with his companions and having enough of such
fellowship, he would stand and spend the rest of the time talking to the crowd -- not before noon but whenever possible during
the quiet of the noon-hour. And when he felt he had carried on
sufficient dialogue he would have himself smeared with oil,
given a massage, and throw himself into cold water, calling the
warm public baths "necessary for the senile among men."

   (A little after this, Philostratus gives the follow-
   description of Apollonios as a public speaker.)

I.17   He would not give out a narrow, subtle discussion,
nor talk on and on, nor did anyone hear him use the question-
and-answer method like Socrates, as if he were ignorant, nor
instruct his pupils like the Peripatetics. Rather, as if
delivering divine truth,[1] he would say when discussing, "I
know..." and "It seems to me..." and "Where are you going?" and
"It is necessary to know that...". And his sayings were short
and hard as steel, authoritative words that went straight to
the point. Indeed, his words sounded as if they were the ordinances of a king. Once some heckler asked him why *he* never
asked about anything. "Because," said he, "when I was a little
boy I asked questions, but now I must not ask but teach what I
have found out." "How, then, O Apollonios, will the wise man
speak?" he asked again. "Like a lawgiver," he said, "for in
those things wherein the lawgiver has convinced himself, he
must enjoin upon the people." This is the way he seriously
discoursed while in Antioch, and he converted even the most
vulgar people to himself.

---

[1]Lit. "as if from a tripod" -- a reference to the peculiar
three-legged stool-like arrangement upon which the seeress sat
in the Temple of Apollo at Delphi as she gave inspired answers
in response to various questions.

(Philostratus then relates Apollonios' decision
to travel to India to visit the world-famous sages
living there. This immense and dangerous journey
Apollonios undertook in stages. He first traveled
north-east to the upper reaches of the Euphrates and
the ancient capital city Nineveh. There he picked up
the faithful disciple, Damis, who stayed with him the
rest of his life, and whose diaries and notebooks
later allegedly served Philostratus as the main source
for this account. Apollonios made a deep impression
upon him right away, says Damis, when he assured him
he would not need Damis as an interpreter since he
already understood all languages even though he had
never studied any! But Philostratus seems to forget
this later on when he portrays Apollonios regularly
using an interpreter. This is only one of many such
anomalies in the writing.

They set off downstream for the great city of
Babylon and after various adventures, reach it and
are welcomed by the king himself. The keeper of the
city gate sends out the "good news" (*evangelion*) that
a man had come who is "wise and a Greek and a good
counselor."

Apollonios stays more than a year, and Philostratus uses the opportunity to portray Apollonios
taking part in various philosophical debates with
the king -- all of which are intended to show how
"philosophical" Apollonios was. The following excerpt is typical.)

I.38   Once when the king showed him the tunnel which
crossed under the Euphrates (the only one of its kind in the
world at that time; see I.25) and asked, "What do you think of
this marvel?" Apollonios made light of the wonderful construc-
tion saying, "It would be a marvel, O King, if you walked on
foot through a river as deep and impassible as this one is."
And when the king pointed out the walls in Ekbatana[1] and said
they were a dwelling-place of the Gods, he replied, "For the
Gods it is not a dwelling-place at all. Whether of men, I do
not know; the Spartans have no walls of any kind around the

---

[1]The ancient northern capital of the Persians, more than 250
miles to the northwest.

city where they dwell." Another time after the king had
decided a certain law-suit between some villages and was boasting to Apollonios that he had carefully listened to the law-
suit for two whole days, Apollonios remarked, "You certainly
are slow to find out what is just." Once, as vast amounts of
tax money were pouring in from his subjects, the king opened
his treasure room and showed Apollonios the money, tempting
him to desire wealth. But he was not impressed with anything
he saw, saying, "To you, O King, this is money. To me, garbage."
"What then is the best use I may make of it?" he asked. "By
spending it," he said, "for you are King."

> (Eventually, the two set off for India with the
> king's blessing. The following is a typical passage
> from Philostratus' descriptions of their trip.)

II.4   As they were passing over the Caucasus mountains,[1]
they say they saw men eight feet tall, who were black, and
others, when they crossed the Indus River, who were ten feet
tall. But during the journey to the river they saw the following thing worth telling. They were going along at night by the
light of the moon, when suddenly the ghost of a hobgoblin rushed
upon them changing from one horrible shape into another and even
becoming invisible. But Apollonios recognized what it was and
he shouted curses at the goblin and commanded those with him to
do the same, for this is the remedy for such an attack, and the
ghost took to flight in the shape of a bird, as spectres often
do.

II.5   As they were crossing over the very highest peak of
the mountain range and going slowly since it was so steep,

---

[1]Philostratus' geographical references are quite vague and
inaccurate. Perhaps he means here the mountain range lying
along the east side of the Tigris River, the Zagros Mountains,
which he passed over on the way to India. The Caucasus are far
to the north and lie on an east-west line between the Black
Sea and the Caspian.

Apollonios began to discuss the following with Damis:

"Tell me," he said, "where were we yesterday?"

"On the flatlands," Damis replied.

"And today, O Damis, where are we?"

"In the Caucasus Mountains," he said, "unless I have completely forgotten myself!"

"Were you down rather low, yesterday?" he asked again.

"That," said the other, "is not worth asking! For yesterday we were traveling down through the hollow of the earth, but today we are up next to heaven."

"Are you sure then, O Damis," he said, "that yesterday the journey was low but today it is high?"

"As sure as God makes little green apples!"[1] said the other, "unless I'm crazy."

"How do you think the roads differ from each other," asked Apollonios, "or what is better to you today than yesterday?"

"Well, yesterday I was walking where there were many people," said he, "but today, where there are few."

"What?" replied Apollonios, "Is it not possible, Damis, by turning aside from the thoroughfares in a city to walk where there are few people?"

"That's not what I said," he replied. "Yesterday we journeyed through villages and people, but today we have climbed up into a somewhat empty and sacred region, for you heard the guide say the barbarians consider it the home of their Gods," and as he said this, he gazed up at the peak of the mountain.

But Apollonios brought him to what he had been driving at from the beginning; "Can you tell me, Damis, what sort of communion with the supernatural there is if you walk close to heaven?"

"None," he said.

"And yet surely you should now, having stood upon a

---

[1] Lit. "By Zeus!"

mechanism so high and divine as this mountain, with new clarity
expound teachings concerning heaven and the sun and the moon,
which you probably think you can touch with a pole standing
this close to them!"

"What I knew yesterday about the supernatural," Damis
replied, "I also know today. A new thought concerning it still
has not hit me."

"Then, Damis," he returned, "you must still be low
down, and have received nothing from the height, but are as far
from heaven as you were yesterday. Thus what I asked you in
the beginning was reasonable after all, only you thought it was
a foolish question."

"Well, I certainly thought, Apollonios, that I would
be wiser when I went down from this mountain, because I've
heard that Anaxagoras of Klazmenion examined things in heaven
from Mt. Mimas in Ionia and Thales the Milesian from Mt. Mykale
near his home, and they say some use Mt. Pangaios for an obser-
vatory and others Mt. Athos. But I myself, having now gone up
on a height greater than all of these, am going down nothing
wiser."

"Nor were they," said Apollonios, "for such vistas
display a brighter heaven and bigger stars and the sun rising
out of the night, things already known to shepherds and goat-
herds. But in what way God cares for the human race and in
what way he rejoices to be served by it, what true virtue is
and what righteousness and moderation are, Athos will not show
to those who climb it, nor the Olympus esteemed by the poets,
unless the soul itself discerns them. And if it, pure and uncorrupted, can 'touch' these things, I would say it soars up
much higher than this old Caucasus peak!"

> (From this point on, until Apollonios and his
> companions arrive at the Indian imperial city of
> Taxila, "the greatest city in India," and King
> Phraotes (a successor of King Porus who had fought
> Alexander the Great), Philostratus' narrative begins
> to read like the National Geographic Magazine as he
> describes the interesting regions and strange animals
> they encountered. Such "travelogues" were just as

popular in Greco-Roman times as in our own and
Philostratus plays this favorite theme to the hilt.

Before long, Apollonios arrives at another
large mountain reputed to be the shrine of the Indian
Dionysos, and this allows Philostratus to discuss the
conflicting claims made regarding the two Dionysos's,
Indian and Greek. Then they finally reach the Indus
River and see herds of elephants. A small boy riding
an elephant provides Apollonios with an illustration
for a tirade against slavery. Philostratus then
offers some information of his own, and inserts a
little treatise on different kinds of elephants,
their uses in warfare, their incredible longevity,
types of tusks, and how affectionate they are toward
their young. This leads to a whole series of anecdotes telling of fierce animals' instinctive tender
care for their young. Then Philostratus begins to
describe the Indus River (about 1/2 mile wide where
they cross), its periodic flooding, its similarities
to the Nile, speculates as to why both India and Egypt
[thought to be on the two edges of the earth] are
peopled by dark-skinned races, and so on.

They finally arrive at Taxila, the royal city,
"about the size of Nineveh," where they are welcomed
by the king, Phraotes. Apollonios' first interest
is in the monuments to the climactic battle between
Alexander the Great and the earlier Indian king,
Porus. Alexander had defeated Porus, but found him
such a gallant opponent that he returned his kingdom
to him as a tribute to his bravery. When news of
this astonishing gesture reached the Greek homeland,
it caused widespread comment and resulted in a general
curiosity about this Indian king for whom Alexander
had shown such admiration. Thus, Philostratus pauses
to recount a string of anecdotes about Porus revealing
his character and wit.)

II.21   My story will not let me pass by in silence what they
write about this Porus. Once when Alexander was about to cross
the Indus River and attack him and some were advising Porus to
make allies of certain kings on his eastern boundary beyond the
Hyphasis and the Ganges Rivers, saying that Alexander would
never attack a coalition of all the Indians drawn up against
him, Porus replied, "If the loyalty of my people is such that
I can not be saved without allies, then it were better that I

should not rule!" Another time when someone announced to him
that Alexander had captured Darius the Persian king, he remarke
"Darius may have been king, but he wasn't a man!" When the
elephant groom had decked out the elephant upon which he was
about to do battle, he said, "This one, O King, will carry you.
Whereupon Porus replied, "I, rather, will carry him -- if I stil
am the man I used to be!" Advised that he should make sacrific
to the Indus River so that it would not accept the Macedonian
rafts nor be easily crossed by Alexander, Porus said, "It is no
right for those who can use arms to rely on magical curses."
After the battle when he seemed even to Alexander to be divine
and beyond human nature, one of his relatives said, "If you had
paid homage to him when he crossed over, O Porus, you would not
have been defeated in battle nor so many Indians killed or your
self wounded." "But I heard that Alexander cherished honor
above all," said Porus, "and I realized that if I abased myself
he would consider me a slave, whereas if I fought him, a king.
And I thought his esteem more worthy than his pity, nor was I
deceived, for by representing myself such as Alexander saw, I
both lost and gained everything in one day." Such are the
things they tell of this Indian, and they say he was the hand-
somest of all the Indians and taller than anyone since the
Trojan men, but that he was quite young when he fought Alexande

> (Philostratus follows his account of the sayings
> of Porus with a rather mediocre imitation of a Pla-
> tonic dialogue on the question whether art can be
> taught -- itself already a time-worn debate, nor is
> Apollonios' conclusion very original. What is
> interesting in the dialogue is the point where
> Apollonios happens to describe the way artists por-
> tray an "Indian", mentioning the following features:
> "the flatness of nose and kinky hair and protruding
> jaw and a certain flashing look about the eyes giving
> a black look to the appearance, and indicating an
> Indian to the eyes of those not ignorant." But this
> is, to us, a perfect description -- not of an Indian -
> but a black African! It comes as no surprise then
> when Philostratus later on refers to the Ethiopians
> as "an Indian race" (3.20). These ethnic labels are,
> of course, not Philostratus' own, but ones typically
> in use in his time, just like our own references to

the American "Indian." But this is just another
indication that one must be cautious in reading this
account's many obsolete geographical and ethnic
observations.

When Apollonios finally meets King Phraotes, he
is surprised to find him living as ascetically as a
Pythagorean philosopher despite his great wealth.
They soon become close friends, as Phraotes tells
Apollonios how young Indian boys are made into
philosophers, while Apollonios helps him solve a
difficult legal dispute. Following a very unphilo-
sophical, enormous banquet, and an interminable
debate concerning the effects of heavy drinking on
the art of divination, King Phraotes sends Apollonios
on his way toward the Brahmin sages living not far
away.

This gives Philostratus the opportunity to resume
his "travelogue," and so the reader hears about the
great river Hyphasis. But the identity of this river
is unclear -- especially when he says it "goes across
India" and is as large as the Ister (=Danube), the
greatest of all the rivers in Europe. But Philostratus is relying on second or third-hand geographical notions of India, which were highly inaccurate.
In any case, many marvelous sights are to be seen
along its banks: unicorns, cinnamon groves, pepper
trees tended by trained apes, corn growing twenty
feet high, fields of enormous beans, sesame, and
millet, as well as other unnamed exotic fruits
"sweeter than all the others the seasons bring."
But most exciting of all was a dragon hunt that our
travelers happened to see. Philostratus briefly
digresses to inform the reader of the numerous
varieties of dragons in India. For example, there is
the small black marsh dragon not more than 60 feet
long. Then there are the plains dragons, silvery
and "as fast as the swiftest river." But the real
monsters were the mountain dragons. They had golden
scales, eyes of fiery stone, bushy beards, could spit
fire and made a horrible, brassy clashing noise when
they burrowed under the earth. This beast is so
fearsome everything stays clear of it, although there
are fabulous riches and magic charms inside its head
for those who catch it. Thus the Indians have devised
a secret method of capturing it, says Philostratus,
and he proceeds to describe it.)

III.8   They sew golden letters on a scarlet cloth and place
it in front of its hole after placing a sleep-charm upon the

letters so that they will overcome the irresistable eyes of the
dragon. And they chant many forbidden mysteries over the
letters which will cause it to stretch its neck out of its hole
and sleep upon the letters. Then the Indians fall upon the
dragon lying there, striking its neck with axes, and when they
have cut off its head, they ravage it for the stones inside, for
they say hidden inside the heads of the mountain dragons are
stones in the shape of flowers flashing forth every color in
the rainbow and having a mystical force like the ring they say
Gyges had. But frequently *it* catches the Indian with his axe
and secret art and carries him back into his burrow, all but
shaking the mountain down. These are also said to live in the
mountains around the Red Sea (=Indian Ocean), and they say they
hear them hissing terribly and going down to the sea and far
out into the ocean. How long these beasts live is impossible
to know and unbelievable if I did say. This is what I know
about dragons.

   (After traveling about a week, Apollonios and
Damis reach the "heart of India" and the sacred
mountain whereon the sages live, which the latter
regarded as "navel of the land" -- i.e., the exact
center. The travelers were met on the road by the
sages' personal envoy, a youth who was "the blackest
Indian of all" (3.11), who invites Apollonios up to
the palace of the sages, asking the others to wait
below. The days following are spent learning about
the fabulous qualities of the mountain, e.g., auto-
matic robot tripods serving different dishes at meal
time, large stone jars containing rain or winds and
clouds which the sages release when the farmers need
them, the mysterious weapons the sages have with
which to defend their mountain fortress, and so forth.
Just as marvelous is the daily life and religious
ritual of the eighteen sages. Apollonios is astonished, for example, to find statues not only of
Indian and Egyptian Gods but also of the older Greek
Gods, Athena Polias and Apollo of Delos. He is
gratified to see that the main part of their worship
was devoted to the sun, to which they sung praises
at noon and at midnight while suspended in mid-air
several feet off the ground. Naturally there were
no sacrifices of any sort. Each day began with
exercises followed by rubbing with a heat-producing

ointment, and then a dip in a cold pool. After this, the rest of the day was passed in philosophical debate, settling the disputes of kings who came for advice, and healing the sick and afflicted.

Such well-thumbed philosophical topics as "knowing oneself," the nature of the soul, transmigration of souls, of what the cosmos was composed, whether there is more land or water on the earth, and so on, are related by Philostratus. The general tenor of these discussions is indicated by the following:)

III.18   Thereupon he asked another question, namely, whom did they think themselves to be? "Gods," came the answer. When he asked why, the reply was, "Because we are good men." This answer seemed to Apollonios to be so full of sound education that he said it later about himself in his defense before the Emperor Domitian.

(Philostratus periodically interrupts the philosophical discussions in order to liven things up. He first has a local king appear who exaggeratedly slanders the Greeks. Naturally Apollonios leaps to the defense and in the ensuing argument, the king is easily defeated and then reduced to tears. Of course, the whole thing is artificial, for Philostratus is just shrewdly playing upon his readers' prejudices. Then after more discussion, several sick are suddenly brought in to be healed. The contrived character of the whole outline should not escape our notice; (1) a series of debates concerning familiar themes of philosophy is interrupted by; (2) a comic-serious dramatic confrontation with the visiting king (pointing forward to the final clash with Domitian). This is followed by; (3) a sumptuous, incredible feast; (4) two more philosophical arguments, then; (5) a clump of healing accounts, followed by; (6) more philosophical and natural-history discussions. After all this, Philostratus says in a final summarizing statement, "In such communion with the sages Apollonios passed *four months* there in discussion" (III.50). These are the healing stories:)

III.38   In the midst of these words, the messenger of the sages appeared bringing in Indians needing help. And he led up

a little woman pleading for her boy whom she said was sixteen
years old and who had been possessed by a demon for the past
two years, and that the character of the demon was that of a
deceiver and a liar. When one of the sages asked why she said
these things, she replied, "Because my boy is most beautiful,
the demon has fallen in love with him and does not let him be
in his right mind, or permit him to walk to school or to arche:
class or stay at home but drives him out into deserted regions
And the boy does not have his own voice but speaks in a deep
and hollow voice, like a man. And he looks at you with other
eyes than his own. I constantly weep because of these things
and beat myself and chastise my son as much as is fair, but he
does not recognize me. But when I decided to come here -- I
decided to a year ago -- the demon confessed himself using the
child as a mouthpiece, and -- would you believe it -- began
telling me that he was the ghost of a man who died once in a
battle, dying while loving his wife, but that she outraged the
marriage by taking another after he had been dead only three
days. And so because of this he hated the love of women and
changed over to this boy. But he promised, if I would not tel
you about him, to give my child many good and wonderful things
I was really persuaded by these promises, but he has put me of
for so long now, taking over my whole house, it's obvious he
intends to do nothing reasonable or true." Then the sage aske
again if the boy were nearby, but she said he wasn't, although
she had tried all sorts of things to bring him, "but the demon
threatened to hurl me over steep banks and into pits and to
kill my son if I brought him here for judgment, so I left him
at home." "Be of good cheer," said the sage, "for he will not
kill him after he has read these." And pulling out a certain
letter from his robe he gave it to the woman, and indeed, the
letter was addressed to that very ghost and filled with the
most terrifying threats (unless he left the boy alone).

III.39-40   And someone limping also came up, who was already
thirty years old, a mighty hunter of lions. Once a lion sprang
and landed upon his back and he twisted his leg. But after
they stroked his hip with their hands, the youth went away
walking perfectly. And someone who was flowing pus from his
eyes went away completely cured of his disease, and another
man who had a paralyzed hand departed with its strength returned.
The husband of a certain woman who'd had seven painful preg-
nancies begged their aid in easing her birthgiving, and she was
healed in the following way: they commanded the husband, when
his wife was about to give birth, to carry a live rabbit under
his shirt into the room where she was giving birth and, walking
around her, at the same moment when she strained to push the
baby out to release the rabbit. Then the baby would easily come
out, only they warned that the whole womb would be expelled
together with the baby unless he shooed the rabbit outside the
door immediately.

         (Philostratus concludes these stories by saying
    "and the men were astonished at the manifold wisdom"
    of the sages. They resume the account of their
    philosophical discussion, this time focusing chiefly
    on the art and benefits of divination of the future.
    Iarchus, the chief sage, assures Apollonios, "Those
    who delight in divination, my friend, become divine
    from it and contribute to the salvation of mankind"
    (III.42), since it included, among others, the art
    of healing as the most important (III.44). There is
    a comical moment when Iarchus playfully asks Damis
    whether Apollonios' gift of foretelling the future
    has rubbed off on him a little, after all this time.
    But Damis' answer is quite revealing. It is not so
    much divination he is after, says Damis. Rather,
    since he is an Assyrian by birth, he hopes that by
    associating constantly with Apollonios and imitating
    everything he did, to learn manners and philosophy
    and, in short, "mix freely with Greeks and with his
    help become a Greek" (III.43).

         Finally Apollonios asks about the stories he has
    heard of the fabulous animals living in India. That
    is, Philostratus is ready to interject some more of
    his "travelogue" material, and so he has Iarchus
    relate strange and marvelous accounts of huge man-
    eating porcupines, giant birds that quarry gold with

their beaks, the immortal phoenix which sets fire to
its own nest and then sings a funeral dirge to itself,
only to come to life again as a worm, and so on.

When the time for parting came, after "four
months" of such discussions, the sages embrace
Apollonios and solemnly assure him that he "will
seem to be a God to many not only after he is dead
but even while living." (III.50) He heads southwest toward the coast, and boards a ship bound for
Babylon. Philostratus relates bits and pieces of
geographical and mythological lore as Apollonios
sails along the Red Sea (=Persian Gulf) and then the
Euphrates River until he finally reaches Babylon.
From there he retraces his steps to his homeland of
Ionia, and Ephesus.

When he arrived, says Philostratus, there was
great rejoicing in Ephesus and invitations from
numerous other cities asking him to come as soon as
possible to set their affairs in order. So Apollonios
begins a tour, only to return in great haste to Ephesus after an epidemic breaks out there, caused by a
demon which had infiltrated the city.)

IV.10   With such words as these he restored harmony to the
city of Smyrna. But when the plague struck the Ephesians and
nothing could control it, they sent a delegation to Apollonios,
asking him to become the healer of their suffering. He, thinking it unnecessary to be delayed by using the road, said, "Let
us go," and was instantly in Ephesus, something Pythagoras also
did, I believe, when he was once in Thurii and Metapontum at
the same time. Then, calling the Ephesians together, he said,
"Be of good cheer, for today I will stop this plague," and so
saying he led the whole body to the theater, where they later
set up the statue of the Averting God Heracles in memory of the
event about to happen. There they found an old man who seemed
blind, craftily blinking his eyes, and carrying a sack with a
piece of bread in it, wearing rags, and his face was very dirty.
Standing the Ephesians around him, he said, "Gather as many
stones as you can and throw them at this enemy of the Gods."
But the Ephesians were amazed at what he said, and thought it

a terrible thing to kill a stranger as wretched as this, for he of course was beseeching them and begging for mercy. But Apollonios vehemently urged the Ephesians to throw their stones and not to let him escape. And when some used their slings on him, he who seemed before to be blinking as if blind, suddenly glared around showing eyes full of fire. The Ephesians then realized it was a demon and showered him with their stones so that they heaped up a large pile on top of him. After a short wait, Apollonios ordered the stones removed and the beast which they had killed to be recognized. When it appeared, uncovered of what had been thrown at it, it had disappeared! Instead the form of a dog was seen, similar to those from Molottos, as big as the biggest lion in size, crushed under the stones. It had vomited foam like a mad dog. And so they erected the statue of the Averting God, that is of Heracles, over the place where the apparition was stoned.

("Having had enough of the Ionians," says Philostratus, Apollonios "set out for Hellas" -- the Greek territory on the other side of the Aegean. On the way, Philostratus capitalizes on the popular interest in Homer's *Iliad*, by having Apollonios stop at the grave of Achilles and call up his ghost one midnight. When Achilles appears, he grows and grows until he is over twenty-five feet tall. Nothing daunted, Apollonios greets him in a friendly way and Achilles on his part seems glad to have someone to converse with at long last. In return for Apollonios' promise to have the customary offerings at his grave restored, Achilles agrees to answer any five questions about the Trojan War. These turn out to be cocktail-circuit bon-bons, such as, was Polyxena, supposedly the lover of Achilles though never mentioned by Homer, really sacrificed to Achilles on his grave? And was Helen really abducted to Troy, i.e., wasn't the whole story simply invented out of whole cloth by Homer? And so on.

When he arrives at Athens, he is once again immediately recognized and acclaimed by one and all. The only sour note is a refusal by the chief priest of the mystery at Eleusis to initiate Apollonios during a current festival, on the grounds that he was a wizard and an associate of foul demons. Apollonios of course puts the priest down, to the

delight of the crowd. On another occasion he is
lecturing the crowd on the proper way to pour out
libations to the Gods, when he is interrupted by a
heckler -- only Apollonios immediately perceives a
deeper danger, i.e., the heckler is possessed by a
demon.)

IV.20   And when he told them to have handles on the cup and
to pour over the handles -- this being a purer part of the cup
since no one's mouth touched that part -- a young boy began
laughing raucously, scattering his discourse to the winds.
Apollonios stopped and, looking up at him, said, "It is not you
that does this arrogant thing, but the demon who drives you
unwittingly," for, unknown to everyone, the youth was actually
possessed by a demon, for he used to laugh at things no one
else did and would fall to weeping for no reason and would talk
and sing to himself. Most people thought it was the jumpiness
of youth which brought him to do such things, and at this point
he seemed carried away by drunkenness, but it was really a demon
which spoke through him. Thus, when Apollonios began staring
at it, the phantom in the boy let out horrible cries of fear
and rage, sounding just like someone being burned alive or
stretched on the rack, and he began to promise that he would
leave the young boy and never possess anyone else among men.
But Apollonios spoke to him angrily such as a master might to
a cunning and shameless slave, and he commanded him to come
out of him, giving definite proof of it. "I will knock down
that statue there," it said, pointing toward one of those around
the Porch of the King. And when the statue tottered and then
fell over, who can describe the shout of amazement that went up
and how everyone clapped their hands from astonishment! But
the young boy opened his eyes, as if from sleep, and looked at
the rays of the sun (i.e., at Zeus, who had delivered him).
Now all those observing these events revered the boy, for he
no longer appeared to be as coarse as he had been, nor did he
look disorderly, but had come back to his own nature nothing

less than if he had drunk some medicine. He threw aside his fancy soft clothes and, stripping off the rest of his luxuriousness, came to love poverty and a threadbare cloak and the customs of Apollonios.

> (Shortly after this Philostratus records some surprisingly harsh threats Apollonios levels at the Athenians because of their lust for bloody gladiatorial shows. One is reminded of similar threats uttered by the Jewish prophets.)

IV.22   He censured the Athenians for something else also. They would gather in the theater of Dionysus below the Acropolis and watch men butcher each other, enjoying it more than they do in Corinth today. For they would buy men for high prices, namely those who had committed crimes such as adultery or fornication or burglery or purse-snatching or kidnapping, people who had received the death-sentence, and, arming them, would command them to attack each other. Apollonios rebuked these practices and when he was invited to the city assembly of the Athenians, he replied that he would not enter such a filthy place, filled with the defilement of blood. Once he said in a letter that it was amazing "Athena had not already abandoned the Acropolis because of the blood you pour out there. For it seems to me that, before long, when you celebrate the Pan-Athenian Festival, you will no longer use bulls but sacrifice hundreds of men to the Goddess. And you, Dionysios, will you continue to come to your theater, now that it is filled with blood and gore? Do the sages of Athens perform religious ceremonies to you there? Go somewhere else, Dionysus! You are too pure for that!"[1]

> (Apollonios then went around to the Greek temples, correcting their practices. In Corinth he frees a young man from the clutches of a vampire masquerading

---

[1] Apollonios makes a pun on Dionysios' symbol, the sacred zither, which cannot be translated. Lit. - "Your zithering is more pure."

as a beautiful young woman who was fattening him up
for the kill.

Eventually he goes to Crete for a tour of that
island, and from there to Rome. Having landed in
Italy, he receives word that Nero is terrorizing Rome
making a special target of philosophers. The famous
Stoic philosopher Musonius was already in prison.
This news comes as a shock to many of the followers
in Apollonios' train, and, as Damis observes, a numbe
began finding pretexts to turn back, thus "running
away from both Nero and philosophy" (IV.37). But the
remainder are ready to stick it out, "being unified
by the encouragement of Apollonios, they desired both
to die on behalf of philosophy and to appear better
than those who had run away" (IV.38), and so they
finally reach Rome.

Before long, reports of Apollonios' scorn at
Nero's shameless posturing as a popular singer reache
the attention of the police and he is arrested and
brought up for trial. However, he gets off because
for some mysterious reason the scroll upon which the
grounds for his arrest had been written is suddenly
found to be blank. Apollonios is clearly superior
to his foes, and they are now afraid to attack someone with such mysterious powers. Not much later, he
works another even more miraculous feat.)

IV.45   A young girl seemed to have died in the very hour of

her marriage, and the bridegroom was following the bier weepin

over his unfulfilled marriage. Rome mourned also, for it

happened that the dead girl was from one of the best families.

Apollonios, happening to be present where they were mourning,

said, "Put down the bier, for I will end your weeping for this

girl," and at the same time he asked what her name was. The

bystanders thought that he was going to give a speech like

those which people give at burials to heighten everyone's

sorrow. But he didn't; instead he touched her and saying some

thing no one could hear, awakened the girl who seemed dead.

And the girl spoke and went back to her father's house, just

like Alcestis who was brought back to life by Heracles. And

when the relatives of the girl offered Apollonios 150,000 silv

pieces as a reward, he replied that he would return it to the

child as a gift for her dowry. Now whether he found a spark of
life in her which had escaped the notice of the doctors -- for
it is said her breath could be seen above her face as it rained
-- or whether, her life actually being completely extinguished,
she grew warm again and received it back, no one knows. A grasp
of this mystery has not been gained either by me or by those
who chanced to be there.

> (Nero soon prohibits all philosophical activity
> throughout the city, and Apollonios decides to leave
> such an inhospitable locale and visit the "pillars of
> Hercules" at the western end of the Mediterranean
> Sea, i.e., the Straits of Gibraltar.

V.   After passing several months in the region of
Gibraltar, Apollonios and Damis voyage to Sicily and
thence back to Greece. Once again he spends the next
months touring Greece, reproving and correcting the
priests in the various temples. Then, in the spring,
he sets off for Egypt. As before, while Apollonios
and Damis travel along, Philostratus uses this
"travel" setting to provide Apollonios with little
speeches or tirades on a number of conventional
subjects, such as the folly of bloody sacrifices,
the futility of greed, horse racing, and so forth.

He meets Vespasian in Egypt (it is the winter
of 69) -- after refusing to see him in Judaea, "a
country which those who dwelt in it have polluted
as much by what they do as what is done to them"--
and assures him he should seek to be the next
Emperor. There then follows a lengthy debate on the
popular question of how a sovereign ought to rule.
Of course, Philostratus' speeches, put in the mouth
of Apollonios, as well as speeches for the opposition (given to a rival named Euphrates), contain
nothing original or remarkable -- in fact the way
Apollonios is portrayed unabashedly playing up to
Vespasian's ambitious desire for power is rather
shocking. Of interest to us, however, is another
appearance of second-century Roman anti-Jewish hatred
similar to the comment of Apollonios just mentioned.
In the course of his argument Euphrates says -- and
the others readily agree -- that Vespasian would have
done better to use his army to invade Rome and depose
Nero instead of wasting it in suppressing the Jewish
rebellion. For the Jews, says Euphrates, "have long
since stood aloof, not only from Romans but from all

men, they who seek an 'unspotted life' -- to whom no
fellowship with men at table or in libations or in
prayers or sacrifices is welcome. Let them remove
themselves from us farther than Susa or Bactria or
the Indians beyond! There was certainly no good
reason to punish this standoffish nation, whom it
were better never to have taken over in the first
place." (V.33). This statement is significant as
it indicates the growth of the first, minor stages
of Greco-Roman anti-semitism. This new phenomenon
seems to have been provoked partly by Jewish exclu-
sivism, as is clear from Euphrates' specific reasons
why Gentiles resented this stubbornly aloof nation.
With the rise of Christianity, however, a whole new
religious dimension is added. But it is clear that
there was already present a sort of low grade, international hostility toward the Jews, triggered by the
rebellion of 67-70, upon which Christianity could
capitalize -- as we can see it did in such virulently
anti-semitic writings as the Gospel of Peter and the
Acts of Pilate. Following the conference with Vespasian, Apollonios and his followers depart for upper
Egypt and the famous naked sages living in the desert.

VI.   At this point, a geographical comment by Philostratus provides us with a fascinating glimpse of the
naive, ill-informed way in which an educated Roman
thought of the world: "Ethiopia is the western end
of everything under the sun just as India lies on the
eastern and is bounded by Egypt at Meroē and touching
an unknown region of Libya, comes to an end at the
sea which the poets call Ocean, thus naming what goes
around the entire mass of dry land" (VI.1). It is a
flat, roughly circular earth having a rim of water
("Ocean") and three or four inland seas, lying beneath the curved bowl of heaven to which were fastened
sun, moon and stars. Of lower Africa, or eastern Asia,
much less the Pacific and the New World, there is no
awareness.

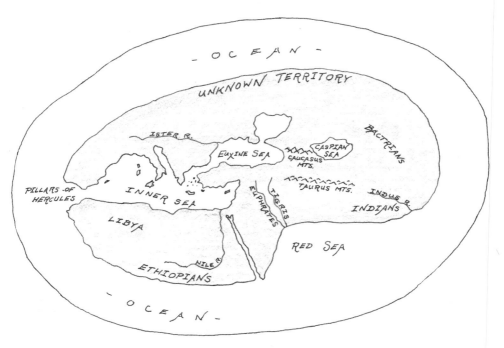

(Adapted from "The World According to Herodotus
430 B.C." in J.O. Thomson, *Everyman's Classical
Atlas*, 3rd ed. 1966, p. 2.)

When Apollonios and Damis reach the territory
where the naked sages live, they find an unfriendly
reception. It seems a stranger has come just before
to warn that the Apollonios who will soon visit them
is a wizard and an evil man. In this way Philostratus
begins to weave into the plot the theme of intrigue
against our hero-saint, a theme which will reach a
mighty crescendo in the final act when Apollonios,
betrayed by this same stranger (it is actually the
jealous Euphrates), at last must answer to charges
of sorcery and treason before the Emperor Domitian
himself. Euphrates, whom Apollonios bests in the
debate on kingship with Vespasian, mentioned above, is
from the first portrayed by Philostratus as a sinis-
ter, evil person. Thus, it is possible that this
character is someone Philostratus invented and worked
into his plot to give it more excitement -- just like
the little erotic touches inserted here and there to
spice up the story (e.g., the beautiful young boys

Apollonios keeps meeting and virtuously refraining
from seducing, although they are completely under
his power). Details like these heighten the reader's
interest in the story. Anyone can enjoy philosophy
when it is spiced up with a little intrigue and sex!

But we have gotten ahead of our story. When the
identity of the malicious stranger is revealed,
Apollonios gives a lengthy defense of his way of life
to the Egyptian sages. This is followed by several
debates, one of which expresses the popular Greco-
Roman scorn at the animal Gods of the Egyptians.
Other typical discussions touch on the nature of the
soul, the nature of justice and the structure of the
cosmos.

But the visit is not a happy one, and before
long Apollonios and Damis and the rest decide to
search for the fabled sources of the Nile, another
popular bit of geographical lore. Proceeding up-
stream, says Philostratus, they finally came to the
first of several huge, roaring cataracts or water-
falls. Then they pass two more, and with each one,
the noise and confusion becomes more deafening and
terrifying. Finally they find themselves in an in-
credibly dense, mountainous region, with giant geysers
of water gushing forth out of the sides of sheer
cliffs all around them. Fearing permanent deafness
and nearly paralyzed with terror because of the
horrible demons which lurked all around (for all the
demons and devils in the world gathered here, says
Philostratus), they hastily retrace their steps.

After briefly recounting episodes in their stay
among some Ethiopian villages, Philostratus abruptly
drops the thread of the Egyptian journey and, using
a common Hellenistic literary gimmick to speed up
the passage of time and shift the scene of action,
he suddenly describes the contents of some letters
that passed between Titus, Vespasian's son, and
Apollonios (cp. 1 Maccabees 12 & 14). Using this
change of subject as a springboard, Philostratus
then jumps the story forward several years to an
occasion when Titus and Apollonios meet each other
in Tarsus, describing what they said to each other
on that occasion. Of course, Egypt and Ethiopia are
all forgotten now, and Philostratus, in rough summary
fashion, fills the rest of Book VI with disconnected
anecdotes of Apollonios' activities when he is back
in the region of his boyhood -- Cilicia. The main
thing Philostratus wants to do is to hurry time
along, i.e., both to introduce and get rid of Titus,
so that his wicked younger brother Domitian can then

be brought onto the stage -- and everything set up
for the mortal clash between him and Apollonios that
occupies so much of Books VII and VIII, and concludes
Philostratus' tale.

VII.   Book VII, which might be titled "The Martyrdom
of Philosophers," contains Philostratus' efforts to
set Apollonios' clash with the ruthless emperor
Domitian in the best possible light. First Philostratus lists all other examples where philosophers
have faced death at the hands of a tyrant, e.g.,
Zeno, Plato, Diogenes, Crates. Then he finds fault
with each one in such a way as to show that, not only
was Apollonios' bravery, wit, and power superior to
theirs, but he also confronted a tyrant who ruled
the whole world -- not just some petty island king or
ruler of an obscure country.

          Next Philostratus takes pains to show that
Apollonios came to this clash quite voluntarily; he
was not dragged thither by Domitian's superior might.
Thus, when Domitian decides to arrest Apollonios
(who is in Asia at the time), Philostratus says
Apollonios knew of it by his powers of foresight and
immediately began his trip to Italy before the orders
for his arrest had even reached the provincial
governor of Asia.

          Then Philostratus heightens the dramatic tension
by emphasizing the base cowardice of even the closest
of Apollonios' disciples. Meeting him when he
arrives in Italy, they all try to dissuade him from
throwing his life away. This, of course, provides
"Apollonios" (=Philostratus) with several occasions
to deliver ringing speeches on the duty of the philosopher to die unafraid for the sake of liberty,
rather than cravenly preserve his freedom while
tyranny makes slaves of everyone.

          There is a curious ambiguity in Philostratus'
portrait of Apollonios, however. On the one hand
he is shown unceasingly pressing forward into danger,
speaking of the need for bravery in the true philosopher, his patience under tribulation, his manliness,
and the like. But on the other hand, there are places
where Philostratus makes it equally clear that Apollonios is not really in any danger, either from Domitian
or anyone else. For example, on one occasion Apollonios says, "I myself know more than mere men do, for
I know all things....and that I have not come to Rome
on behalf of the foolish will become perfectly clear;
for *I myself am in no danger with respect to my own*

body nor will I be killed by this tyrant...." (VII.14)
If this be true, what is the point of resounding
phrases such as "it is especially fitting for the
wise to die for the sake of the things they practice"
(VII.14) and "death on behalf of friends...(is) the
divinest of things human" (VII.14)? How can Philostratus have Apollonios say later on to an agent of
Domitian's: "It will be enough for me to leave,
having saved myself and my friends, on behalf of whom
I am here *in danger*" (VII.38)? Either Apollonios is
in danger or he isn't! Well, as the outcome will
show, he was not in any danger at all. But then what
is the point of all these fine speeches concerning
risking death at the hands of tyranny? Apparently,
that is all they are -- fine speeches, rather the
rhetorical product of an author primarily concerned
with their immediate effect, but who had not thought
out their place in his story as a whole. For if all
Apollonios' friends had had the same powers he did
(such as being able to remove iron shackles at will),
then obviously none of them would have been afraid
of Domitian either. Thus, when Philostratus describe
Apollonios being led through the streets of Rome unde
heavy guard from the prison to the palace for trial,
and how "everyone turned to see Apollonios, his appea
ance attracting admiration, for he seemed so god-like
that those standing about were astonished, while his
having come to risk danger on behalf of men made
those who formerly slandered him now friendly" (VII.3
...at this point it becomes clear that Philostratus'
vanity and facile ability to conjure up a touching
scene with his pen, regardless of its inconsistency
with the rest of the story, has gotten quite out of
control.

VIII.   In any case, the grand climax to Philostratus'
story is at hand. The final test has come; the vindi
cation (or collapse) of everything Apollonios has
trained for and practiced all his life will now be
revealed. Either he will "be true to himself" now,
in the moment of supreme crisis, or all will brand
him a coward and a traitor to philosophy.

          There has already been a preliminary hearing at
which Domitian became enraged when Apollonios would
not buckle under his threatening. This was followed
by a period of solitary confinement, and the shaving
off of his hair, intended to soften Apollonios up.
During this time, various soldiers or spies, secretly
sent from Domitian, harass Apollonios and his seeming
helplessness. But Apollonios withstands it all, seeing through all the stratagems to intimidate him.

Finally the day of the trial dawns, and the final
struggle begins. The audience hall is jammed with
people as the procedure begins. There is a brief
preliminary skirmish with some minor official (a
skillful touch to delay the action, thus heightening
the suspense), and then his old enemy, the philosopher
Euphrates, who is now his chief accuser, loudly de-
mands that Apollonios stop ignoring the king and give
his full attention to "the God of all mankind." Thereupon Apollonios, who had been standing with his back
to the emperor, ostentatiously looks up towards the
ceiling (i.e., towards Zeus). This bold affront so
enrages Euphrates that he begs the king to get on
with the accusations so that they could end the trial
and begin the punishment Apollonios clearly deserves.

Domitian accordingly reads out the first charge:
Apollonios dresses differently than everyone else.
He does not wish to bother the animals to get wool or
skin, replies Apollonios skillfully. Then Domitian
reads the second charge: Why do men consider Apollonios equal with the Gods? This, declares Apollonios,
is simply because they see in him a good man (lifting
a line from the Indian sages). Third, how could he
predict the plague that struck Ephesus if he were not
a wizard? Apollonios explains that his light diet
enables him to sense harmful pestilences in the air
before other men do. Finally, the accusation of
sedition comes up. Domitian asks whether Apollonios
had plotted to help Nerva overthrow the government,
and to this end had he not sacrificed a young boy and
examined his entrails for signs of a favorable omen
for the plot? What of that? Apollonios scornfully
rejects the whole accusation as a blatant lie, and
dares anyone to come forward with proof that he did
any of these things. The gallery unexpectedly
applauds loudly and -- wonder of wonders -- the emperor
seems to be impressed himself! But suddenly, something totally unexpected happens --.)

VIII.5   When Apollonios had said these things, the crowd indi-

cated its approval more loudly than was customary in the court

of the king. Thereupon, Domitian, considering those present to

have born witness together in Apollonios' favor, and, being

somewhat influenced himself by his answers -- for when questioned

he seemed to have given logical answers -- declared, "I acquit

you of these charges! But, you must stay here so that we may

meet you privately." But Apollonios took courage and said, "I
thank you, O King, but because of these sinful (courtiers) here,
the cities are being destroyed, the islands are full of fugi-
tives, the mainland full of weeping, your soldiers are cowardly
and the senate is suspicious. Give me my freedom, if you will,
but if not, then send someone to imprison my body, for it is
impossible to imprison my soul! Indeed, you will not even take
my body, 'for you can not kill me since I am not a mortal man,'
and, saying this, *he vanished from the courtroom*! --which was a
smart thing to do at the time, for it was obvious that the tyrant
was not going to question Apollonios sincerely but just detain
him by various pretexts. For he boasted later in not having
killed the sage. But Apollonios did not want to be dragged into
further confinement and, anyway, he considered it more effective
if the king were not ignorant of his real nature, that he could
never be taken captive involuntarily!

> (And so, Apollonios suddenly appears out of the
> blue to Damis and a friend in a small town by the sea,
> where he had sent Damis several days before the trial.
> At this point, however, Philostratus breaks into the
> narrative with a long speech he says Apollonios had
> composed to give before the king -- but, due to his
> sudden departure he didn't have an opportunity, the
> king having restricted him to the four accusations.
> So Philostratus gives it (for Apollonios) in its
> entirety (it runs to more than 800 lines!). It is
> clearly intended to be a final *testament*, summariz-
> ing and defending his whole life's work. Its artifi-
> ciality can scarcely be doubted. Otherwise, what is
> the meaning of Apollonios' earlier word to Damis that
> he was *not* going to prepare just such an oration in
> defense of his life, but speak extemporaneously
> (VIII.30)? Philostratus, following the time-honored
> methods of Hellenistic historiography, has here
> simply fabricated the speech Apollonios *ought* to have
> given on this momentous occasion --with all the rhe-
> torical skill he can muster. It is largely a rehash
> of all that has gone before, and there is little
> point in asking how much of it goes back to Apollonios
> and how much is from Philostratus' fertile imagination
> (i.e., what he considered it 'fitting' for Apollonios

---

[1] Homer, *Iliad* 22.13.

to have stood for -- or just anything that would be
popular with his readers. We have already seen evidence that Philostratus was closely attuned to what
was palatable fare as far as his readers were concerned!) In any case, we may conclude that this
speech is largely the work and expresses the viewpoint of Philostratus; perhaps here and there are
fragmentary reminiscences of Apollonios' actual
teachings.

     Of particular interest, therefore, is a fasci-
nating, brief description of Apollonios' (=Philostra-
tus') theory as to just what kind of being this
Apollonios supposedly was, right in the middle of
this great speech. That is, Philostratus gives a
short, tantalizing glimpse of what he understands
the "divine man's" role to be, as a savior among
men -- precisely the image in which Philostratus is
laboring to portray Apollonios. The passage in
question starts off with Philostratus having Apollonios compare the Egyptian sages' view of God with the
Indian sages'.)

VIII.7.7   As for the Indians and the Egyptians, the
Egyptians condemn the Indians about other things and find fault
with their teachings about conduct, but as for the explanation
which is given about the Creator of all things, in this they
more or less agree with them, because, in fact, the Indians
taught it to them. This explanation of the origin and being
of all things recognizes God as Creator, the cause of this
creating being His yearning for the good. Since moreover these
things are interrelated, I go on to say that those who are good
among men have something of God in them. Now, of course, it is
thought that the realm (kosmos) which is dependent upon God the
Creator includes all things in heaven, in the sea and on the
land, in which there is equal participation by men -- except
for Fortune's decree.[1] But then there is also a certain realm
(kosmos) constituted by the criteria of Wisdom which is revealed
by the good man, and even you yourself, O King, say there is

----

[1]What is described here is the natural realm of Divine Providence, equally benefitting all men alike, more or less. "The
sun shines on the just and the unjust...."

need of a man resembling God. But what is the manner of the
(third kind of) realm (*kosmos*) all around us? Deranged souls
insanely grabbing for every passing fad, our laws obsolete to
them, having no common sense, their piety toward the Gods sheer
disgrace, loving idle chatter and luxury, from which springs
wicked laziness as the advisor of their every act. Other
drunken souls rush in all directions at once, nothing restrain-
ing their frenzy, even if they should take every pill thought
to bring sleep. Therefore a man is needed who will take care
of the realm in which these people live, a God under the guidance of Wisdom. For this man will be able to urge and to lead
them from the passions by which they are so violently carried
away in their everyday behavior, and from their desire for
material possessions, because of which they will tell you they
have nothing as long as they can't hold their mouths open under
the stream of wealth pouring down. To curb them, so that
they do not commit murder,is perhaps not impossible for such a
man, although to wash away the guilt of murder once committed
is not possible, either for me,or for the God who is Creator
of All.

　　　　(It is a most interesting three-"realms" conception which emerges here. Furthermore, the second
realm, the God-man mediator, is clearly Apollonios'
own conception of himself, i.e., *Philostratus' conception of Apollonios* -- as the use of the first person at the very end reveals, and as he says explicitly
a little later: "I do all things for the salvation
of men" (VIII.7.10). Just before this passage,
"Apollonios" explains why the cities he has visited
think him a God and it forms a good summary of his
whole "mission" on behalf of the salvation of men:
"Indeed, I have been worthy of much honor in each
of the cities which needed me, performing such things
as healing the sick, making more holy those being
initiated into the mysteries or offering sacrifice,
rooting out pride, and strengthening their laws"
(VIII.7.7). This is what is meant by "taking care
of the realm in which men live" (above).

　　　　After giving his version of Apollonios' self-
defense at his trial (shades of Socrates!), Philostratus tells how he suddenly appeared to Damis in

Dicaearchia, the small town on the seacoast where the
other was waiting for him. So Apollonios emerges
from the hour of peril unscathed. Indeed, says
Philostratus, he made "the tyrant a plaything by his
philosophy" (VIII.10). Where is all the talk of
"risk" now? In any case, Damis is naturally startled
to see him, and asks if he is a ghost. "Apollonios
put out his hand saying, Touch me and if I escape
you I am a ghost come from Persephone's realm
(VIII.12). Damis is overjoyed to see it is really
his master, though completely mystified how he came
from Rome so quickly.

Apollonios decides to leave Italy that same day
for Greece, and so they set sail for Sicily and thence
to the Peloponnese. Upon arrival they settle in the
temple of Zeus at Olympia. Instantly word gets around
that Apollonios is not at Rome in prison, or dead, but
has just arrived at Olympia. At this, "the whole of
Greece came together to see him as never before for
any Olympic festival" (VIII.15). The question on
everyone's lips was, how had he gotten away from
Domitian? Apollonios would only "say that he had
given his defense and was saved." But when several
Italians come, they tell the whole story of what
happened in the courtroom. "At this Greece was moved
to near worship of him, believing him to be a divine
man for this reason above all -- that he did not
indulge in loud boasting about any of his deeds"
(VIII.15).

After forty days of discussions and debates at
Olympia, Apollonios proclaims to all that he will
now depart and "converse with you in each of your
cities, in the festivals, the religious processions,
mysteries, sacrifices, libations -- for they have need
of a knowledgeable man" (VIII.19). He then visits a
shrine of Apollo where, after staying in its sacred
cave seven days (longer than anyone ever had before),
he emerges with an authentic book of the teachings
of Pythagoras, which, Philostratus adds, is preserved
to this day at Antium in the palace of Hadrian.

A band of disciples now goes everywhere with
Apollonios, and Philostratus describes one of his
sermons to them, an attack on lawyers who will argue
any case before the judges for money, calling them
"people who welcome enmity, indeed (their vocation
is) the same thing as selling hatred" (VIII.22).

After two years, Apollonios sails for Ionia,
and while staying in Ephesus, he sees as in a vision
(while giving a lecture) the sudden assassination of

Domitian taking place in Rome. No one is willing to
credit Apollonios' vision, although they would like
to. But before long, envoys come with the news that
the Emperor Domitian has been murdered, and Nerva is
now on the throne. A sudden wave of awe sweeps the
city at Apollonios' pre-vision. The Emperor Nerva
then sends for Apollonios to come assist him in
ruling the empire, but Apollonios refuses for the
curious reason that he knew Nerva would die in less
than two years. Sending Damis to Nerva with his
letter of apology, Apollonios himself "dies" not
long after. Of the circumstances surrounding Apollonios' passing, Damis preserves no mention (because he
was in Rome), says Philostratus, but he has found
three other accounts of it, and he relates all three.)

VIII.30   Some say he died in Ephesus, while being served
by two slave women, the two male slaves I mentioned at the
beginning having died already. He freed one of them but not
the other, having a reason in mind, for Apollonios said, "If
you serve her you will benefit from her, for it will be the
beginning of a good thing for you." Thus, after he died, one
served the other until one day, on a whim, the latter sold her
to a merchant, and then someone else bought her from him, even
though she was not good-looking. But he was in love with her
and being quite wealthy he both made her his wife and inscribed
in the public archives the children he had by her.

        But others say he died in Lindos; that is, he entered
the temple of Athena and just disappeared once he got inside.
Those who live in Crete say he died in a more remarkable way
than the people of Lindos tell. For they say that Apollonios
lived in Crete, an object of greater veneration than ever
before, and that one day he came to the temple of Dictynna
(Artemis) at a deserted hour. Dogs are kept there as a guard
for the temple, keeping watch over the riches inside it, and
the Cretans consider them as fierce as bears or other wild
beasts. But when he came up, they did not bark but came up to
him wagging their tails, something they would not do even to
those very familiar to them. The temple attendants thereupon

arrested and bound Apollonios as being a wizard and a thief,
claiming he had thrown the dogs something to soothe them.
But, around the middle of the night, he freed himself and,
after calling to the men who had tied him up so as not to be
unobserved, he ran up to the gates of the temple, which immediately opened by some unseen power, and when he had gone inside,
the gates closed together again (as they were shut originally).
Then the voices of young women singing came forth from inside
the temple and the song was, "Come from earth, come to heaven,
come;" or, "come up from the earth."

> (Of course, when the attendants got the door
> open, Apollonios had disappeared; he was "in Heaven".
> Although gone from the realm of mortal men, he was
> clearly not "dead". To show this, Philostratus
> finishes his biography with a story of a doubting
> disciple who refused to believe that Apollonios
> really was still alive. Thus, Apollonios appears
> to him to remove his doubts.)

VIII.31   This young boy would never agree to the immortality
of the soul. "I, my friends, am completing the tenth month of
praying to Apollonios to reveal to me the nature of the soul.
But he is completely dead so as never to respond to my begging,
nor will I believe he is not dead." Such were the things he
said then, but on the fifth day after that[1] they were busy with
these things and he suddenly fell into a deep sleep right where
he had been talking. Now, the rest of the youths studying with
him were reading books and busily incising geometric shapes on
the earth, when he, as if insane, suddenly leaped to his feet,
still seeming to be asleep, the perspiration running off him,
and cried out, "*I believe you!*" When those present asked him
what was wrong, he said, "Do you not see Apollonios the sage,
how he stands here among us, listening to the argument and
singing wonderful verses concerning the soul?" "Where is he?"

---

[1]After what? The "fifth day" has symbolic significance.

they said, "for he has not appeared to us, even though we wish
this more than to have all mortal wealth." But the youth
replied, "It seems he came to discuss with me alone concerning
the things which I would not believe."

(And the youth goes on to sing the verses of
Apollonios concerning the immortality of the soul,
and with this pious note, Philostratus concludes
his biography.)

63. PHILO OF ALEXANDRIA: ABOUT THE LIFE OF MOSES

(Trans. and notes, D.L. Dungan)

(Introduction: Philo's *Life of Moses* is of special interest for two major reasons; (1) in type of writing it is remarkably similar to the nearly contemporary Christian Gospels and Acts of the Apostles, and displays in a conspicuous way the religious conceptions and impulses which guided Hellenized, Diaspora Judaism, out of which also grew Luke-Acts and the Gospel of John. (2) We have the major source used by the author, namely, the Septuagint (or Greek translation of the Hebrew Bible), and therefore are in a position to compare source-material with finished product, obtaining thereby priceless information (because so rare) concerning the methods of composition of this type of work. Aspects of this will be pointed out along the way.

One rather disconcerting feature of this writing to modern readers is the unabashed superiority Philo claims for Moses at every opportunity. While this may seem obnoxious to us, it is clear that Philo did not intend it to have that effect. To understand what sort of effect he originally intended, we need to remember that this writing, although filled with data about Moses' life and activity, is not a "biography" in the sense we are accustomed to think of it. Despite the narrative framework visible in Book I and in patches of Book II, Philo is not really presenting a chronicle of Moses' life, but assembling episodes which, taken together, form a mosaic disclosing Moses' character.

This writing was part of a larger scheme of several such "biographies", in which Philo writes about the major figures in the Pentateuch: Abraham, Joseph, Isaac, Jacob, and Moses; all as illustrating certain basic types of the spiritual life. Philo alludes to this at one point in the *Life of Moses* (see I 76). Of these various types of the spiritual life, Moses was for Philo the most important, since he was the one man in human history who achieved full communion (*epopteia*) with God, or the Divine Reason that governs the world (which Philo refers to by many terms, especially *Logos*), and, being completely filled by it, was himself divine. This then showed itself in Moses' actions; hence the biographical format, and Philo recounts anecdotes (not necessarily in the order of his source) from Moses' life under the headings of what he did by way of kingship, lawgiving, priestcraft, and prophecy. Naturally, since Moses' actions in all these realms were completely under the guidance of total divine inspiration, they necessarily had to be superior to anything any mere mortal had achieved, before or since.

Living from about 20 B.C.E. until around 50 C.E. in
Alexandria, this writing belongs to what is usually called
Philo's "apologetic" writings, that is, those efforts at expounding the most attractive aspects of Judaism (as he understood it) for his serious-minded, inquiring Gentile friends.)

BOOK I

1   I have decided to write on the life of Moses,
the man whom Gentiles know to have been the lawgiver of
the Jews while the Jews acknowledge him to be the interpreter of the sacred laws, a man in every respect the
greatest and most perfect who ever lived.

               The story of his life should be familiar to
2   all who deserve to know it, but even though the fame of
the laws which he left behind has already gone out through
the whole world, ranging even to the uttermost corners of
the earth, what sort of man he himself really was is not
known to many people, since the historians among the
Greeks did not consider him worth remembering, no doubt
out of jealousy and because not a few of the commandments
3   of the lawgivers of their cities are the opposite of his.
Instead they waste the talents they have acquired through
education in composing poems and long-winded narratives
that are supposed to be funny, filled with voluptuous
licentiousness, notoriously shameful, whereas they should
have fully employed their natural abilities on the instruction to be gained from good men and their lives,
lest anything that is good, ancient or recent, once it
is consigned to silence, be deprived of the light it
might give. Moreover, they would not seem so consistently
to ignore the better themes in order to fasten attention
on things not worth hearing about, telling wicked stories
elegantly, just for the sake of revealing disgusting
things.

4   But I, on my part, ignoring their insulting
silence, will make known the facts concerning the man,

namely what I have learned both from the sacred books
which he left behind as marvelous memorials of his wisdom,
as well as other things from some of the elders of the
Jewish people, for by thus painstakingly melding together
the oral accounts with the written, I think I understand
more accurately than anyone else the facts concerning his
life.

Moses the King

5   I will begin at the point where one must begin.
Although Moses was Chaldean by race, he was born and
raised in Egypt because his ancestors had migrated there
during a time when a protracted famine was destroying
Babylon and the neighboring peoples. They and their
families moved to Egypt to find food, since it was a
broad and verdant land, most productive of eveything the
6   human body requires, especially grain. For the river of
this country, during the hottest part of the summer, when
other rivers, whether caused by springs or rainfall, begin
to dry up, it increases and overflows, flooding the fields
and turning them into lakes. Thus, without needing any
rain, they produce bountiful crops of all kinds year after
year, unless perchance the wrath of God strikes instead
to punish the inveterate irreligiousness of the Egyptians.
7   For a father and mother he was given the best
there was, who, although of the same clan, were drawn
together by likemindedness more than by race. Moses was
the seventh generation from Abraham, the original settler
in Canaan and founder of the whole Jewish nation.
8   Moses was honored with a royal upbringing
through the following circumstances. The king of the
Egyptians feared that the Jewish immigrants (who were
steadily increasing in number) might surpass the native
people and become strong enough to wrest the supremacy
from them, so he devised wicked schemes to diminish their
strength. He ordered the Jews to rear the female babies

born to them (since a woman is weak by nature and afraid
to fight), but to kill all the male babies, lest they
continue to multiply in every city, for the power of an
abundance of good men is a fort in enemy territory hard
to conquer or overthrow.

9   As soon as the child was born, he seemed more
beautiful than an ordinary child, so his parents ignored
the proclamations of the tyrant as much as possible,
and -- though no one knew it -- kept him at home for
three successive months while his mother breast-fed him.

10   But, since in monarchies there are people always trying
to pry into everything, even nurseries, in order to carry
some new rumor to the king, his parents began to fear
that in their concern for saving one, more should perish
instead, namely, they themselves with him.

And so, weeping bitterly, they put Moses out
to die beside the riverbank and departed groaning in
anguish, pitying themselves because of what they were
compelled to do -- calling themselves "Murderers!" and
"Child-killers!" -- and pitying their child also for so

11   meaningless a death. Moreover, as often happens in
terrible situations, they began to accuse themselves as
being the cause of an even greater tragedy; "Oh, why did
we not put him out to die as soon as he was born?" they
said. "It is said that an infant who has not partaken
of his first feeding is not human (and can legitimately
be allowed to die). But we, matchless parents!, actually
nursed Moses for three whole months, thereby making sure
to bring a greater weight of grief upon ourselves and for
him torture, in that, having grown completely aware of
pleasure and pain, he died fully conscious of more
grievous wretchedness."

12   And so, ignorant of what was about to happen,
they departed mourning and filled with sadness, but a
sister of the abandoned child, still young herself but
compelled by familial devotion, stood a little way off,

anxiously watching to see what would happen -- all this
taking place, it seems to me, in accordance with God's
foreknowledge concerning the boy.

13   Now the king of the country had a single,
beloved daughter. They say she was married a long time,
but could not bear children, although as usual she especially longed for a male offspring who would receive the
wonderful inheritance of her father's dominion, which
was liable to fall into a stranger's hands for want of

14   a male heir. Always sad and sighing, on this day especially she sank under the weight of her anxieties and,
although she habitually remained at home and never even
crossed the threshhold, she went out with her maids (to
purify herself) at the river where Moses had been abandoned. And just when she was about to begin using the
sprinkling vessels to pour out prayer-libations (to her
Gods to remedy her sad condition) her eye fell upon Moses
in the densest thicket of the marsh, and she commanded
him to be brought to her.

15   After she had examined him from head to foot,
she rejoiced at his beauty and good health and, seeing
him begin to cry, began to pity him, her soul already
having been turned within her toward motherly affection
as if he were her own baby. Then, realizing that it was
a Hebrew child, (and had been cast away out of) terror
of the king's decree, she began to consider what she
might feed him, for she thought it not safe to take him
immediately to the palace.

16   While she was still uncertain what to do, the
baby's sister, who guessed the meaning of this hesitation
as if from a watch-tower, ran up and asked if she wanted

17   the baby nursed by a Hebrew woman who had been pregnant
not long before. When the princess said that was what
she wanted, the girl's (and the child's) mother was
brought as if she were a stranger, and she very quickly

and gladly promised to nurse him, on the pretext that she needed the wages. And so, through this strategy, God brought it about that the child's first nourishment shoul be from his own mother. Then the princess gave him the name Moses (Greek: *Mōusēs*), which she did because he was actually taken up from the water, for the Egyptians call water *mōu*.

18   When Moses began growing steadily and filling out, even more quickly than might be expected, he was weaned, and his combined mother and provider of nourishment presented him to the princess, since he no longer needed to be nursed, but had become a princely, beautiful

19   child. And she, seeing him more perfect to the eye than others of his age, took a liking to him even greater than before, and made him her son, having already beforehand artfully fashioned some padding for her body in order to seem pregnant, so that everyone would think the child was really her own and not a substitute secretly brought in, for God makes whatever he wills easy to do, even that which seems impossible.

20   Now, even though he began to be provided with the kind of food and servant-help customary for a prince, Moses did not give himself up completely to childish habits, teasing and mocking and infantile behavior, even though those who had been appointed to care for him were quite lenient and not at all strict. Instead he displaye a precociously serious and respectful attitude, paying attention only to those things which he heard or saw that were likely to benefit his soul.

21   Different teachers immediately appeared from everywhere, some of their own accord from the districts of Egypt and neighboring regions, while others were

summoned from Greece at high salaries.[1] But thanks to
his superbly gifted nature, before long his powers excelled theirs and he began to discover things by himself
before they could be taught -- as if he were just remem-

22   bering, not learning for the first time. In fact, he
would even think up more difficult questions himself.
For great natures discern many new things in the field
of knowledge, and just as the bodies of wrestlers which
are healthy and agile in every part need no special
attention from their trainers, or at any rate, very
little, so also the farmer devotes little care upon plants
growing vigorously and becoming well-formed, improving by
themselves. In the same fashion, a well-formed soul begins to flourish by itself and benefits more from things
said beforehand by itself than what is said by its
teachers. Taking its own starting point in intellectual
inquiry, it plunges forth eagerly, as the proverb says,
"like a duck to water."

23   The scholars of the Egyptians instructed him in
arithmetic and geometry, both rhythm and harmony, the
theory of metre, and the whole of music, both as to the
use of instruments as well as textbooks on the simpler
techniques and more advanced treatises. Besides this,
they taught him their philosophy, contained in the symbols displayed in their so-called sacred hieroglyphic

---

[1]Philo's desire to show how Moses mastered all the wisdom of
of the world of his, i.e., Philo's, day is responsible for this
glaring anachronism. Of course, in Moses' day, Greece did not
even exist, much less have an international scholarly reputation.
Although we may be surprised at this remarkable departure from
his source (Ex. 2:10), it would be incorrect to conclude that
Philo is simply inventing this out of whole cloth. Rather, he
is relying, to some extent, on the oral traditions he referred
to earlier, as we can see from their appearance elsewhere, in
Josephus, *Antiquities* II 232-237, in the Tannaitic midrash on
Ex. 2:10 (see quote in H. St. J. Thackeray, *Josephus* Vol. IV.
265, note c), and in Christian literature, Acts 7:22, "he was
instructed in all the wisdom of the Egyptians."

writing and through the adoration of animals which they
even worship as Gods. The other courses of learning the
Greeks taught, but those from the neighboring regions
taught Assyrian writing and Chaldean astrology.

24   This branch of mathematics he also learned from
the Egyptians, who especially pursue such things. Indeed
he accurately mastered everything from both, where they
agreed as well as where they disagreed, but his mind rose
above their rivalry since he was not fond of contention,
and sought only the truth -- his mind being incapable of
accepting any falsehood, as is so often true of the
quarrelsome philosophical sects who will support and
contend for any doctrine whatever without questioning it
to see if it is valid or not, the same as lawyers do who
argue any case at all for money, never caring at all
about justice in their disputes.

25   Moses soon passed beyond the limits of childhood and, consequently, he increased his vigilance, not
letting his youthful lusts run unchecked as some do, even
though there were the numberless provocations abundantly
available that palaces offer. Instead, he bound on the
reins of self-control and patience, as it were, and
26   restrained their impetuous force. Each of the other
passions, also, which are by nature frenzied and riotous
he made gentle, taming and civilizing them, and if somehow one only so much as began to stir or flutter awake,
he would provide a harsher remedy in punishment than mere
verbal scolding. In general, he carefully watched for
the first signs of rebellion in the soul, as if it were
a wayward horse, fearing lest it run away from the
rationality which ought to hold the reins, turning everything into chaos. For these passions are the causes
of both good and bad; good when they are obedient to the
leadership of reason (*logos*), but the opposite when they
turn from regular paths to anarchy.

27   Of course, those who associated with Moses and
all others were amazed, being astonished by this remarkable phenomenon and closely examining what it might be
which inhabited his body or what sort of imprint he
carried in his mind, whether human or divine or a mixture
of both, for it was in no way like a common man's but
stood above that, being lifted up toward more majestic
things.

28   For example, he would give his stomach nothing
more than the minimum amount nature has decreed, while
as for the region below the stomach, he did not even
29   think of it, except to conceive his children. He undertook an unusually austere way of life, holding luxury in
greater contempt than anyone else ever had. Instead, he
yearned to live for the soul alone, displaying through
his actions each day the teachings of philosophy, as he
would state what he knew and then do those things which
accorded with what he had said, so that there was a harmony between reason (*logos*) and life. Whatever reason
dictated, his life reflected, and whatever his life was,
it was shown to be rational, both harmoniously blending
together like a musical instrument.

        (At this point Philo digresses to assert that
        when Fortune exalts other men to the level of
        prosperity Moses now enjoyed, they quickly
        forget their friends and ancestral ways, be-
        coming cold and arrogant, as if they them-
        selves were somehow the cause of their new-
        found wealth.)

32   But Moses, having already reached the pinnacle
of human good fortune, and, indeed, being considered the
son of the present king's daughter and being expected by
almost everyone to accede to his grandfather's dominion --
all but being named "the new king," nevertheless, Moses
remained loyal to his own ancient, native culture, while
the benefits of his adopted family, even if temporarily
more brilliant, he considered false, but the virtues of

his natural parents, even if at the moment they were not
very evident, were at any rate a genuine part of his
heritage. Like an impartial judge, he fairly repaid both
his family and his foster parents, the former with kindness and devoted loyalty, the latter with gratitude for
all they had provided, and he would have gone on being
grateful thenceforth had he not noticed a grave new sin
begun in the country by the king.

> (The king singles out all Hebrew men to be
> forcibly enrolled in state-controlled building
> projects. Philo digresses to recall for the
> reader's sake that the only reason the Hebrews
> were in Egypt in the first place was the great
> famine long before, and now the king was
> wickedly beginning to treat the Hebrew people,
> who were really guests and refugees, like
> slaves and enemies of the state.)

37   Then the king gave orders for impossibly heavy
tasks, piling up labor upon labor for the Hebrews, and
the iron fist was ready for those who sank down due to
weakness, for the king appointed as overseers of the
tasks, merciless, savage men who had no compassion toward
38   anyone, men who earned the label "slave drivers" by what
they did. The Hebrews were put to work, some shaping clay
into bricks, others bringing straw from everywhere to mix
in and strengthen the bricks. Others were set apart to
rebuild houses, city buildings, town walls, and irriga-
tion canals, carrying building materials themselves every
day and night without a break, given no chance to rest,
not even being allowed to sleep, but forced to do everything at once, fetching materials as well as building, so
that before long their bodies became exhausted since the
39   souls had already yielded to despair. Naturally, scores
upon scores died, as if under the onslaught of a terrible
plague, and their corpses were just thrown aside and left
unburied outside cities, not being allowed even a little
dust to cover them up or relatives and friends to come

and mourn those so pitiably destroyed. And even the un-
constrained passions of the soul, which are more nearly
free than anything else in nature, these wicked men sought
to crush under tyrannical pressure more powerful than
they.

40   Witnessing these things, Moses became alternate-
ly depressed and then angry, since he was not in a position either to punish the wrongdoers or to help those
being wronged. He did what he could verbally, such as
it was, advising those in charge to be more lenient, to
give up or at least abate such excessively harsh commands,
while he exhorted the Hebrew workers to bear their present condition nobly, to take it like men, not to let
their souls have any sympathy for their bodies -- but to
41 hope for better things from such evil conditions, since
everything in the world sooner or later changes into its
opposite: clouds into empty air, violent winds into
quiet breezes, stormy seas into tranquillity, while human
affairs are even more changeable since they are least
42 stable. Repeating such things as these, Moses sought,
like a good doctor, to ease their heavy affliction. But
after a brief respite, the Egyptians only returned with
vigor renewed from their pause, laying wholly new out-
43 rages upon the people, more intolerable than before.
For some of the overseers were exceptionally harsh and
unrestrained, no better than savage, carnivorous beasts
or venomous reptiles, animals in human form, treacherous
beasts in human bodies so as to appear deceptively civilized, but underneath more hard-hearted than iron or
steel.

44   One of the most violent of these taskmasters,
a man who had mercy on no one, whom entreaty made even
harsher, flogging those who didn't obey him with breath-
less haste, tormenting them to death, outrageously torturing his workers -- this man Moses did away with,

justifying his action as the right thing to do, and it
was rightly done that a man who lived to destroy others
should himself be killed.

45   Now when the king heard of it, he became very
angry, not asking whether someone had killed or slain
unjustly or justly, but because his grandson did not
agree with him and did not have the same enemies and
friends as he. Instead Moses hated the people he liked,
but loved those whom the king detested, showing concern
for those toward whom the king was indifferent and
inexorable.

46   Given this opportunity, various officials who
had long been suspicious of the youth, and who feared
that in due time (after he came to power) he would
remember the evil and injurious things they had done in
the past and avenge himself on them -- these courtiers
began pumping thousands of rumors into the king's open
ears, some on one side, others on the other side, trying
to instill in him the fear that Moses was planning to
seize power, saying, "He will attack you! He will stop
at nothing! He is forever hatching new schemes because
he wants to be king before the proper time! He flatters
some, threatens others, kills without a trial, and
despises those especially who are friendly toward you.
What are you waiting for? Cut the ground out from under
him and his plots! Any delay on the part of the victim
gives the advantage to the attacker!"

47   Because such slanders were circulating everywhere, Moses withdrew into the neighboring country of
Arabia, where he would be able to live safely, at the
same time crying aloud to God to deliver the Hebrews from
their helplessness as well as deservedly to punish those
who let no opportunity pass by to insult them, and, moreover, that He double His gift by permitting Moses to see
these both take place.

God heard his prayers, noting Moses' character-
istic love of the good and hatred of evil, and not long
48   after, He brought judgment upon Egypt, as it was proper
for Him to do. Before this came about, however, Moses
was exercising in the contests of virtue, having as a
trainer his own special rationality, under whose guidance
he was being trained for the best careers, the theoretical
and the practical. He regularly sought to disentangle the
doctrines of philosophy, easily resolving them with his
soul and depositing them indelibly in his memory, then
bringing his own personal, wholly admirable, actions into
conformity with them. Nor did he allow mere appearances
to deceive him, but held only to the truth, keeping one
guide before himself, namely, the right reason of nature
(*ho orthos tēs physeōs logos*), which alone is the source
and fountain of virtues.

> (At this point, Philo illustrates his argument
> by introducing a story based on Ex. 2:15-22.
> Once in Arabia, says Philo, Moses did not
> merely hide nor did he seek to ingratiate him-
> self with local officials for the sake of
> protection, should the Egyptians come after
> him. Instead, he fearlessly intervened in the
> affairs of others when the "healthy impulses
> of his soul," namely, "his love of the good,"
> prompted him to do so.)

51   I will describe something he did at this time
and, although it might seem a trivial thing, nevertheless
it did not spring from a trivial spirit. The Arabs
raise cattle and appoint as shepherds not only men but
also women, youths and maidens among them, nor are these
52   only of the less important, lower classes, but even
members of the very best families. Thus, seven maidens,
whose father was a priest, had led their flock of sheep
beside a certain fountain, and, having tied buckets to
the draw-ropes, they were taking turns in pulling up the
water, quickly filling the drinking-troughs which lay
53   nearby. Now there were other shepherds also who

constantly came and took advantage of these young maidens
roughly driving them away with their flock, in order to
bring up their own animals to the already prepared water
benefiting from the labors of others.

54   This happened once when Moses was nearby, and
when he saw it, he ran over and confronted them, saying,
"Why do you do wrong, just because the place is isolated
Are you not ashamed to be so lazy and spineless? You ar
beautiful long hair and fat -- not men! These girls worl
like youths, willfully doing whatever needs to be done;
are you going to mince around like girls? Why don't you

55   go somewhere else? Give the water back to those who cam
here first and drew it. You should have filled the
troughs for them in order that the water be more plenti-
ful, and here you are trying to snatch what little has
been prepared! By the Heavenly Eye of Justice, you will
not get away with it, for It sees everything, even in

56   the most deserted places! It has appointed me their
unexpected ally, and I assuredly am a co-fighter with
the Great Hand of Justice on behalf of those who are
wronged! While it is not fitting for the greedy to see
that Hand, you will feel it invisibly wounding you unles
you change!"

57   As he spoke, they became terrified of him, sin
his appearance was transformed as he became infused with
the Spirit, and they feared that he was about to cast a
spell or utter an oracle (destroying them), so they gave
in and led the flock of the young maidens back to the
troughs, having moved their own aside.

58   The girls returned home jubilant, and related
the unexpected news to their father, which created in hi
an ardent longing to see the stranger. He upbraided his
daughters for their ingratitude, saying, "What is the
matter with you? Why did you just let him go? You shou
have brought him back with you immediately, and if he wa

reluctant, insisted on it! Or did you suspect that I
would be inhospitable? Do you think you will never run
afoul of evil men again? Those who forget favors done
for them certainly soon lack allies! But never mind;
your transgression can still be healed. Quickly run back
and invite the stranger both to visit us and to accept
some reward, for a favor is owed to him."

59   The girls ran back and overtook Moses not far
from the well. Explaining the message from their father,
they begged him to return home with them. Their father
was immediately struck by his beautiful appearance and a
little later by his character, for great natures are conspicuous and need little time to make themselves known,
and forthwith gave Moses his prettiest daughter as a
wife, through this one deed giving evidence of all the
qualities which exhibited his noble goodness, and goodness is worthy of our love, for there is no need of
supporting testimony from other virtues, for goodness
carries within itself sufficient indications to make
itself known.

60   After the wedding, Moses took charge of the
herds, and in herding sheep was first being instructed
in leadership; for practice in shepherding was also a
preliminary exercise in the expected rule Moses was one
day to exert over the civilized herd of men.

> (Philo continues to dilate on this theme,
> arguing that "the only perfect king is one
> well-versed in knowledge of shepherding."
> He realized this may sound a bit ridiculous,
> and warns the reader, "you can laugh if you
> want" -- but it is still the truth. He then
> goes on to describe in detail how Moses'
> phenomenal way with sheep led to never-ending,
> daily improvement in the size and quality of
> his flocks, to the astonishment and envy of
> his neighbors. It is equally astonishing to
> us what Philo can find in a single verse of
> his source, namely, Ex. 3:1. After this,
> Philo takes up the story of the Burning Bush.)

65   One day, as Moses led the flock to a place with
plenty of water and grass, being especially abundant in
sheep fodder, there came to pass in a certain glen, a
marvel which he saw, most astonishing. A bramble bush,
the sort full of thorns and frail-looking, suddenly
caught on fire, although no one had set it on fire, and
became wrapped in a sheet of flame from roots to branch-
tips, just as if it were spewing forth from a fountain;
nor was the bush burnt up but it remained whole, seeming
to use the fire for food, as it were, instead of itself
66   being fuel for the fire. And in the midst of the flame
there appeared a figure of wondrous beauty, unlike anything ever seen, a most divine image, flashing forth
light more brilliant than the fire itself. Some might
suspect it was the very form of Him Who Is, but let it
be called an angel, which silently announced the things
soon to happen more clearly than if they were spoken,
by means of this glorious vision of the great things to
be done.

> (Philo's point is that the flaming but not
> consumed bush is a symbol of the persecuted
> but not destroyed Hebrew people, while the
> angelic being in the center is a sign --
> unmistakeable without needing any words -- of
> God's imminent deliverance.)

71   After revealing this portent and miracle to be
performed, God addressed Moses with utmost clarity concerning the things about to be accomplished and through
oracles began to urge him to hurry back to care for his
people, not only in order to be a partial cause of their
freedom, but also to be the leader of their settlement
elsewhere, to take place not far away, promising to
72   assist him in all things. "For since they have suffered
much evil and endured intolerable arrogance, there being
no one among men to relieve nor have mercy on their mis-
fortunes, I myself have had pity on them," God said.

"For I know that each by himself and all with one accord
have turned to prayers and supplications in hopes of
assistance from me, and I, being kind by nature, am
favorable to genuine prayers. Therefore, go to the king
of that country, and have no concern whatever about anything, for the former king, from whom you fled on account
of fear of a plot against you, has died and the country
has been entrusted to another, who remembers nothing
evil of your past deeds. Take with you the elders of
your people and tell the king that the Hebrew nation has
been summoned by me through an oracle to make a three-
days' journey outside the country, where they will
sacrifice according to the rites of their fathers."

But Moses, not ignorant that his own people as
well as all others would disbelieve the things told them,
said, "If, however, they inquire what the name is of him
who sent me, and I myself am not able to tell them, will
I not seem to deceive?"

God said, "First, tell them that I am He Who
Is,[1] in order that, having learned the difference between
what is and what is not, they may be taught in addition
that absolutely no name applies to me literally, to whom
belongs being as such (*to einai*). But if their natures
are too weak to be satisfied with that and if they still
seek some further designation, explain only this much to
them: I am God, God, that is, of the three men named
after a virtue, the God of Abraham, the God of Isaac, and
the God of Jacob, of whom the first is the standard of
wisdom gained by teaching, the second is the standard of
wisdom acquired by nature, and the third is the standard
of wisdom achieved through training. But if they should

Greek: *ego eimi ho ōn*; a well-known etymology based on the
umption that the Hebrew Tetragrammaton יהוה came from the
b היה 'to be'. Of course, Philo is following the LXX here.

still disbelieve, let them be taught once more by these
three signs, and then they will change their minds, for
these will be signs which no man has ever seen or heard
of before."

77   And these were the signs: the rod which Moses
was carrying God commanded him to cast to the ground,
where it instantly came alive by itself, and turned into
the largest of the reptiles, a full-grown, enormous snak
At this, Moses quickly retreated from the animal, and out
of fear was desperately looking for a way to escape wher
God called him back and ordered him to pick it up by the
tail, at the same time giving him the courage to do so.

78   It was writhing about, but at Moses' touch, it stood
straight up, stretched out tight to its full length and
immediately transformed its essential nature by itself
back into a staff, so that Moses marveled at the double
change, unable to decide which of the two was more
staggering, his soul dumbfounded by the two equal mirac.

79   That was the first, and before long God worked
another miracle as well. He ordered Moses to conceal on
of his hands in his tunic and a little later to bring i
forth. When he did what was commanded, the hand sudden
appeared whiter than snow; and when he once more replac
his hand in his tunic and brought it forth again, it ha
turned back to the same color it was, regaining its pro
appearance.

80   These things God taught him, while they were
face to face, as a friend with a pupil, while Moses had
with him the instruments for the miracles to be perform

81   namely, his hand and the staff with which he was provid
The third miracle was not portable nor could it be taug
beforehand, but it was to be just as astonishing, havin
its occurrence in Egypt. It was this: "When you have
drawn some water from the river," said God, "pour it upo
the earth and it will become the reddest of blood, bein

changed both in appearance and internal property into
something completely different."

82   Apparently this also seemed believable to
Moses, not only because of the undeceitfulness of the
speaker, but also because of the miraculous deeds that
83   he had already been shown, the hand and the staff. But
although he believed, nevertheless, Moses begged God concerning the mission, saying that he stuttered and was
slow of tongue -- and this especially since he had just
been hearing God Himself speaking, for Moses considered
human eloquence to be speechlessness by comparison with
divine; and at the same time Moses was cautious by nature,
shrinking back from overly grandiose things, judging that
such exceeding great tasks were not for the likes of him.
Instead, he urged God to choose another who could easily
84   accomplish each of the things commanded him. But God,
although approving of his modesty, said, "Are you ignorant
of Who it is that gives man a mouth and fashions the
tongue and throat and the whole mechanism of rational
speech? It is I! Therefore fear nothing. At my indication, everything will be strengthened and transformed into
good working order, so that the streams of words will flow
beautifully and smoothly from a clean fountain with nothing still hindering it. And if there be need of an interpreter, you will have for a subordinate speaker your
brother, in order that he might announce to the people
your messages, while you repeat the divine messages to
him."

        (And so, Moses starts on his way back to Egypt
        with Aaron, prepared for a showdown with the
        pharoah. Needless to say, Philo does not men-
        tion the strange little episode in Ex. 4:24-26,
        where the Lord tries to kill Moses. As is
        familiar to us all, the Egyptian monarch only
        reacts to Moses' announcement with angry con-
        tempt, so that Moses unleashes the ten plagues
        upon Egypt. Philo here rearranges his source
        slightly, so that Aaron performs three plagues

(water into blood, frogs, and gnats), Moses
three (rainstorms, locusts, darkness), both do
one (boils), and God does the last three
(horseflies, death of cattle, death of first-
born). The reason for this rearrangement of
the biblical account is not clear, although
later Philo emphasizes that the very elements
of nature are under Moses' control (see I 156).
The Egyptians finally surrender and permit the
Hebrews to leave. At this point, when they
are finally about to set off for the Promised
Land with Moses at their head, Philo inter-
sperses a long, lyrical passage, sounding the
dominant theme of this whole first movement:
Moses the Perfect Leader; Moses the God-King!)

148   Moses was appointed the leader of all these
(emigrants and refugees), having received dominion and
kingship, not in the way those do who force their way
into royal office by means of armies and armored cavalry
and powerful infantries and navies, but because of his
virtue and noble goodness and consideration for all,
149   which he never failed to exhibit. Furthermore, the God
who loves virtue and goodness granted it as a prize
worthy of him, since Moses had given up the Egyptian
leadership, even though he was the daughter's son of the
previous king. But because of the injustices occurring
throughout the country, he bid good riddance to hopes of
succeeding those in office, due to his nobility of soul
and good judgment and natural hatred of evil. Thus it
seemed fitting to Him who is the President and Manager
of all things to repay Moses with the kingship of a more
populous and powerful nation. It was soon to be made
holier than all others, so that it might forever offer
prayers on behalf of the race of men, for the prevention
of evil and participation in good things.

150   Once Moses had received the dominion, however,
he did not, as some, desire to exalt his own household
and promote his own sons, although he had two, to greater
power, so as to display them as his partners in the present and successors thereafter, for his mind was guileless

and pure toward everything, small as well as great. Thus
he conquered his natural tender affection toward his
children like a good judge by the impartiality inherent
151   in his rationality. For he had set one supremely important goal (*telos*) for himself, namely, to help his subjects, taking in hand everything whether by word or by
deed which might be for their benefit, overlooking no
opportunity in his endeavors for the common prosperity.
152   Only he of all those who had ever yet led (nations) did
not treasure gold or silver, did not levy taxes or
acquire houses or possessions or cattle or household
servants or public revenues or anything else conducive
to an expensive and luxurious life, even though he could
have.

153   Instead, he considered the effort to acquire
wealth of material possessions to reflect a poverty-
stricken soul, scorning it as a kind of blindness; on
the other hand, he held in high esteem that natural
wealth which is not blind, being more zealous for it than
anyone else I ever heard of. He would not worry about
his clothing or food or other things pertaining to daily
life, for the sake of living in greater pompous conceit.
Instead, he lived with the thrift and simplicity of a
common citizen.

         But as for those things in which a ruler *ought*
154   to be lavish in his desires, Moses truly was -- namely,
in self-control (*enkrateia*), patience, moderation,
shrewdness, judgment, understanding, industry, suffering
hardship, scornful of pleasures, righteousness, advocat-
ing excellence, lawfully censuring and punishing wrongdoers, praising and honoring the upright, again according
to the law.

155   Consequently, having bid good riddance to great
wealth and to the riches mankind pants after, God honored
him in return with the greatest and most perfect of

riches, that is, the wealth of the entire earth and sea,
rivers, and all other things, the elements and their
combinations. For inasmuch as God thought him worthy
to be made known as a partner in His province, Moses was
given the whole world as property prepared for the heir.
156   Consequently, each of the elements obeyed him as its
master, taking on other qualities in obedience to his
commands. Nor should we be surprised at this, for if,
as the proverb says, "Friends share all things in common,"
and the prophet is said to be the friend of God, it follows that he would participate also in His possessions,
157   as much as is needful. For since God possesses everything, He needs nothing, and while the good man rightly
possesses nothing, not even himself, yet he receives a
share of the treasures of God, as much as he may. And
is that not only fair? For he is a citizen of the world
(*kosmopolitēs*), not a citizen of any of the individual
cities found in the inhabited world; and, as such,
necessarily has as his "estate," not some piece of land
158   in this or that country, but the whole world! Is that
not true? And was it not still grander than being partner with the Father and Maker of All to have the joy of
being considered worthy of His own Name? For Moses was
in fact called God and King of the whole nation![1] It is
said that Moses entered into the very same darkness within
which God was; that is, into the formless, invisible, non-
corporeal, original pattern of being of existing things,[2]
where he perceived what is forever invisible to natural,
mortal sight.

Then, putting himself and his life among us

---

[1] See Ex. 4:16.

[2] ...*aeidē kai aoraton kai asōmaton tōn ontōn paradeigmatikēn
ousian*.... This is not a reference to God in Himself, but,
according to Philo's ontology, to the Logos, which was the
rational pattern of nature.

like a beautiful work of art, he set up this wholly
noble and divinely-formed work as a model (*paradeigma*)

159 for those who wish to imitate it. Blessed indeed are
those who stamp his pattern (*typos*) into their own souls,
or desire that it were so stamped! For above all, let
our minds bring forth (his character) -- the perfect configuration of virtue[1] -- but if we cannot, at least may
we have the resolute desire to acquire that configuration.

> (In these last sentiments, Philo clearly
> enunciates what one of the fundamental notions
> of Hellenistic biography was all about: by
> relating the *acts* of someone dear to the Gods
> and more than human, lesser men could see
> reflected the pattern or form of a life truly
> pleasing to the Gods, and imitate it. It was,
> therefore, as a kind of exhortation that Moses
> or Apollonios or Pythagoras were described in
> biographies. On the other hand, these biog-
> raphies are powerfully consoling at the same
> time, for they reveal such "great natures" as
> these men selflessly giving of themselves for
> the betterment of lesser men's lot. As Philo
> says, Moses made this his supreme goal, toward
> which he devoted every effort.[2] For these
> reasons, such biographies engendered both love
> and gratitude coupled to a new desire to mend
> one's ways.
>
> Philo will play other chords in the other
> sections of his biography; but now he will
> tell of Moses' deeds which show him as the
> resourceful Leader, as the wise General, as
> the loving-yet-stern Father of his erring
> children -- in short, as the ideal King.)

163   And so, having received dominion over the
people voluntarily, God having directed them and assented
to it, Moses set off for their new home in Phoenicia and
Lower Syria and Palestine, which at that time was called
the land of the Canaanites, the boundaries of which used
to stand at a distance of three days' journey from Egypt.

---

[1] *to eidos teleion aretēs.*

[2] And Apollonios says nearly the same thing; see p. 292.

164   But he did not lead them up by the short way, on the one
      hand fearing that the inhabitants (of the regions along
      the way) might become hostile at the threat of destruc-
      tion and slavery and come forth to attack them, forcing
      the Hebrews to turn around, to take the same road back to
      Egypt, enemy for enemy, new for old, mocked and scoffed
      at, finally being captured and subjected to more grievous
      injury than before. On the other hand, Moses desired to
      lead them through a long stretch of desert to test their
      obedience when their daily needs were not abundantly
165   available but slightly wanting. So he immediately turned
      off onto an oblique road, thinking it might extend to the
      Red Sea, and began to travel along it. At that moment,
      it says, a marvel came to pass, a portent of nature which
166   no one remembers happening before. A cloud shaped into
      a good-sized pillar went before the caravan, shining by
      day with light like the sun, at night like fire, in order
      that they might not wander off the road during their
      march, but follow the inerrant Guide along the way.
      Perhaps it was one of the subordinates of the Great King,
      an invisible angel, a guide concealed in the cloud, whom
      it were not lawful to look upon with the eyes of the
      body.

167   Meanwhile, the king of Egypt, as soon as he saw
      them turning off into what he thought was an impassable
      desert, walking into the rocky and trackless wilderness,
      was delighted at this false step in their journey, be-
      lieving that they were hemmed in with no way out. Then
      he became sorry that he let them go in the first place,
      and made ready to pursue them, intending to force the
      multitude to return out of fear and enslave them, or on
      the other hand, just to kill them on the spot, obliterat-
      ing them from the youths on up.

              (The King of Egypt pursues them with his whole
              army and "six hundred of his finest scythed

chariots," hoping to trap them beside the sea. The Hebrews, suddenly caught unprepared and unarmed, take panic and loudly bewail their fate, accusing Moses of leading them by deceit into a fate worse than slavery, namely, certain death. But Moses rises to the occasion.)

173   When Moses heard (their desperate cries) he excused them, remembering the oracles; and dividing his mind from his speech, he simultaneously interceded silently with God to deliver them from this helpless predicament, while at the same time he cheered up and exhorted those who were bewailing their fate, saying, "Do not be dejected! God's method of defense is not

174   like man's! Why do you leap to merely probable or likely conclusions? God's assistance has no need of advance preparations! When there is no way, God finds his own way. Things impossible to all else are possible for Him alone, and easy."

175   He said these things, still in a calm way, but soon he paused, and then, becoming possessed by God, inspired by the Spirit which customarily often visited him, he uttered this prophetic oracle, "Those fully armed troops which you now see you will see no longer drawn up in battle formation, for they will all fall headlong and disappear into the ocean depths, so that no remnant of them will still appear upon the earth -- and this not in a long time, but in this very night!"

(And sure enough, at sundown a mighty wind began to blow and under cover of pitch darkness, pushed back the waters of the Red Sea. Moses then struck the sea with his staff, and miraculously, the waters parted, piling up in two, high, sheer cliffs on either side. The Hebrews quickly passed through as if on dry ground, but when the Egyptians attempted to pursue them, the great walls of water suddenly buckled and came tumbling down upon them, drowning them all.)

180   This great and marvelous (disaster) astonished
the Hebrews, who thereby gained an unexpected, bloodless
victory. Seeing their enemies destroyed in a moment,
once and for all, they set up two choirs there on the
beach, one of men and the other of women, and sang hymns
of thanksgiving to God, Moses leading the men and his
sister the women (see Ex. 15:20-21).

> (Freed of their Egyptian menace at last, the
> Hebrews set out toward "Phoenicia" -- Philo
> regularly uses the Greco-Roman designation so
> that his Gentile readers would understand.
> Next come various adventures in the desert,
> as the Hebrews successively ran out of fresh
> water (Ex. 15:22-26), food (Ex. 16), and water
> again (Ex. 17:1-7; cp. also Num. 20:1).

> Using the last episode as a springboard, Philo
> jumps over a great portion of his source
> material to Num. 20, which contains the same
> story as Ex. 17:1-7. Philo uses the rest of
> Ex. 17 in the first of the battles he recounts,
> then switches to Num. chs. 20 ff. for the
> successive episodes to the end of Book I. This
> manner of drastically reducing a larger source
> by epitomizing little sections of it, even
> weaving together the incidents taken over into
> a different order than that of the original --
> all without any warning or indication of what
> is going on -- was perfectly acceptable Hellen-
> istic "history" writing. For example, Philo
> skips over the entire Mt. Sinai account, al-
> though parts of it are used later in Book II.
> But here in Book I, it is as though it never
> happened, and Moses is simply portrayed as
> going in a round-about way from Egypt through
> the desert to Canaan. Besides omitting as
> irrelevant great sections of legal and cultic
> material in his sources, it is also clear that
> Philo is quietly covering up some dirty linen.
> For example, nothing whatever is said about
> Aaron's leading role in the Golden Bull debacle
> (Ex. 32:19-35), or the Lord's angry decree
> that neither Moses nor Aaron may enter into the
> Promised Land (Num. 20:12). In fact, Philo
> skillfully tells the story in such a way as to
> give the unmistakable impression that Moses
> actually did enter the Promised Land in the
> triumphant conclusion of Book I. Of course,
> the Bible describes the possession of

trans-Jordan lands by the tribes of Reuben and
Gad -- but the way Philo suppresses any mention
of the fact that it was Moses' *successor* who
conquered the rest of the territory on the other
side of the Jordan creates the impression that
Moses successfully completed his great task.

But we are getting ahead of the story. After
these trials in the wilderness, the Hebrews
reach the "Phoenician" regions, and immediately
are attacked by the forces of Amalek (Ex. 17:
8-16). As will be remembered, according to
Exodus this battle was won because Aaron and
a friend held Moses' arms up over the battle-
field long enough for the Hebrews to win.
That version was apparently not acceptable to
Philo, who tells the story this way.)

16   (Having sent his soldiers on ahead), Moses
first sprinkles himself round about with his customary
purification rituals, then runs up quickly onto a nearby
hill to beseech God to shield and preserve victory and
dominion for the Hebrews, whom He had already delivered
from more grievous battles as well as other evils, namely,
driving away catastrophes threatened by men, but also
from the revolutionary alterations of the natural elements
in Egypt and the constant famine during their travels.
17   Then, when they are about to join in battle, something
extraordinarily marvelous takes place affecting his
hands; for they are first very light and then very heavy,
and when they are lightened and taken up on high, his
fellow fighters are strong and fight gloriously like
stout men, but when they are weighed down, the enemies
are strong, God thereby recalling through symbols that
the earth and all the nether regions are the proper portion of the one group, while the most holy air belonged
to the other, and just as Heaven reigns and rules the
earth in all things, so also this nation will conquer
all its opponents.

8   As long as his hands, like balances, continue
first to get lighter and then heavier, during this time

the contest is undecided. But suddenly they become
weightless, the fingers fluttering like wings, and they
are lifted up on high into the air, like the winged
creatures that fly through the air, and they remain
lifted up until the Hebrews win a total victory, their
enemies being slaughtered from the youths on up, which
indeed was brought about so that they justly suffered
what they wrongly desired to inflict on others.

> (Next Philo turns back to Numbers 13-14 and
> recounts the story of the spies sent into
> Canaan. Moses wanted a more exact description
> of the "Phoenician" countryside, so he sent
> out twelve men to survey the land, in order to
> decide what to do next. When the spies came
> back, ten of them told fearful tales of the
> gigantic size of the inhabitants and their
> huge walled cities, while Joshua and another
> described a bountiful land, easily to be taken.
> The ten cowardly scouts persuaded the people
> not to try an invasion, and so the whole people
> turned away to do some more wandering in the
> desert. Philo does not mention the biblical
> explanation of this additional 40 years' wan-
> dering, namely, the anger of the Lord at the
> disobedience of the people (see Numbers 14:26-
> 35); he merely says the people cravenly decide
> not to enter the land for the time being.
>
> When they eventually did try again, more con-
> flict awaited them. Their first battle is
> against the Edomites (Num. 20:14-21), and then
> another king, whom Philo calls "Chananes,"
> rushed into battle against them, only to be
> resoundingly defeated like his predecessors
> (Num. 21:1-3).
>
> After this, Philo skips over the story of Moses
> and the bronze serpent (Num. 21:4-9), and picks
> up the brief account of the stop at a certain
> well in the wilderness, where the Lord had
> promised to give water to them (Num. 21:16-18).
> Of this minor story, Philo skillfully makes a
> glorious event, indeed a sort of joyous, anti-
> cipatory celebration of the conquest of the
> Promised Land itself.)

255   A little later, the Hebrews discovered a spring
of sweet water which bountifully provided enough drink

for the whole multitude -- for the spring was in a well
on the borders of the country. They drank it not as if
it were water but pure wine, so that their souls over-
flowed and in their festivity and joy, the choirs dear
to God formed a circle around the well and sang a new
hymn to the God who apportions land in a foreign country,
to the true Leader of settlers, because here for the
first time since they had left the long stretch of desert
and were about to take possession of inhabited territory,
they had found abundant water, and felt it appropriate
not to pass by the spring unnoticed.

>(Book I concludes with the telling of two more
>battles; a minor conflict with the Amorite
>King, Sihon (Num. 21:21-26), and, finally, the
>great battle against Balak, king of the Moabites,
>who had hired the "far-famed Mesopotamian pro-
>phet, Balaam" to help him. Of course, the Lord
>thwarts all of Balaam's spells, and makes him
>prophesy against Balak (Numbers 22-24). In the
>process of rewriting his material, Philo con-
>verts the contents of Numbers 25, an unrelated
>account of certain Hebrew men who cohabited
>with the Moabite women and the resultant wrath
>of the Lord, into a devilish plot suggested by
>Balaam to Balak, after everything else had
>failed. Balak carries it out, with terrible
>consequences to the Hebrews, until Phinehas
>leads a purge of the offending Hebrews, slaugh-
>tering them wholesale. After this, Moses goes
>to battle against Balak and utterly defeats
>him, capturing immense booty (cp. Numbers 31).

>Finally, as in Numbers 32, two of the tribes,
>Reuben and Gad, decide to settle down where
>they are and not cross the Jordan River. This
>causes immediate suspicion, since the other
>tribes conclude that these two will not help
>in the fight to conquer the main part of the
>land, and Moses has to quell the dissension
>and reach a compromise satisfactory to every-
>one. With this, Philo ends Book I.)

334   The matters pertaining to Moses' kingship have
now been recalled, and it is right to speak next also of
the things he did through his high priesthood and lawgiving, for he was granted these powers as especially

most appropriate to his kingship.

BOOK II

Moses the Lawgiver

1   The first composition (*syntaxis*) is about the
birth and nurture of Moses, also about his education and
rulership, in which he ruled not only blamelessly but
very commendably, and about the things done by him in
Egypt and on the journeys, both beside the Red Sea and
in the desert -- things which surpass the power of all
speech to describe -- and furthermore about the hardships
which he straightened out and about the allotment of the
foreign districts which he partly divided up among his
soldiers. That which is here composed concerns things
2   which came after and are related to them. For some say,
and they are not far wrong, that cities advance toward
excellence only in this way: if the kings practice philosophy or if philosophers are kings. Now Moses appears
to have displayed to an uncommon degree not only these
two qualities within himself, namely, the kingly and the
philosophical, but also three others, of which the first
is his efforts concerning lawgiving, the second concerning
the high priesthood, and the last concerning prophecy.
3   I have decided to speak now concerning these
three, necessarily supposing them to be quite appropriate
combined in the same person, for by the foreknowledge of
God he became king and lawgiver and highpriest and prophet
4   and in each he carried off first prize. But why all are
to be combined in the same person must be made clear. It
befits kings to command what is necessary and to forbid
what is wrong, but the ordination of things to be done
and the prohibition of things not to be done is a property
of the law, so that the king is immediately a living law
5   (*nomos empsychos*), and the law a just king. Further, the
king and lawgiver should be in charge, not only of human

affairs, but also divine, for without divine protection,
the affairs of kings and subjects will not prosper. For
this reason, such a person needs to be foremost in priestcraft, in order that, on the basis of perfect rituals and
perfect understanding of the worship of God, he might seek
the prevention of evils and the bestowing of good things,
both for himself and for his subjects, directing such
petitions to the Gracious One who responds to prayers.
For how can He Who is favorable by nature, Who considers
worthy of privilege those who sincerely serve Him, not
bring such prayers to perfect fruition?

6   Nevertheless, myriads of human and divine
matters are unclear to the king and lawgiver and highpriest, for Moses was nothing less; for even though such
great offices had been successfully invested in him, he
was mortal and necessarily therefore also obtained prophecy, in order that whatever could not be discovered by
rational means, could be learned from the foreknowledge
of God, for those matters which surpass the mind, prophecy
anticipates beforehand.

7   How beautiful and harmonious is the union of
these four qualities! Intertwined and sharing in each
other, they dance in rhythm, receiving and repaying
benefits, imitating the Virgin Graces[1] -- whom an immut-
able law of nature ordains shall never be disunited,
concerning which it may be rightly said what one often
hears pertaining to virtue, "to have one is to have all."

8   To begin with, let us consider the virtues
belonging to the context of giving laws. Now I am not
ignorant of the fact that it is fitting for him who is
to become the best of lawgivers to be in full and complete
possession of all virtues. But since as in households

---

[1]In Greek mythology, three daughters of Zeus: Beauty, Charm,
Wisdom.

there are some who are the most closely related members
of the family, while others are more distantly related,
although all are relatives of each other, so also some
virtues are understood to stem more directly out of
certain situations, while others are not so directly in-

9   volved. In the legislative context, we may distinguish
four brothers or close relatives: love of mankind, love
of justice, love of the good, and hatred of evil. Each
of these is demanded of everyone into whom enters the
zeal for giving laws: love of mankind, or presenting to
the public an exposition of one's maxims (*gnōmai*) concerning the common good; righteousness, or honoring equality
and distributing (justice) to each according to his just
deserts; love of the good, or approving everything
naturally noble and unrestrainedly providing them to all
worthy of their abundant use; and, finally, hatred of
evil, or rejecting those who dishonor virtue and regarding them with suspicion as enemies of the human race.

10   It is a great thing indeed if someone obtains
even one of the virtues here described, and certainly
marvelous if anyone can grasp them all at once, yet it
seems Moses alone succeeded in doing this, plainly displaying all the above-mentioned virtues in the things he

11   ordained. This would not be so unless Moses had written
under the guidance of God and handed his writings down
to be used by those who were worthy, as the most beautiful
of their possessions, duplicates and copies of the pat-
terns (of the Logos) carried about in our souls like
images in a shrine, and those who have the sacred writings
know that the laws he revealed manifest most clearly the
virtues just described.

12   The following consideration will make particularly credible our contention that Moses became the best
of all the lawgivers anywhere, whether among the Greeks
or the barbarians, and that his laws are the best and

are truly divine since they omit nothing that is needed.
3   If anyone objectively surveys other nations' customs, he
will find them (continually) changed due to all sorts
of causes: wars, tyrannies, and numerous other unavoidable
things heaped upon them by fickle chance. Oftentimes
excessive affluence brought about by an overabundance of
money and possessions has overthrown the laws, the masses
being unable to bear "too much of a good thing," and as
a result of intemperance become arrogant, and arrogance
subverts law and order.
4   Only the laws of Moses have remained as stead-
fast, unshaken, immovable, as if stamped with the seal
of nature herself, remaining firm from the day he wrote
them until now, and hopefully they will continue to
endure throughout all eternity as if immortal -- as long
as the sun and the moon and all heaven and earth exist.
5   Although our nation has experienced various changes, both
of good fortune and the opposite, nothing -- not even the
least of the commandments -- has been altered, for it
seems that everyone highly honors their majestic, godly
character.

> (Philo goes on to assert that there is yet
> something still more wonderful about them.
> Peoples the world over, who care little
> enough for each others' laws, are unanimous in
> their sincere and profound admiration for the
> laws of the Jews. These have attracted the
> "attention of all, barbarians, Greeks, inhabi-
> tants of the continents, of the islands, of
> the nations to the east, those to the west,
> Europe, Asia, the whole inhabited world
> (*oikoumenē*) from end to end" (II 20). As
> evidence, Philo points to the widespread
> Gentile concurrence in the Jewish custom of
> the Sabbath, and reverence for their annual
> Passover festival.[1]

---

[1]To understand how Philo could assert this bold claim without
ear of ridicule, it is necessary to remember the privileged
osition the Jews as a nation actually occupied in Imperial
oman policy during this period. See further V. Tcherikover,
ellenistic Civilization and the Jews (1959) pp. 306-308.

He then goes on to relate a story, which is
not in his main source for the life of Moses,
the point of which is to prove the fully inspired character of the *Greek translation* of
the Hebrew scriptures. This is a rather strange
idea when you stop to think about it, but we
should remember that Philo and many other
Diaspora Jews could not read Hebrew (or
"Chaldaean" as they called it), and therefore
had to rely on this Greek translation as their
Holy Word, much as modern fundamentalist Pro-
testants rely on the King James Version.

Although the origin of this story is a fascinating question in itself,[1] let it suffice for
the moment to say that the chief reason Philo
repeats it here is because, according to the
story, the translation was eagerly sought
by a famous *Gentile* king, because *Gentiles*
wanted to read this famous law-code. The ensuing story has to do with Ptolemy II Philadelphus, the second of the Ptolemaic dynasty in
Egypt, who ruled from 285-246 B.C.E. It is
probably true that he encouraged the enterprise
here described, though hardly to the glorious
extent Philo claims.)

25   That the sacred quality of Moses' legislation

has seemed marvelous not only to the Jews but also to all

others is clear both from what has already been said and

also from what I am about to relate.

26   In ancient times, the laws were written in the

Chaldaean language, and they remained for a long time in

the same dialect without changing, as long as their beauty

27   had not appeared to other men. But when, due to the care-

ful and continuous observance every day by those using

them, others also became aware of them, and their fame

spread in all directions -- for although excellence can

be hidden for a short time by envy, in due time it will

shine forth once again thanks to the benevolence of

nature. Eventually, some thought it a shame that the

---

[1]The earliest version of the story Philo tells here is to be
found in a writing called *The Letter of Aristeas*, written ca.
175 B.C.E.

laws had been drawn up only for half of the race of mankind, namely the barbarians, while none of the Greeks
had any share in them, and so they turned to the task of
translating them.

28   Since this was an important task for the common
good, it was not entrusted to private citizens or public
officials, of whom there were a great number (willing to
do it), but to kings, even to the most highly regarded of
29   kings. Ptolemy, called Philadelphus, was the third in
succession from Alexander the Great, who had conquered
Egypt, and as far as virtues in leadership are concerned,
he was the best not only of his contemporaries, but also
of those who ever were in ancient times. Even today, so
many generations later, his fame is still sung for the
many evidences and memorials of genius that he left behind
in cities and countries, as the proverbial expression
shows, when deeds of great distinction and large public
30   buildings are called "Philadelphian" after him. In short,
just as the dynasty of the Ptolemies flourished more
grandly than all other royal dynasties, so also among
the Ptolemies, Philadelphus stood out; for the praise-
worthy things this one man achieved were more than all
the rest put together, so that just as the head is the
leader of a living body, he became, after a fashion, the
head of kings.

31   Such a man as he had a zeal and longing for
our legislation and decided to adapt the Chaldaean to the
Greek language, and immediately sent off ambassadors to
the highpriest and king of the Jews (they were the same
person), explaining his plan and urging him to choose
some according to merit who might translate the Law.
32   The highpriest was naturally pleased and, considering
that the king would not have been eager to undertake
such a task without divine wisdom (guiding him), carefully sought out those Hebrews most highly approved by

him, who, in addition to their ancestral, also had a Greek
education, and joyfully sent them to Ptolemy.

33   When they arrived they were hospitably received
with courteous and warm speeches and as their host sump-
tously entertained them, they entertained him in return,
for he was testing the wisdom of each one by proposing
new instead of the customary problems, and they cleverly
and precisely solved them, not turning to lengthy speeches
but just as the occasion required, in terse, pointed
aphorisms (*apophthegmata*).

34   Being approved as fit, they immediately began
to complete their noble mission. Reckoning the task of
translating the laws divinely uttered in oracles to be
so important, since they were required neither to sub-
tract nor add nor alter anything, but to preserve the
original form and image, they sought out the purest of
the places in the region around the outside of the city.
For inside the walls there was every kind of living
animal, and because of the disease and death and the
unhealthy behavior of the healthy citizens, they were
suspicious (of attaining their aim there).

35   Now Pharos island lies nearby Alexandria; it
is a long, narrow strip of land pointing toward the city,
surrounded not by deep water close to shore but many
shallows, so that the noise of the waves' roaring and
splashing, being carried over a long distance weakens
36   and becomes indistinct. This made it still and quiet,
and so they decided it was especially suitable as a place
where they could, with the soul alone, commune with the
laws. Thereupon they set up their lodgings and, taking
the sacred books, they stretched them and their hands up
toward Heaven asking God that the project not fail. And
He assented to their prayers, in order that the majority
or even the whole race of mankind might benefit by making
use of these philosophical and wholly noble commandments
for the improvement of life.

37   As each one sat secretly alone, with no one
else around except the four parts of nature: earth,
water, air and heaven, the genesis of which was soon to
be the first part of the sacred mysteries to be expounded--
for the creation of the world is the first chapter of the
laws--as if possessed by God they prophesied, not each
one different things, but each one the very same words
and sentences, as if each were being guided by an
invisible prompter.

38   Now who does not know that every language, and
especially Greek, has many words and that the same thought
can be shaped in many different ways by changing the word-
ing or the sentences, each expression being appropriate
to the matter at hand? But this did not happen to this
legislation, it is said, for the words corresponded
exactly, the Greek with the Chaldaean, perfectly corresponding to the things they indicated.

40   Thus if Chaldaeans know the Greek language or
if Greeks have learned the Chaldaean, and obtain both
copies, the Chaldaean and the translation, they are
astonished, revering them as sisters or rather as being
one and the same in contents and in words, for these men
were not considered translators but expounders of sacred
mysteries (*heirophantēs*) and prophets, to whom it was
granted by means of their uncorrupted rationality, to
collaborate with the purest spirit of all, Moses.

41   For this reason, to this day a feast and a
celebration is held every year on Pharos island, to
which not Jews only but all kinds of others cross over,
to magnify the place in which the splendor of that translation first shone forth, and also to give thanks to God
for His good service in times past but ever anew.

43   ....This is why the laws of Moses are seen to
be blessed and are eagerly desired by all, common citizens and rulers alike, and this even though our nation

has not prospered for a long time, for things can not
blossom into their prime if somewhat over-shadowed.
44   But if some new start toward better times would take
place, how much progress there would no doubt be!   I
believe that every man would abandon his own customs and,
bidding good riddance to his ancestral ways, change over
to honor these laws alone!   For if our nation should
prosper, our laws would shine out once again, darkening
all others just as the rising sun does the stars!

> (This story is a priceless gem from the brief
> but dynamic period when Hellenized Judaism,
> especially in Alexandria, was slowly transform-
> ing itself from a nationalistic into a universal
> religion, a process eventually partly subsumed
> and partly shouldered aside by Christianity's
> meteoric ascent as *the* Hellenistic universal
> religion *par excellence*.   In the closing lines
> is one of the rare, vestigial traces of the
> older nationalistic messianic expectation --
> i.e., the restoration of the Palestinian nation-
> state.   But if the true worshipper is a citizen
> of the world, like Moses, to belong to any par-
> ticular country would be superfluous.
>
> The rest of the section on Moses as lawgiver
> would no doubt be equally fascinating, if we
> still had it.   However, a major segment (about
> one-third) seems to have disappeared from the
> text.   At this point, Philo is explaining that
> Moses initiated his legislation, perhaps un-
> expectedly, with an account of the creation of
> the world, in order to show that "the Father
> and Maker of the world was also truly its law-
> giver."   By thus describing "the creation of
> the Great City (*megalopolis*)", i.e., the world,
> says Philo, Moses intended to assert that "his
> laws are the image most resembling the govern-
> ment of the world itself.   Therefore, if anyone
> wishes to examine carefully the qualities of
> the laws commanded, he will find them tending
> toward the harmony of all existence, being in
> accord with the Reason of everlasting nature"
> (II 52).
>
> Philo then makes a very quick synopsis of
> material from Genesis, passing from the creation
> narrative to the account of the destruction of
> Sodom.   He then goes back and retells the story

of the Flood, perhaps getting ready to tell of
the laws Moses gave for the "second generation
of mankind," -- but here the manuscript breaks
off.)

Moses the Highpriest

56   We have already fully recounted two parts of
the life of Moses, namely the royal and the legislative;
the third, concerning his priestcraft is to be added to
these.
         The most important and most necessary quality
which must belong to a highpriest is piety (*eusebeia*).
This Moses practiced in the highest degree, at the same
time making use of the other good gifts given him by
nature, which philosophy took over like good soil, making
him even better by the attention he paid to its wholly
noble teachings; nor did it cease before the fruits of
virtue were perfectly formed through word and deed.

57   For this reason, Moses came to love God and be
loved by God as few others, becoming inspired by the love
of Heaven, to a remarkable degree honoring the Ruler of
All and being honored by Him in return. Now wisely
serving Him Who truly exists is appropriate to honoring,
and it is the practice of priestcraft to serve God. It
was this privilege, than which there is no greater good
in existence, of which Moses was considered worthy, being
taught through oracles each of the rituals and sacred
duties.

58   However, first of all he had to be pure in soul
and in body, meddling with none of the passions, but keeping himself pure from all things whatever pertaining to
mortal nature -- eating and drinking and association with
59 women. This last in particular he despised for a long
time, from the time when he first began to prophesy and to
be possessed by God, thinking it proper always to keep
himself prepared for oracles from God. On one occasion

he disregarded food and drink for forty successive days,
doubtless because he had better food through his soul's
contemplation, coming from Heaven above. It made him
better, first in mind, then also in body, advancing in
each one to such strength and health that those seeing
70   him later did not believe it. For in obedience to divin
commands, Moses had ascended the loftiest and most sacre
mountain in that area, where it was unapproachable and
impassable, and remained there for the period just mentioned while partaking of none of the necessary benefits
of food, and, forty days later, it is said he descended
with an appearance much more beautiful than when he went
up, so that those who saw him were amazed and astounded,
their eyes being unable to long withstand the assault of
71   the sun-like brightness flashing forth from him. While
he had been staying up on the mountain, he had been in-
ducted into the mysteries (*mystagōgeō*), being taught all
things concerning priestcraft, the first in order concer
ing instructions about the temple and the furnishings in
it.

> (Philo now recapitulates in considerable detai
> parts of the priestly instructions in the book
> of Exodus (though not in the order found there
> namely, the structure and layout of the tent o
> meeting, the ark of the covenant, the high-
> priest's vestments, the sacrificial vessels
> and utensils -- all these he describes at so
> much length we begin to wonder what the purpos
> is. Then we see why; the whole business reall
> contains profound allegorical symbols of deepe
> mysteries. For example, the instructions con-
> cerning the central position of the altar of
> incense symbolizes thankfulness for the earth,
> since it occupies the middle of the universe.
> The seven-branched candlestick symbolizes the
> sun and the six planets. The table of show-
> bread, situated on the north side of the sacre
> enclosure, is a figure of the north wind since

---

[1]He takes up the material in Exodus in this order: chs. 26,
27, 25, 30, 28, 38.

it provides man with the most beneficial atmos-
pheric conditions for growing wheat, i.e.,
bread, and so on. Then in the midst of these
speculations, Philo warns that the outward
performance of these rituals was never intended
by Moses to be sufficient. Accompanying them
had to be a sincere, inward purity of heart.
"For true worship is nothing else than the
piety of a soul loved by God. The thanksgiving
of such a soul is given immortality and, being
inscribed in the records before God, lives on
eternally with the sun and the moon and the
whole world." (II 108). We now give an excerpt from this section, for Philo was particularly impressed with the significance of the
highpriest's vestments.)

118   (The robe of the highpriest) is a representation
and copy of the world, a part corresponding to each of its
parts. Beginning with the full-length robe, this gown is
completely violet in color, which is a counterpart of the
air, for air is by nature black and, after a fashion, a
robe all about us, being stretched out from above near
the region of the moon down to the earth, and spreading
out everywhere. Whence also the gown spreads from the
119 chest to the feet all around the body. At the ankles are
embroidered knobs shaped like pomegranates and flowers
and bells. The flowers are a symbol of the earth, for
flowers and all things grow from it. The pomegranates
symbolize water, aptly said because of their flowing
juice, while the bells symbolize the harmony and symphony
of these things, for nothing at all could begin if the
earth were without water or the water without earth, but
only if they come together and form a mixture of both....
122   Reason suggests that the ephod (shoulder cape)
is a symbol of heaven, by the following likely conjectures.
First of all, the two emerald stones carried on the points
of the shoulders recall, as some think, the major leading
stars of day and night, the sun and the moon, although one
might argue, coming somewhat closer to the truth, that
they are each of the hemispheres.... (The twelve stones

fastened) on the breast, not alike in color, and being
divided up into four rows of three, what else do they
indicate but the twelve signs of the zodiac?

131 ....Such riddles does Moses indicate through
the sacred vestments. By placing a turban instead of a
crown on his head, he thinks it right that while the one
consecrated to God is worshiping, he surpasses all men,
132 not common citizens only but even kings. On top of the
turban is the gold plate (*petalon*) on which is carved
the marks of four letters, said to recall the name of Him
Who Is, meaning that without invocation of God, nothing
of what exists will be sustained, for His good and gracious
power brings about the harmonious existence of all things.
133 Dressed in this fashion, the highpriest is sent
to the sacred tasks, in order that, whenever he enters
into the temple to offer the ancestral prayers and sacrifices, the whole world goes in with him, being carried in
by these likenesses: the robe, of the air; the pomegranates, of water; the flowers, of the earth; the scarlet
(thread in the ephod), of fire; the ephod, of heaven; the
emeralds carried on the shoulders, the form of both hemispheres, ...the twelve stones on the breast in four rows
of three, the zodiac, and (the *petalon*) that Reason
(*Logos*) which connects and administers the whole together.
134 For it is necessary for him who is consecrated to the
Father of the world to make use of that most perfect
advocate of virtue, namely his Son, in order to obtain
forgiveness of sins and provision of abundant good things.[1]

---

[1] Referring to the world by "Son". Just as the Maker of the
world could be called the Father of All, so his creation might
be called "his Son". And the thought is, where the Father
might not listen to the prayers of the highpriest alone, when
the highpriest comes before Him *as the world*, the Father can
hardly spurn him then; and so the world becomes symbolically a
kind of intercessor.

.35   Perhaps, moreover, Moses is teaching the servant
of God that he should attempt to be invariably worthy of
the world, even if he cannot always be such of the world's
Maker. For, dressed in a replica of the world, he himself, carrying about like an image in a shrine this pattern
(of the world) in his mind, ought to be transformed
from human nature into the nature of the world, as it
were, and, if it is permitted to say so, but it is certainly permitted not to lie when speaking of the truth!,
to be a miniature world.

> (After this section, Philo describes how Moses
> established the Hebrew priesthood under divine
> direction. Aaron, Moses' brother, is chosen
> to be the first highpriest, and as a confirma-
> tion, the first sacrifice is blessed by a par-
> ticularly striking miracle: an unearthly fire
> suddenly shoots out of the sanctuary and con-
> sumes the offering in an instant (cp. Ex. 29;
> Lev. 8; 9:24).
>
> Philo then takes up the next logical subject,
> the divinely guided selection of attendants
> to help the highpriest. But here Philo must
> have experienced some difficulties, for in the
> Bible this is precisely the story of mass apos-
> tasy, i.e., the worship of the Golden Bull
> while Moses is up on Mt. Sinai with God. And
> who led the apostasy? None other than the newly
> chosen highpriest, Aaron (see Ex. 32). It is
> a laundering job of major proportions, but Philo
> is equal to the task. His Gentile readers would
> never know that Aaron had anything to do with
> it.)

.61   After Moses had ascended the mountain nearby
and was alone with God for many days, some men of un-
stable natures, thinking his absence to be a perfect
opportunity for causing anarchy, unrestrainedly rushed
headlong into impiety, and utterly forgot their reverence
for Being Itself (*to on*), becoming zealous worshippers of
.62 Egyptian idols. Having fashioned a golden bull, a replica
of the animal considered to be the most sacred in that
country, they offered sacrifices not fit to be offered,

set up ill-suiting choirs, sang hymns in no way differin
from dirges, and were completely carried away, being ove
powered by a double drunkenness of strong alcohol, the
one from the wine and the other from foolishness. They
carried on carousing and debauchery the whole night long
mingling together in enjoyment of wickedness, while un-
foreseen Justice, which sees what is not seen and what i
worthy of punishment, was lying in wait ready to strike.

163   When the continuous shouting in the camp, because of the crowds of people carousing together, began
to spread over a great distance, so that the echo even
reached the top of the mountain and struck the ears of
Moses, he was undecided what to do because of his love
for God and his love for man, for he could neither endur
to abandon his fellowship with God in which he conversed
privately with Him, one to one, nor could he ignore the
multitude below, filled with the evil results of anarchy

164   For he understood that awful din, perceiving in the confused and indistinct noise what is unclear and unapparer
to others, namely, the typical passions of the soul, and
that the continual uproar was a drunken melee, intemperance begetting gluttonous satiety, satiety insolence.

165   Pulled this way and tugged that way toward each side,
Moses remained still, being at a loss what to do.

While he was thinking it over, the following
was uttered in an oracle to him: "Go there quickly.
Descend. The people are hurrying into lawlessness, and
are worshipping and sacrificing as to a God the form of
a bull fashioned by hands -- which is not God -- having
utterly forgotten all the things which they have seen

166   and heard tending towards piety." Astonished and necessarily believing these unbelievable events, like an arbi
trator or mediator, Moses did not immediately rush off bu
first made an appeal and pleaded on behalf of the natior
asking for pardon of their sins. When the guardian and

intercessor had reconciled God, he went down, simultaneously rejoicing and downcast, for he was full of joy
that God had accepted his supplication, but he was plunged
into anxiety and sorrow upon seeing the lawlessness of the
multitude.

167   Arriving in the middle of the camp and being
amazed at the sudden change of habits of the multitude,
and how great a lie they had exchanged for so great a
truth, he observed that not everyone had been infected
by the disease, but there were some healthy people still
possessed of a passionate hatred of evil. Desiring to
distinguish those who were incurable from those who
despised the things being done, and to see if any sinners
should repent, he announced a proclamation (*kerygma*) --
it was in fact an accurate test of each mind, to determine
168   its degree of holiness or the opposite -- for he said, "If
anyone is for the Lord, let him come to me!" Little enough
said, but indeed the point was important, for this is what
was being made clear: "If anyone considers nothing made
by hand nor any creature to be Gods, but that there is One
Ruler of all that is, let him come to me."

169   Out of all who were there, some, who were the
rebels devoted to the Egyptian vanity, did not pay any
attention to what he said, while others, out of fear of
punishment perhaps, (also did not have enough) confidence
to draw near, either fearing some sort of punishment from
Moses or an attack from the mob, for the multitude always
170   sets upon those who do not share its folly. One tribe
out of all of them, called the Levites, as soon as they
heard the proclamation, eagerly ran up to him as if given
a signal, their swiftness displaying zeal and their haste,
their souls' eagerness for piety.

        (Moses orders the Levites immediately to slaugh-
        ter all of the offending Hebrews, and before
        long, 3,000 are dead. As a reward for their
        zeal, they are appointed Aaron's assistants.

Finally, Philo tells the story of Aaron's Rod --
an account of the dissension which arose because
of Moses' picking his own brother to be the
highpriest. Moses also handles this accusation
of favoritism characteristically (see Num. 16:
1-3; 17).)

Moses the Prophet

187   Since we have said that it is necessary to include four things in the most perfect leader, namely
kingship and lawgiving and priestcraft and prophecy, in
order that through lawgiving he might ordain what is
necessary and forbid what must not be done, through
priestcraft he might manage not only human affairs but
also divine, and through prophecy whatever cannot be com-
prehended by rational processes he might announce through
oracles -- having fully treated of the first three and
shown that Moses was the best king, lawgiver and highpriest, I come to the final section in order to show that
he became the most highly approved prophet also.

188   Now I am not ignorant that they are all divine
oracles (*chrēsmoi*) which are written in the sacred books,
announced through Moses. I will speak here of those more
especially his own, but first let me clarify: of all the
oracles (*logia*), some are said to come from the presence
of God through a prophet as the interpreter of God; others
are uttered in response to questions, as answers; and
others are from Moses himself when possessed by God and
carried out of himself.

          (That is, Philo enumerates three kinds of
          divine utterance (*logion*) in the sacred writ-
          ings: those where Moses is simply God's mouth-
          piece (or interpreter, *hermeneutēs*), and two
          other kinds, in which he is, strictly speaking,
          a prophet (*prophētēs*). Of these, one kind
          involves questions put to the Deity which are
          answered in oracles, and another kind occurs
          when the prophet is filled with the divine
          spirit and gives an oracle foretelling some
          future event. Philo says he will restrict

himself to examples of these latter two kinds
of "prophecy".

Of the first sort, where Moses was confronted
with a difficult situation and had to inquire
of God what to do, Philo gives four examples.
The first concerned a man who cursed God (Lev.
24:10-16); the second, a man who profaned the
Sabbath rest (Num. 15:32-36); the third, a
complicated problem concerning conflicting
ritual obligations (Num. 9:1-14); and the
fourth, a knotty legal question concerning
seven orphaned girls (Num. 21:1-11). In the
first two cases, God orders a stern, inexorable
punishment of the miserable offenders. In the
last two, His boundless mercy and great wisdom
are revealed. Indeed, as Philo tells the story
of the poor orphaned daughters, and God's tender
concern for them, he suddenly bursts into an
unusually exalted passage.)

238   He Who is the Maker of All, who is the Father

of the world, holding together and controlling earth and

heaven, water and air, and whatever comes from each of

these, He Who rules Gods and men, did not disdain to give

an answer to orphaned girls. And having given an answer,

He added something more than a judge would, ...He Who is

kind and gracious, Who fills all things everywhere with

His benevolent power -- He expressed praise of the lowly

239   maidens! O Master, how may one hymn Thee? With what

mouth, what tongue, what instruments of speech, what sort

of reason, the authoritative part of the soul? If the

stars should become a single choir, could they sing a

worthy hymn? If the whole of heaven should resolve it-

self into a single voice, could it describe a single

part of Thy virtues?

(For examples of Moses' accurate prediction of
future events while under divine inspiration,
Philo goes back to the events narrated in Book
I and repeats four cases, in order to show that
Moses' predictions actually did come to pass:
(a) announcing to the Hebrew people by the Red
Sea that they would soon see the oncoming
Egyptian forces totally annihilated; (b) warning
the people not to store the heavenly manna, for

it would rot; (c) calling the Levites to slay
everyone worshipping the Golden Bull; and (d)
predicting the horrible death to befall all
those who dared to question the selection of
Aaron as highpriest. In each case, Philo is
careful to emphasize that Moses made the prediction while out of his normal mind, i.e.,
"no longer being in himself, being carried
away by God and prophesying (*thespidzō*)"
(II 250); or, again, "He no longer remained
his own self and utterly changed both in form
(*eidos*) and mind (*dianoia*), he said, prophesying... etc." (II 272). It was clearly a major
aspect of Hellenistic religious experience that
human beings could become "filled with the
God(s)" and, in that condition, speak divine
truth inaccessible under normal conditions.[1]

At this point, then, Philo has reached the
conclusion of his narrative of various aspects
of Moses' character and life, and there is
nothing left to do but describe the circumstances surrounding Moses' ascension and burial.
It is worthy of the most careful meditation,
that Philo is not in the least perturbed by the
accounts of Moses' death and burial in Deut.
33-34, when it comes to telling his readers
what really happened to Moses when he went up
on the mountain for the last time.)

288   Later on, when he was about to be sent to the
other colony in Heaven and, abandoning mortal life, to be
immortalized, having been called back by the Father, with
his dual being of body and soul now fundamentally trans-
muted into a single entity, wholly and completely transformed into a pure, sun-like mind, at this point Moses
was again carried away (by the Spirit), and no longer
uttered general oracles to the whole nation, but spoke to
one tribe after the other, foretelling the things about to
happen, which thereafter would come to pass. Some of
these have already occurred, while others are still expected, since belief in things about to be is confirmed

---

[1]This is the origin of our term "enthusiasm". It comes from
the Greek term *en-theos-omai* -- "to be inspired, filled with
God."

by what has occurred before.

0   ... (These oracles are) marvelous enough, but
especially marvelous is the conclusion of the holy writings which, as the head is to a living animal, this is
1   chief part of the whole legislation. For when he was
already rising up into the air, standing as it were at
the starting line in order that he might fly straight up
the race-course to Heaven, Moses was inspired and possessed by God so that while still living he prophesied
shrewdly concerning his own death, how he died, although
not yet dead, how he was buried while no one was present,
obviously not by mortal hands but by immortal powers, how
he was not given last rites in a tomb of his forefathers,
obtaining a memorial of special honor which no man has
seen, and how the entire nation was saddened, mourning
him for a whole month, displaying their sadness individ-
ually and collectively on account of his indescribable
kindness and solicitude toward each one and toward all.

2   Such was the life, such also the death of the
king and lawgiver and highpriest and prophet Moses, as
commemorated in the sacred writings.

64. "THE DEEDS OF HERAKLES"

(Diodorus Siculus, *Library of History* 4.9.1-10; 10.7; 11.5;
13.3; 26.1-2; 27.3; 29.3; 38.3-5; 39.1-2; trans. D.R. Cartlidge)

(Introduction: This account of the life or deeds
(*praxeis*) of Herakles is taken from a lengthy "Universal History"
in 40 books, written by an otherwise unknown Sicilian historian
of the first century B.C.E. His monumental work, of which less
than half is still extant, reflects the current Stoic notion of
"one world-one society-one humanity." The individual histories
of the nations comprising the known world (i.e., Spain to India),
are portrayed as all springing from the universal activity of
Divine Providence for the mutual benefaction of the whole world.
Consequently, this is not "secular" history, but history viewed
within a religious perspective in the broadest sense. As a
result, Diodorus goes back to the origin of the Gods and the
creation of the world in his opening books, and then carefully
treats the mythical heroes or demigods of each nation -- Egypt,
Assyria, India, Ethiopia, Atlantis, Greece, etc. -- until
he comes to more recent times. Then his narrative shifts to a
cumbersome annalistic framework wherein the significant events
in every country are treated year by year. Our account comes
from his treatment of the Greek mythical heroes.

Aware that his readers might be inclined to be
skeptical of his description of Herakles, he warns his readers
not to judge Herakles' greatness by their own weakness, lest
they should "forget the good deeds he bestowed upon all humanity,
belittling the praise he used to receive for the noblest deeds,
...[and thus] no longer preserve the religious veneration for
this God which has been handed down from our fathers.")

(Diodorus' account of the birth and labors of
Herakles probably was taken by him mostly from an
earlier writing entitled, *In Praise of Herakles* by
Matris of Thebes, who lived in Alexandria during the
second century B.C.E. This is Diodorus' account of
Herakles' conception and birth, IV.9.1-10.)

They say that Perseus was the son of Danae, who was
the daughter of Akrisios and Zeus. Andromeda, Kepheos' daughter,
lay with him (Perseos) and bore Elektryon; then Euridike, daughter of Pelops, cohabited with him (Elektryon) and gave birth to
Alkmene. Alkmene was taken by Zeus, through a deceit, and she

347

bore Herakles. Thus, the root of his family tree, through both
his parents, is said to go back to the greatest of the Gods
(i.e., Zeus), in the way we have shown.

      The excellence begotten in Herakles is not only seen
in his great acts (*praxeis*), but was known before his birth.
When Zeus lay with Alkmene, he tripled the length of the night,
and, in the increased length of time spent in begetting the
child, he foreshowed the exceptional power of the child who was
to be begotten. All in all, this union was not done because of
erotic desire, as with other women, but more for the purpose of
creating the child. Because he wished to make the intercourse
legitimate, and he did not wish to take Alkmene by force, nor
could he ever hope to seduce her because of her self-control,
therefore, he chose deceit. By this means he tricked Alkmene:
he became like Amphitryon (her husband) in every way.

      When the natural time of pregnancy passed, Zeus, with
his mind set upon the birth of Herakles, announced beforehand,
with all the Gods present, that he would make the child born
that day, king of Perseus' descendants. At that Hera became
jealous and, using her daughter Eileithyia as her helper, she
stopped the labor pains of Alkmene, and brought Eurystheus[1] to
light before his full time. Zeus was out-witted, but he wished
to confirm his promise and to look ahead to the appearance
(*epiphaneia*) of Herakles. Therefore, they say, he persuaded
Hera to agree: Eurystheus was to be king, as Zeus promised;
but Herakles was to serve under Eurystheus and to complete
twelve "labors" which Eurystheus was to devise. When the deeds
were done, Herakles was to obtain immortality.

      Alkmene gave birth, and, because she was afraid of
Hera's jealousy, the child was exposed in a place which to this
time is called the Field of Herakles. Now, at the same time,
Athena, with Hera, happened to go by and was amazed at the

---

[1]A descendant of Perseus by a different family lineage, and
later the king of Argos.

quality of the child. She persuaded Hera to offer her breast.
The child sucked on the breast more violently than a normal
child, and Hera, suffering great pain, tore the child away from
her breast. Athena then took him to his mother and urged her
to nurture him....

After this, Hera sent two snakes to destroy the baby,
but the child did not panic, and he grabbed the neck of each
snake in his hands and strangled them.

> (The most famous deeds of Herakles were his
> twelve "labors" (Gk. *athlos*, root of our word
> "athlete." It means "a contest or struggle for a
> prize.") Diodorus reports that Herakles learned
> what his twelve "struggles" were to be from the
> Delphic Oracle, IV.10.7.)

Zeus sent orders (to Herakles) to serve Eurystheus,
but Herakles went to Delphi and consulted the God (Apollo) about
this. He received an oracle which clearly pointed out that it
was ordered by the Gods he should complete twelve struggles
commanded by Eurystheus, and when they were completed, he would
achieve immortality.

> (Herakles becomes very depressed at this news;
> he does not wish to serve an inferior, yet he could
> not disobey the Gods. He goes mad (at Hera's insti-
> gation) and kills his own children. When he comes
> to himself, he is overcome by grief, but finally
> reports to Eurystheus for his twelve struggles.
> Here are Diodorus' description of a number of them.)

11.5   The second labor he received was to kill the Dernaian
Hydra, whose single body had growing from it one hundred necks,
each with a snake's head. If one of these was cut off, the
place which was cut put out two more. On account of this, it
was held to be invincible, and reasonably so, for the part of
it which was mastered sent out a doubled assistance. Against
such a difficult thing, (Herakles) concocted an ingenious plan.
He ordered Iolaus (his companion) to cauterize the severed part

with a torch, in order to cut off the flow of blood. So, with
the beast mastered this way, he dipped his arrows in the venom,
so that when the arrow was shot, the wound from the arrow-head
would be incurable.

13.3   ...He received from Eurystheus the order to clean
out the stables of Augeas with no one's help. This stable,
over many years, had accumulated a tremendous amount of manure.
It was to insult Herakles' pride that Eurystheus ordered the
cleansing. But Herakles considered it beneath him to do this
thing; he wanted to avoid the shame from the insult. So he
changed the course of the river Alpheios into the stables, and
by means of the river flow he cleaned out the stables. Without
accepting the insult, he completed the struggle in one day.
Therefore, one should be astonished at Herakles' ingenuity;
for he accomplished the dirty work without shame. Nothing
stuck to him which was unworthy of immortality.

26.1   Herakles, according to the myths handed down, descend
into the places of Hades, and being welcomed by Persephone, as
if he were her brother, he led out Theseus and Peirithoös, out
of their bonds. This was accomplished by the good favor of
Kore. He captured the dog (Cerberus), who was delivered up
miraculously, led him out and put him on display for men (to
look at).

26.2   The final struggle which Herakles received was to
bring back the golden apples of the Hesperides, so again he set
sail to Libya. The writers of the myths disagree concerning
these apples. Some say, in certain gardens of the Hesperides
in Libya there were golden apples, guarded always by a most
fearful snake. Some others say the Hesperides had flocks of
sheep distinguished by their beauty, and they were poetically
called "golden apples" because of their beauty, in the way
Aphrodite is called "golden" because of her beauty. Some say

the sheep had a peculiar odor, like gold, and thus earned the
name, and that Drakon (i.e., "snake") was the overseer of the
sheep. He excelled in strength and power of body to guard the
sheep and to kill anyone who dared to steal them. But concerning these things, it is alright for each man to believe as he
is persuaded. Herakles killed the guardian of the apples, and
after he carried them to Eurystheus, thus having completed his
struggles, he waited to have immortality given him, just as
Apollo prophesied.

(Herakles did many other mighty deeds, in con-
junction with his twelve "struggles". They were
examples of how Herakles brought wisdom to men, and
how he "cultivated", i.e., civilized the world.)

27.3   At the time Herakles was completing the last
"struggle"...some pirates seized (Atlas' daughters)...and
immediately fled to their ships and sailed away. Herakles...
killed all the pirates and carried the girls back to their
father, Atlas. At which, because of the good deed, Atlas not
only agreeably gave assistance in the "struggle," but taught
(Herakles) copiously about astrological matters. Atlas had,
better than any man, worked out astrological matters and in-
geniously determined the spheres of the stars, so that the
opinion exists that he bears the whole world on (his) shoulders.
Likewise, when Herakles bore to the Greeks the knowledge of the
sphere, he achieved great honor. Men hinted that what had
happened was (Herakles) took over Atlas' burden of the world.

(The last three sentences of this story are a
good example of "rationalizing" by Diodorus. The
tale did relate what Diodorus says "men hinted at."
Heraklean theology made much of this tale. Herakles,
for example, is called "the Logos scattered in all
things, who gives to nature her power and vigor,"
Cornutus, *Compend of Greek Theology*, 31. With all
these tales in mind, Apuleius says, "Hercules...
traveller around the earth, cleanser of wild places,
tamer of the nations, he is God, while he travels the
earth," *Apology*, 22.)

29.3   When Herakles was still a boy, but was of great
strength, (Thespius, king of Athens) strongly wanted his
daughters to bear children by Herakles. He, therefore, invited
Herakles to a certain sacrifice and they feasted brilliantly.
He then sent his daughters, one by one, (to Herakles). He lay
with all of them and made them pregnant; he became the father
of fifty sons....After they had grown up, (Herakles) decided
to send them to establish a settlement in Sardinia, as the
oracle had ordered.

> (Diodorus then relates a series of exploits, as
> Herakles battles one king after another who won't
> give Herakles the hand of his daughter in marriage --
> on the grounds that Herakles is already married. In
> each case, Herakles takes the daughter by force, after
> killing the father, or brothers, as the case may be.
> The last mentioned was Iolê, the daughter of Eurytus,
> king of a region on the island of Euboea. Following
> his victory, Herakles sends a servant back to his
> wife for his sacred clothes, in order to make thank
> offerings to the Gods. She, hearing of Herakles' new
> paramour, decides to soak the robe in a magic potion
> which will turn his love toward her. However, the
> potion was given to Herakles' wife, Deïneira, by a
> centaur, who is secretly plotting his death. The
> potion is really a deadly poison. When Herakles puts
> on the robe, the poisonous fumes attack his flesh,
> and he begins inexorably to die in horrible torment.
> We resume the story at this point; Diod. Sic.
> IV.38.3-5.)

As he suffered more and more from his sickness, he
sent Likumnios and Iolaos to Delphi to ask Apollo what it was
necessary to do to heal the illness. Meanwhile, Deïneira (his
wife) was so overcome by the severity of Herakles' circumstances
and, being aware that it was her fault, ended her life by hang-
ing.

The God delivered the oracle that Herakles was to be
carried to Oïte with his battle gear; they were to construct a
great funeral pyre near him. The rest, it said, remained for
Zeus to do. When these orders were carried out by Iolaos, and

he had pulled back a way to see what was to happen, Herakles
gave up hope and climbed onto the pyre. He called for someone
to light it. When no one dared to obey, only Philoktetes was
moved to comply. He received, because of his service, the gift
of Herakles' bow and arrows; then he lit the pyre. Immediately,
a lightning bolt fell from the heavens; the pyre was completely
consumed. After this, those who were with Iolaos came to the
bone-gathering, but they found not one bone anywhere. They
supposed that Herakles, as the oracle had proclaimed, had
crossed over from human circumstances to that of the gods.

39.1   ...The Athenians were the first of all to honor, with
sacrifices, Herakles as a God, showing, as an example to other
men, their piety to the God. Thus they persuaded first the
Greeks and, after them, all the men of the inhabited world to
honor Herakles as a God.

39.2   ...after Herakles' apotheosis, Zeus persuaded Hera to
make Herakles her son and from that time to regard him with a
mother's concern. This (second) birth is said to have happened
thus: Hera lay on a couch and took Herakles to her body, letting
him fall toward the earth, miming true birth. Even now, the
barbarians perform this ritual when they wish to adopt a son.
Hera, after the adoption, so the myth-tellers say, united Hebe
with Herakles, concerning whom the poet (Homer) says:

>...the phantom (of Herakles), he makes
>merry in feasts with the immortal gods and
>has (as his wife) Hebe of the beautiful ankles.
>(*Odyssey* 11.602-3.)

They say, therefore, that Herakles was enrolled by Zeus among
the twelve Gods, but he did not accept this honor, for it was
impossible for him to be enrolled unless first one of the twelve
Gods was deposed, and it would have been out-of-place for him
to accept an honor which bore dishonor to another God.

MYSTERY RELIGIONS OF THE GRECO-ROMAN WORLD

A preliminary bibliography of secondary literature in English

(Compiled by Eldon J. Epp)

Note: Some of the best, most useful, or most easily accessible titles are marked with an asterisk *.)

HELLENISTIC RELIGIONS

ANGUS, Samuel. The Religious Quests of the Graeco-Roman World, 1929. Reprint: 1967.

BELL, H. Idris. Cults and Creeds in Graeco-Roman Egypt. Liverpool, 1957.

BEVAN, E.R. Later Greek Religion. London, 1927.

BRADY, Thomas Allen. "The Reception of the Egyptian Cults by the Greeks (330-30 B.C.)," The University of Missouri Studies, Vol. X, No. 1 (Jan. 1935), pp. 1-88.

CUMONT, Franz. After Life in Roman Paganism. New Haven, 1922. Reprint: New York, 1959.

_____. Astrology and Religion among the Greeks and Romans, 1912. Reprint: New York, Dover, 1960.

_____. Lux Perpetua. Paris, 1949.

_____. The Oriental Religions in Roman Paganism, 1911. Reprint: New York, Dover, 1956.

DODDS, Eric R. Pagan and Christian in an Age of Anxiety. Some Aspects of Religious Experience from Marcus Aurelius to Constantine. Cambridge University Press, 1965.

DÖLGER, Fr. J. Sol Salutis. Münster/W., 1920.

FARNELL, Lewis Richard. Cults of the Greek States. 5 vols. Oxford, 1896-1909.

FERGUSON, J. Religions of the Roman Empire. 1970.

FERGUSON, W.S. "The Leading Ideas of the New Period [Hellenistic Period]," Cambridge Ancient History, Vol. VII, pp. 1-40.

*FESTUGIÈRE, A.J. Personal Religion among the Greeks.
    Berkeley: University of California, 1954.

FOWLER, W.W. The Roman Festivals of the Period of the
    Republic. London, 1899.

GAGER, John G. Moses in Greco-Roman Paganism. Philadelphia
    1972.

GASTER, Theodor H. Thespis: Ritual, Myth and Drama in the
    Ancient Near East. New York, 1950.

GILLIAM, J.F. "The Roman Military Feriale," Harvard Theolog
    cal Review 47(1954):183-6.

GLOVER, T.R. The Conflict of Religions in the Early Roman
    Empire. London, 1927. Reprint: Boston, Beacon, 1962

GRANT, F.C. "Greek Religion in the Hellenistic-Roman Age,"
    Anglican Theological Review 34(1952):11-26.

*_____. Hellenistic Religions. The Age of Syncretism. New
    York, 1953.

_____. "Professor Latte's History of Roman Religion,"
    Anglican Theological Review 43(1961):404-9.

_____. Roman Hellenism and the New Testament. New York, 19

GRANT, Michael. Myths of the Greeks and Romans. New York,
    1962.

GRANT, Robert M. Miracle and Natural Law in Graeco-Roman an
    Early Christian Thought. Amsterdam, 1952.

GREENE, William Chase. Moira: Fate, Good and Evil in Greek
    Thought. Cambridge, Mass., 1944. Reprint: New York,
    Harper, 1963.

GUTHRIE, W.K.C. The Greeks and Their Gods. London/Boston,
    1950.

_____. Orpheus and Greek Religion. London, 1935; 2nd ed.,
    1952.

HALLIDAY, W.R. History of Roman Religion. Liverpool, 1922.

JONAS, Hans. The Gnostic Religion. Boston, 1958; 2nd ed.,
    1963.

JUNG, C.G. and K. KERÉNYI. Essays on a Science of Mythology
    The Myths of the Divine Child and the Divine Maiden.
    New York, 1949. Reprint: 1963.

KERÉNYI, Károly. The Gods of the Greeks. London/New York, 1951.

KRAELING, Carl H. Anthropos and Son of Man. A Study in the Religious Syncretism of the Hellenistic Orient. New York, 1927.

LAISTNER, M.L.W. Christianity and Pagan Culture in the Later Roman Empire. Ithaca, N.Y.: Cornell, 1951.

LA PIANA, George. "Foreign Groups in Rome during the First Centuries of the Empire," Harvard Theological Review 20(1927):183-403.

LATTE, Kurt. Römische Religionsgeschichte. München, 1960.

MURRAY, Gilbert. Five Stages of Greek Religion. Oxford, 1925. Reprint: 1951.

NILSSON, Martin P. Geschichte der griechischen Religion. Vol. II: Die hellenistische und römische Zeit. 2nd ed., München, 1961.

*_____. Greek Piety. Oxford, 1948.

_____. A History of Greek Religion. Oxford, 1925; 2nd ed., 1949. Reprint: 1964.

_____. Greek Folk Religion. New York, Harper, 1961. [Original title: Greek Popular Religion. New York: Columbia, 1940.]

_____. "Pagan Divine Service in Late Antiquity," Harvard Theological Review 38(1945):63-69.

_____. "Problems of the History of Greek Religion in the Hellenistic and Roman Age," Harvard Theological Review 36(1943):251-275.

_____. "Psychological Background of Late Greek Paganism," Review of Religion (1947):115-125.

NOCK, Arthur Darby. Essays on Religion and the Ancient World, ed. Zeph Stewart with a bibliography of Nock's writings. 2 vols. Cambridge, 1972.

*_____. Conversion. The Old and the New in Religion from Alexander the Great to Augustine of Hippo. Oxford, 1933. Reprint: 1963.

_____. "Cremation and Burial in the Roman Empire," Harvard Theological Review 25(1932):321-359.

*NOCK, A.D.   "The Development of Paganism in the Roman Empire,"
     Cambridge Ancient History, Vol. XII:409-449.

*_____.   Early Gentile Christianity and Its Hellenistic Back-
     ground. New York, Harper, 1964. [originally 1927]

_____.   "A Feature of Roman Religion," Harvard Theological
     Review 32(1939):83-96.

*_____.   "Religious Developments from the Close of the Republic
     to the Death of Nero," Cambridge Ancient History, Vol. X:
     465-511.

_____.   "The Roman Army and the Roman Religious Year," Harvard
     Theological Review 45(1952):187-277.

_____.   "Sarcophagi and Symbolism," American Journal of
     Archaeology 50(1946):140-70.

_____.   "A Vision of Mandulis Aion," Harvard Theological
     Review 27(1934):53-104.

NORDEN, Eduard.   Agnostos Theos.   Untersuchungen zur Formen-
     geschichte religiöser Rede.   Leipzig, 1913.   Reprint:
     1956.

PETTAZZONI, Raffaele.   Essays on the History of Religions.
     Leiden, Brill, 1954.

_____.   "State Religion and Individual Religion in the
     Religious History of Italy," in Pettazzoni, Essays on
     the History of Religion.   Leiden (1954) pp. 202-14.

RAMSAY, W.M.   "Religion of Greece and Asia Minor," Hastings
     Dictionary of the Bible, Vol. V:109-156.   1904.

RANDALL, John H.   Hellenistic Ways of Deliverance and the
     Making of the Christian Synthesis.   New York, 1970.

ROHDE, Erwin.   Psyche: The Cult of Souls and Belief in
     Immortality among the Greeks.   London/New York, 1925.

SOKOLOWSKI, F.   "Fees and Taxes in the Greek Cults," Harvard
     Theological Review 47(1954):153-164.

_____.   "A New Testimony on the Cult of Artemis of Ephesus,"
     Harvard Theological Review 58(1965):427-431.

_____.   "On Prothipia and Promanteia in Greek Cults," Harvard
     Theological Review 47(1954):165-171.

_____.   "Partnership in the Lease of Cults in Greek Antiquity,'
     Harvard Theological Review 50(1957):133-143.

SOKOLOWSKI, F. "The Real Meaning of Sacral Manumission,"
Harvard Theological Review 47(1954):173-181.

WEINSTOCK, Stefan. "Victor and Invictus," Harvard Theological
Review 50(1957):211-247.

WEISS, H. "The *pagani* among the Contemporaries of the First
Christians," Journal of Biblical Literature 86(1967):
42-52.

YERKES, R.K. Sacrifice in Greek and Roman Religions and Early
Judaism. New York, 1952.

II. MYSTERY RELIGIONS

A. COLLECTIONS OF SOURCES

BEVAN, E.R. Later Greek Religion. London, 1927.

CORNFORD, F.M. Greek Religious Thought from Homer to the Age
of Alexander. London, 1923.

GRANT, Frederick C. Ancient Roman Religion. New York, 1957.

*_____. Hellenistic Religions. The Age of Syncretism. New
York, 1953.

PALLIS, Svend Aage. Greek Religious Texts. Copenhagen, 1948.
[Greek texts only]

B. MYSTERY RELIGIONS IN GENERAL

ANGUS, Samuel. The Mystery Religions and Christianity. New
York, 1925.

_____. The Religious Quests of the Graeco-Roman World. New
York, 1929.

BLEEKER, C.J. [ed.] Initiation. Leiden, 1965.

BOUSSET, Wilhelm. Kyrios Christos. Nashville, 1970. [Orig-
inal: 1913[1]; 1921[2]; 1935[4]]

*CAMPBELL, Joseph [ed.] The Mysteries. Papers from the Eranos
Yearbooks. New York, 1955.

_____ [ed.] Pagan and Christian Mysteries. Papers from the
Eranos Yearbooks. New York, Harper, 1963. [Abridgement
of preceding title]

CUMONT, Franz. After Life in Roman Paganism. New Haven, 1922.
     Reprint: 1959.

*_____. Astrology and Religion among the Greek and Romans.
     New York, 1912. Reprint: 1960.

**_____. The Oriental Religions in Roman Paganism. 1911.
     Reprint: New York, Dover, 1956. [paperback]

_____. "Un fragment de rituel d'initiation aux Mystères,"
     Harvard Theological Review 26(1933):151-160.

*DILL, Samuel. Roman Society from Nero to Marcus Aurelius.
     1904. Reprint: Cleveland, World, 1956.

DOW, Sterling. "The Egyptian Cults in Athens," Harvard
     Theological Review 30(1937):183-232.

EITREM, Samson. Orakel und Mysterien am Ausgang der Antike.
     Zürich, 1947.

ELIADE, Mircea. Rites and Symbols of Initiation. The Myster-
     ies of Birth and Rebirth. New York, 1958. Reprint: 1965.

FRAZIER, J.G. The Golden Bough. 12 vols. 3rd ed., London,
     1911-15. See Part III, IV.

GARDNER, P. "Mysteries (Greek, Phrygian, etc.)" Hastings
     Encyclopaedia of Religion and Ethics, Vol. IX:77-82.

GLOVER, T.R. The Conflict of Religions in the Early Roman
     Empire. London, 1909. Reprint: Boston, 1960.

GOODENOUGH, Erwin R. Jewish Symbols in the Greco-Roman Period.
     12 vols. New York, 1953-65.

_____. By Light, Light. The Mystic Gospel of Hellenistic
     Judaism. New Haven, 1935.

GREENE, William C. Moira: Fate, Good and Evil in Greek
     Thought. Cambridge, Mass., 1944. Reprint: New York,
     1963.

GUTHRIE, W.K.C. The Greek and their Gods. Boston, 1954.

HALLIDAY, W.R. The Pagan Background of Early Christianity.
     Liverpool, 1925.

HARRIS, E. & J.R. The Oriental Cults in Roman Britain.
     Leiden, Brill, 1965. New edition in preparation.

HARRISON, Jane. Prolegomena to the Study of Greek Religion. Cambridge, 1903. 3rd ed., 1922. Reprint, New York, 1955.

_____. Themis. A Study of the Social Origins of Greek Religion. Cambridge, 1912, 1927. Reprint: Cleveland, 1962.

HATCH, Edwin. The Influence of Greek Ideas on Christianity. London, 1890. Reprint: New York, 1957.

HOOKE, S.H. "The Way of the Initiate," in Hooke, The Seige Perilous. London (1956) pp. 74-90.

KERN, Otto. Die griechischen Mysterien der klassischen Zeit. Berlin, 1927.

LEISEGANG, Hans. "The Mystery of the Serpent," The Mysteries (ed. J. Campbell. New York, 1955), pp. 194-260. Also in: Pagan and Christian Mysteries (ed. J. Campbell. New York, 1963), pp. 3-69.

MOORE, Clifford H. "Oriental Cults in Britain," Harvard Studies in Classical Philology 11(1900):47-60.

MORET, A. "Mysteries (Egyptian)," Hastings Encyclopaedia of Religion and Ethics, Vol. IX:74-77.

METZGER, Bruce M. "Methodology in the Study of the Mystery Religions and Early Christianity," in Metzger, Historical and Literary Studies: Pagan, Jewish, and Christian. Leiden (1968) pp. 1-24.

NILSSON, Martin P. Greek Piety. Oxford, 1948.

_____. Greek Popular Religion. New York, 1940. Reprinted as Greek Folk Religion: New York, 1961.

NOCK, A.D. "The Development of Paganism in the Roman Empire," Cambridge Ancient History, Vol. XII:409-449.

_____. "Mysteries," Encyclopedia of the Social Sciences, Vol. VI:172-175.

_____. "Mysterion," Harvard Studies in Classical Philology 60(1951):201-204.

REITZENSTEIN, Richard. Die hellenistischen Mysterienreligionen. Leipzig, 1927[3]. Reprint: 1956.

SCHMITT, Paul. "The Ancient Mysteries in the Society of Their Time, Their Transformation and Most Recent Echoes," The Mysteries. Papers from the Eranos Yearbooks (ed. J. Campbell. New York, 1955) pp. 93-118.

WAGNER, Günter. Pauline Baptism and the Pagan Mysteries.
     Edinburgh/London, 1967.

WILLOUGHBY, H.R. Pagan Regeneration. Chicago, 1929.

ZIELINSKI, Thaddeus. The Religion of Ancient Greece. An
     Outline. London, 1926.

III. SPECIFIC MYSTERY RELIGIONS

     A. MYSTERIES AT ELEUSIS

DODDS, Eric R. The Greeks and the Irrational. Berkeley, 1951.
     Reprint: 1957.

DOW, Sterling, and Robert F. Healey. A Sacred Calendar of
     Eleusis. Cambridge, Mass., Harvard University Press,
     1965.

EITREM, S. "Eleusinia--les mystères et l'agriculture,"
     Symbolae Osloenses 20(1940):140ff.

ELIADE, Mircea. Rites and Symbols of Initiation. The
     Mysteries of Birth and Rebirth. New York, 1958.
     Reprint: 1965.

GUTHRIE, W.K.C. The Greeks and Their Gods. Boston, 1950, 1954

JUNG, C.G., and K. KERÉNYI. Essays on a Science of Mythology.
     New York, 1949. Reprint: 1963.

*KERÉNYI, K. Eleusis: Archetypal Image of Mother and Daughter.
     New York, 1967.

MAGNIEN, V. Les mystères d'Eleusis. Paris, 1950.

*MYLONAS, G.E. Eleusis and the Eleusinian Mysteries. Princeton
     1961.

_____. The Hymn to Demeter and Her Sanctuary at Eleusis.
     St. Louis, 1942.

NILSSON, M.P. Greek Popular Religion. New York, 1940.
     Reprinted as Greek Folk Religion: New York, 1961.

*OTTO, Walter F. "The Meaning of the Eleusinian Mysteries,"
     The Mysteries. Papers from the Eranos Yearbooks (ed.
     J. Campbell. New York, 1955) pp. 14-31.

ROHDE, Erwin. Psyche: The Cult of Souls and Belief in
     Immortality among the Greeks. London, 1925. Reprint:
     1966.

SCHMITT, Paul. "The Ancient Mysteries in the Society of their
    Time," The Mysteries. Papers from the Eranos Yearbooks
    (ed. J. Campbell. New York, 1955) pp. 93-118.

ZIELINSKI, Thaddeus. The Religion of Ancient Greece. An
    Outline. London, 1926.

ZUNTZ, Gunther. Persephone. Three Essays on Religion and
    Thought in Magna Graecia. Oxford, 1972.

    B. CULTS OF DIONYSUS

DAVIS, G.M.N. The Asiatic Dionysos. London, 1914.

ELDERKIN, George W. Kantharos. Studies in Dionysiac and
    Kindred Cult. Princeton, 1924.

FESTUGIÈRE, A.J. "Les mystères de Dionysos," Revue Biblique
    44(1935):192ff., 366ff.

GRANT, Michael. Myths of the Greeks and Romans. New York,
    1962.

GUTHRIE, W.K.C. The Greeks and Their Gods. Boston, 1954.

HARRISON, Jane. Prolegomena to the Study of Greek Religion.
    Cambridge, 1903. 3rd ed., 1922. Reprint: New York,
    1955.

NILSSON, Martin P. "The Bacchic Mysteries of the Roman Age,"
    Harvard Theological Review 46(1953):175-202.

_____. Dionysiac Mysteries of the Hellenistic and Roman Age.
    Lund, 1957.

NOCK, A.D. "A Cult Ordinance in Verse," Harvard Studies in
    Classical Philology 63(1958):415ff.

*OTTO, W.F. Dionysus: Myth and Cult. Bloomington: Indiana
    University, 1965.

ROHDE, Erwin. Psyche. The Cult of Souls and Belief in Immor-
    tality among the Greeks. London, 1925. Reprint: New
    York, 1966.

ZIELINSKI, Thaddeus. The Religion of Ancient Greece. An
    Outline. London, 1926.

[SEE also the general works on Mysteries]

C. ORPHISM

GUTHRIE, W.K.C.   The Greeks and Their Gods. Boston, 1950, 1954

*_____. Orpheus and Greek Religion. A Study of the Orphic
     Movement. London, 1935. 2nd ed., 1952.

HARRISON, Jane. Prolegomena to the Study of Greek Religion.
     Cambridge, 1903. 3rd ed., 1922. Reprint: New York,
     1955.

KERN, Otto. Orpheus. Eine religionsgeschichtliche Unter-
     suchung. Berlin, 1920.

_____. Orphicorum Fragmenta. Berlin, 1922. [Sources]

LAGRANGE, M.-J. Les Mystères: L'Orphisme. Paris, 1937.

LEISEGANG, Hans. "The Mystery of the Serpent," The Mysteries.
     Papers from the Eranos Yearbooks (ed. J. Campbell.
     New York, 1955) pp. 194-260.

*LINFORTH, I.M. The Arts of Orpheus. Berkeley: University of
     California, 1941.

MACCHIORO, Vittorio. From Orpheus to Paul. A History of
     Orphism. New York, 1930.

*NILSSON, M.P. "Early Orphism and Kindred Religious Movements,"
     Harvard Theological Review 28(1935):181-230.

NOCK, A.D. "Orphism or Popular Philosophy," Harvard Theologica
     Review 33(1940):301-315.

ROHDE, Erwin. Psyche.... London, 1925. Reprint: New York,
     1966.

*WILI, Walter. "The Orphic Mysteries and the Greek Spirit,"
     The Mysteries. Papers from the Eranos Yearbooks (ed. J.
     Campbell. New York, 1955) pp. 64-92.

ZIELINSKI, T. The Religion of Ancient Greece. An Outline.
     London, 1926.

[SEE also the general works on Mysteries]

D. CULT OF THE GREAT MOTHER (CYBELE/ATTIS)

CHADWICK, H. "An Attis from a Domestic Shrine," Journal of
     Theological Studies 3(1952):90-92 + 3 plates.

DILL, Samuel. Roman Society from Nero to Marcus Aurelius.
     1904. Reprint: 1956.

FISHWICK, Duncan. "The *cannophori* and the March Festival of
     Magna Mater," Transactions and Proceedings of the Ameri-
     can Philological Association 97(1966):193-202.

GOW, A.S.F. "The Gallus and the Lion," Journal of Hellenic
     Studies 80(1960):89 ff.

KÖVES, Th. "Zum Empfang der Magna Mater in Rom," Historia
     12(1963):321-347.

NOCK, A.D. "Eunuchs in Ancient Religion," Archiv für Religions-
     wissenschaft 23(1925):25 ff.

*SHOWERMAN, G. The Great Mother of the Gods. 1901. Reprint:
     1970.

*VERMASEREN, Maarten J. The Legend of Attis in Greek and Roman
     Art. Leiden, 1966.

TAUROBOLIUM:

DUTHOY, R. The Taurobolium. Its Evolution and Terminology.
     Leiden, Brill, 1969.

MOORE, C.H. "The Duration of the Efficacy of the Tauro-
     bolium," Classical Philology 19(1924):363-365.

_____. "On the Origin of the Taurobolium," Harvard Studies
     in Classical Philology 17(1906):43-48.

[SEE also the general works on Mysteries; also see Magna Mater
 in indexes]

     E. CULT OF ISIS (and OSIRIS/SERAPIS)

ALFÖLDI, Andrew. A Festival of Isis in Rome under the Christian
     Emperors of the Fourth Century. Budapest, 1937.

*BELL, H. Idris. Cults and Creeds in Graeco-Roman Egypt.
     Liverpool, 1953.

BRADY, T.A. "The Reception of the Egyptian Cults by the Greeks
     (330-30 B.C.)." University of Missouri Studies 10(1935):
     1-88.

BUDGE, E.A. Wallis. Osiris. 2 vols. London, 1911. Reprint:
     1961.

DILL, Samuel.   Roman Society from Nero to Marcus Aurelius.
    1904.   Reprint: 1956.

DOW, Sterling.   "The Egyptian Cults in Athens," Harvard
    Theological Review 30(1937):183-232.

FESTUGIÈRE, A.J.   "À propos des arétalogies d'Isis," Harvard
    Theological Review 42(1949):209-234.

*_____.   Personal Religion among the Greeks.   Berkeley, 1954.
    Reprint: 1960.

GRIFFITHS, J.G.   The Origins of Osiris.   Berlin, 1966.

_____.   Plutarch's De Iside et Osiride.   University of Wales
    Press, 1970.

MOEHRING, H.R.   "The Persecution of the Jews and the Adherents
    of the Isis Cult at Rome A.D. 19," Novum Testamentum
    3(1959):293-304.

*NAGEL, G.   "The 'Mysteries' of Osiris in Ancient Egypt," The
    Mysteries.   Papers from the Eranos Yearbooks (ed. J.
    Campbell.   New York, 1955) pp. 119-134.

PETTAZZONI, R.   "Sarapis and his 'Kerberos'," in Pettazzoni,
    Essays on the History of Religions.   Leiden (1954) pp.
    164-170.

SCHMITT, P.   "The Ancient Mysteries in the Society of Their
    Time, Their Transformation and Most Recent Echoes," The
    Mysteries.   Papers from the Eranos Yearbooks (ed. J.
    Campbell.   New York, 1955) pp. 93-118.

SCHWARTZ, J.   "La Fin du Serapeum d'Alexandrie," Essays in
    Honor of C. Bradford Welles.   New Haven (1966) pp. 97-111

VIDMAN, L.   Isis und Sarapis bei den Griechen und Römern.
    Epigraphische Studie....   Berlin, 1970.

_____.   Sylloge inscriptionum religionis Isiacae et Serapiacae.
    Berlin, 1969.

WELLES, C.B.   "The Discovery of Sarapis and the Foundation of
    Alexandria," Historia 11(1962):271-298.   Cf. p. 512.

WITT, R.E.   Isis and the Greco-Roman World.   London, 1971.

[SEE also the general works on Mysteries]

F. MITHRAISM

BETZ, H.D. "The Mithras Inscriptions of Santa Prisca and the New Testament," Novum Testamentum 10(1968):62-80.

BOON, G.C. "A Temple of Mithras at Caernarvon-Segontium," Archaeologia Cambrensis (1960):136-172.

BRANDON, S.G.F. "Mithraism and Its Challenge to Christianity," Hibbert Journal 53(1955):107-114.

*CAMPBELL, Leroy A. Mithraic Iconography and Ideology. Leiden, Brill, 1968.

_____. "Typology of Mithraic Tauroctones," Berytus 11(1954): 1-60.

CUMONT, Fr. et. al. "The Mithraeum," Excavations of Dura-Europos. 7th and 8th Seasons.... New Haven, 1939.

CUMONT, Franz. Textes et monuments figurés relatifs aux mystères de Mithra. 2 vols. Brussels, 1895-1899.

*_____. The Mysteries of Mithra. New York, Dover, 1956 [Original: 1903]

DILL, Samuel. Roman Society from Nero to Marcus Aurelius. 1904. Reprint: 1956.

GEDEN, A.S. Select Passages Illustrating Mithraism. New York, 1925. [Sources]

GERSHEVITCH, I. (trans. & ed.). The Avestan Hymn to Mithras. Cambridge, 1959.

GRIMES, W.F. "Excavations in the City of London," Recent Archaeological Excavations in Britain. Selected Excavations 1939-1955.... (ed. R.L.S. Bruce-Mitford. London, 1956)

HALLIDAY, W.R. The Pagan Background of Early Christianity. London, 1925.

LAEUCHLI, Samuel (ed.). Mithraism in Ostia. Mystery Religion and Christianity in the Ancient Port of Rome. Evanston, 1967.

LAEUCHLI, Samuel. "Urban Mithraism," Biblical Archaeologist 31(1968):73-99.

MEIGGS, Russell. Roman Ostia. Oxford, 1960.

MENASCE, Jean de. "The Mysteries and the Religion of Iran," The Mysteries. Papers from the Eranos Yearbooks (ed. J. Campbell. New York, 1955) pp. 135-148.

METZGER, B.M. "The Second Grade of Mithraic Initiation," in Bruce M. Metzger, Historical and Literary Studies: Pagan, Jewish and Christian. Leiden (1968) pp. 25-33.

*NOCK, A.D. "The Genius of Mithraism," Journal of Roman Studies 27(1937):109-113.

PETTAZZONI, R. "The Monstrous Figure of Time in Mithraism," in Pettazzoni, Essays on the History of Religions. Leiden (1954) pp. 180-192.

RICHMOND, I.A. "The Cult of Mithras and Its Temple at Carrawburgh...," Recent Archaeological Excavations in Britain. Selected Excavations 1939-1955... (ed. R.L.S. Bruce-Mitford. London: 1956).

_____. "Mithraism in Roman Britain," Durham University Journal 36:1(Dec. 1943).

_____, and J.P. Gillam. "The Temple of Mithras at Carrawburgh Archaeologia Aeliana 39(1951):1-92.

THIEMS, P. "Mitra and Aryaman," Transactions of Connecticut Academy of Arts and Sciences 41(1957):1-96.

TOYNBEE, J.M.C. A Silver Casket and Strainer from the Walbrook Mithraeum in the City of London. Leiden, Brill, 1963.

VERMASEREN, M.J., and C.C. van Essen. "The Aventine Mithraeum Adjoining the Church of Sa. Prisca...," Antiquity and Survival, I:I,3-36 (1955).

VERMASEREN, M.J. Corpus Inscriptionem et Monumentorum religionis Mithraicae. The Hague, 1956-60. 2 vols. [Sources]

VERMASEREN, M.J., and C.C. van Essen. The Excavations in the Mithraeum of Santa Prisca in Rome. Leiden, 1965.

*VERMASEREN, Maarten J. Mithras, The Secret God. New York, 1963.

ZAEHNER, R.C. The Dawn and Twilight of Zoroastrianism. New York, 1961.

[SEE also the general works on mysteries]

G. THE MYSTERIES AND CHRISTIANITY

ANGUS, Samuel. The Mystery Religions and Christianity. New York, 1925.

BOUSSET, Wilhelm. Kyrios Christos. Nashville, 1970. Original: 1913[1], 1921[2], 1935[4].

BRANDON, S.G.F. "Mithraism and Its Challenge to Christianity," Hibbert Journal 53(1955):107-114.

BROWN, Raymond E. "The Semitic Background of the New Testament Mysterion," Biblica 39(1958):426-448, 40(1959):70-87. Also in Catholic Biblical Quarterly 20(1958):417-443.

CAMPBELL, Joseph (ed.). The Mysteries. Papers from the Eranos Yearbooks. New York, 1955. [See various articles]

CLEMEN, Carl. Primitive Christianity and Its Non-Jewish Sources. Edinburgh, 1912.

GRANT, Frederick C. Roman Hellenism and the New Testament. New York, 1962.

HALLIDAY, W.R. The Pagan Background of Early Christianity. Liverpool, 1925.

HATCH, Edwin. The Influence of Greek Ideas on Christianity. 1888. Reprint: New York, 1957.

HOOKE, S.H. "Christianity and the Mystery Religions," in Hooke, The Seige Perilous. London (1956) pp. 91-101.

KENNEDY, H.A.A. St Paul and the Mystery-Religions. London, 1913.

KNOX, Wilfred L. Some Hellenistic Elements in Primitive Christianity. London, 1944.

_____. St. Paul and the Church of the Gentiles. Cambridge, 1939.

LOISY, Alfred. Les Mystères païens et le mystère chrétienne. Paris, 1913. 2nd ed., 1930.

*NOCK, Arthur Darby. Conversion. The Old and the New in Religion from Alexander the Great to Augustine of Hippo. Oxford, 1933. Reprint: 1952.

*_____. Early Gentile Christianity and Its Hellenistic Background. New York, Harper, 1964. [Original, 1927]

NOCK, A.D.   "Hellenistic Mysteries and Christian Sacraments,"
     Mnemosyne, Series IV:5(1952):177-213.

RAHNER, Hugo.   Greek Myths and Christian Mystery.   New York,
     1963.

SCHÜTZE, Alfred.   Mithras-Mysterien und Urchristentum.   Stutt-
     gart, 1960.

WAGNER, Günter.   Pauline Baptism and the Pagan Mysteries.
     Edinburgh/London, 1967.

METZGER, Bruce M.   "Methodology in the Study of the Mystery
     Religions and Early Christianity," in Metzger, Historical
     and Literary Studies: Pagan, Jewish, and Christian.
     Leiden (1968) pp. 1-24.

III.   HELLENISTIC HEALING

     SEE: PHILOSTRATUS, Life of Apollonios of Tyana

ACHTEMEIER, Paul J.   "Gospel Miracle Tradition and the Divine
     Man," Interpretation 26(1972):174-197.

AFRICA, Thomas W.   Rome of the Caesars.   New York, 1965.
     See Ch. 7: "The Wizard--Apollonius of Tyana," pp. 122-139.

BEHR, C.A.   Aelius Aristides and the Sacred Tales.   Amsterdam,
     1968.

CASE, S.J.   "The Art of Healing in Early Christian Times,"
     Journal of Religion 3(1923):238-258.

CATON, R.   The Temples and Ritual of Asklepios at Epidaurus
     and Athens.   London, 1900.

DODDS, Eric R.   The Greeks and the Irrational.   Berkeley, 1951.
     Reprint: Boston, 1957.

DUPREZ, A.   Jésus et les dieux guérisseurs à propos de Jean, V.
     Paris, 1970.

*EDELSTEIN, Emma J. and Ludwig.   Asclepius.   2 vols.   Baltimore:
     Johns Hopkins, 1945.

*FESTUGIÈRE, A.J.   Personal Religion among the Greeks.   Berkeley
     1954.

GESSLER, J.   "Notes sur l'incubation et ses survivances," Le
     Muséon 59(1946):661-670.

GRANT, Robert M. Miracle and Natural Law in Graeco-Roman and Early Christian Thought. Amsterdam, 1952.

GUILMOT, M. "Le Sérapeion de Memphis. Étude topographique," Chronique d'Égypte 37(1962):359-381.

HAMILTON, Mary. Incubation, or the Cure of Disease in Pagan Temples and Christian Churches. London, 1906.

HERZOG, R. Die Wunderheilungen von Epidaurus. Leipzig, 1931.

*KERÉNYI, Károly. Asklepios: Archetypical Image of the Physician's Existence. New York, 1959.

KOENIG, J. "Sourciers, thaumaturges et scribes," Revue de l'Histoire des Religions 164(1963 B):16-38, 165-180.

LEFORT, T. "Notes sur le culte d'Asclépios; Nature de l'incubation dans ce culte," Musée Belge 10(1906):21-37, 101-126.

McCASLAND, V. "The Asclepios Cult in Palestine," Journal of Biblical Literature 58(1939):221-227.

_____. "Religious Healing in First-Century Palestine," Environmental Factors in Christian History (eds. McNeill, Spinka, and Willoughby) Chicago (1939) pp. 18-34.

NEILL, S.C., and A.D. Nock. "Two Notes on the Asclepius Cult," Journal of Theological Studies 26(1924/25):173-176.

REITZENSTEIN, R. Hellenistische Wundererzählungen. Leipzig, 1906.

WALTON, Alice. The Cult of Asklepios. Ithaca: Cornell, 1894. Reprint: 1970.

WEINREICH, Otto. Antike Heilungswunder. Untersuchungen zum Wunderglauben der Griechen und Römer. Giessen, 1909.

EE also items on SARAPIS under Isis Cult.]

V. MAGIC IN THE HELLENISTIC WORLD

BELL, H. Idris. Cults and Creeds in Graeco-Roman Egypt. Liverpool, 1953.

_____., and A.D. Nock, and Herbert Thompson (eds.). Magical Texts from a Bilingual Papyrus in the British Museum. London. [From Proceedings of the British Academy, Vol. 17] 54 pp.

BONNER, Campbell. Studies in Magical Amulets, Chiefly Graeco-Egyptian. Ann Arbor, 1950.

BUDGE, E.A. Wallis. Amulets and Supersititions. London, 193

_____. Egyptian Magic. London, 1899.

GAGER, John G. Moses in Greco-Roman Paganism. Philadelphia, 1972.

GRANT, Robert M. Miracle and Natural Law in Graeco-Roman and Early Christian Thought. Amsterdam, 1952.

GUTHRIE, W.K.C. The Greeks and Their Gods. Boston, 1950, 19

NILSSON, Martin P. Die Religion in den griechischen Zauber-papyri. Lund, 1948.

NOCK, A.D. "Greek Magical Papyri," Journal of Egyptian Archaeology 15(1929):219-235.

_____. "Paul and the Magus," in F.J. Foakes Jackson and Kirsopp Lake, The Beginnings of Christianity, Vol. V: 164-188.

REES, B.R. "Popular Religion in Graeco-Roman Egypt," Journal of Egyptian Archaeology 36(1950):86-100.

REISS, Ernst. "Religious Gleanings from the Magical Papyri," Classical Weekly 28(1934-35):105-111.

SEE: McCartney, Eugene S., and Richard S. Crum, Classical Weekly 40(1946-47):99-101, 42(1948-49):234-236, for a bibliography on Greek and Roman magic.

[SEE also general works on Greek and Roman religion.]

V. ASTROLOGY IN THE HELLENISTIC WORLD

BOLL, Fr., and C. Bezold. Sternglaube und Sterndeutung: Geschichte und Wesen der Astrologie. 4th ed. Berlin, 1931.

CUMONT, Franz. After Life in Roman Paganism. New Haven, 192 Reprint: New York, 1959.

*_____. Astrology and Religion among the Greeks and Romans. 1912. Reprint: New York, Dover, 1960.

_____. L'Égypte des astrologues. 1937.

*DODDS, Eric R. The Greeks and the Irrational. Berkeley, 1951.
    Reprint: Boston, 1957.

FESTUGIÈRE, A.J. Epicurus and His Gods. Oxford, 1955. See
    Ch. 5, pp. 73-93.

GRESSMANN, Hugo. Die hellenistische Gestirnreligion. Leipzig,
    1925.

LINDSAY, J. The Origins of Alchemy in Graeco-Roman Egypt. 1970.

MURRAY, Gilbert. Five Stages of Greek Religion. 1925.
    3rd ed., 1951. See Ch. 4.

*NILSSON, Martin P. Greek Piety. Oxford, 1948.

_____. "The Origin of the Belief among the Greeks in the
    Divinity of the Heavenly Bodies," Harvard Theological
    Review 33(1940):1-8.

[SEE also general works on Hellenistic Religions.]

VI. DIVINATION

DEMPSEY, T. The Delphic Oracle. Oxford, 1918.

FLACELIERE, Robert. Greek Oracles. New York, 1965.

HALLIDAY, W.R. Greek Divination. A Study of Its Methods and
    Principles. London, 1913.

NILSSON, Martin P. Greek Popular Religion. New York, 1940.
    Reprinted as Greek Folk Religion. New York, 1961.

*PARKE, Herbert W., and D.E.W. Wormell. The Delphic Oracle.
    2 vols. Oxford, 1956.

PARKE, Herbert W. The Oracles of Zeus: Dodona, Olympia, Ammon.
    Oxford, 1967.

VII. IMMORTALITY

*CUMONT, Franz. After Life in Roman Paganism. New Haven, 1923.
    Reprint: New York, 1959.

GUTHRIE, W.K.C. The Greeks and Their Gods. Boston 1950, 1954.

HALLIDAY, W.R. The Pagan Background of Early Christianity.
    London, 1925.

CULLMANN, Oscar.   Immortality of the Soul or Resurrection of
    the Dead?   London, 1958.

*ROHDE, E.   Psyche.   The Cult of Souls and Belief in Immortalit
    among the Greeks.   London, 1925.   Reprint: New York,
    1966.

WELLES, C.B.   "The Epitaph of Julius Terentius," Harvard
    Theological Review 34(1941):79-102.   See also NOCK,
    pp. 103-109 in same issue of journal.

TEXT EDITIONS USED FOR THE TRANSLATIONS

1. Plutarch, *Vitae Parallelae*, ed. K. Ziegler (Teubner ed.), Leipzig, 1968.

2. Diogenes Laertius, *Vitae Philosophorum*, ed. H.S. Long, Oxford, 1964.

3. Greek text based on Papyrus Bodmer V collated with 83 other MSS by Boyd L. Daniels; see "The Greek Manuscript Tradition of the Protevangelium Jacobi" (unpubl. diss., Duke University), 1956.

4. M.R. James, *Latin Infancy Gospels* (the Arundel MS), Cambridge, 1927.

5. Philostratus, *Life of Apollonios of Tyana*, ed. F.C. Conybeare (Loeb series).

6. Diodorus Siculus, *Library of History*, ed. C.H. Oldfather (Loeb series).

7. Iamblichus, *De vita Pythagorica*, ed. M. von Albrecht, Zurich, 1963.

8. C. Tischendorf, *Evangelia Apocrypha* (1876).

9. The "A" text in Tischendorf, *op. cit.*; pp. 140-157.

10. See #5.

11. Philo Judaeus, *Vita Mosis*, ed. F.H. Colson (Loeb series).

12. G. Delling, *Antike Wundertexte*, 2nd ed. (1960), pp. 20f.

13. See #7.

14. G. Delling, *op. cit.*, p. 8.

15. *Ibid.*, p. 13.

16. P. Fiebig, *Rabbinische Wundergeschichten den neutestamentlichen Zeitalters*, 2nd ed. (1933), pp. 7-9.

17. *Ibid.*, p. 23f.

18. *Ibid.*, p. 10-12.

19. *Ibid.*, p. 10.

20. Vergil, *Georgics* I. 463-488 (Loeb series); Suetonius, *Lives of the Caesars* I. 88-89 (Loeb series).

21. G. Delling, *op. cit.*, pp. 14, 7.

22. *Ibid.*, p. 16.

23. E. Schwartz, *Eusebius Kirchengeschichte*, 5th ed., Leipzig, 1955.

24. See #5.

25. Arrian, *Discourses of Epictetus*, ed. W.A. Oldfather (Loeb series).

26. A.D. Nock, A.J. Festugière, *Hermes Trismégisté* I, Paris, 1960.

27. See #5.

28. See #11.

29. See #7.

30. See #2.

31. Plutarch, *Moralia*, ed. F.C. Babbit (Loeb series).

32. See #25.

33. See #5.

34. See #5.

35. A. Guillaumont et. al., eds., *The Gospel of Thomas*, New York, 1959.

36. *Corpus Fabularum Aesopicarum*, ed. A. Hausrath, 2 vols. (Teubner series), Leipzig, 1940, 1956. Also Emile Chambry ed., *Esope*, *Fables*, Paris, 1927.

37. Plato, *The Republic*, ed. P. Shovey (Loeb series).

38. See #7.

39. R.H. Charles, *The Greek Versions of the Testaments of the Twelve Patriarchs*, 1908 (reprinted Darmstadt, 1966), pp. 171-182.

40. *Pistis Sophia*, ed. C. Schmidt (*Coptica* II), Hauniae, 1925.

41. See #5.

2. See #11.

3. See #2.

4. *Acta Alexandrinorum*, ed. H.A. Musurillo, S.J., Oxford, 1954.

5. M. Hadas, *The Third and Fourth Books of Maccabees* (Jewish Apocryphal Literature), New York, 1953.

6. K. Bihlmeyer, *Die apostolischen Väter*, 2nd ed., 1956.

7. P. Fiebig, *op. cit.*, pp. 13-15.

8. See #5.

9. Ovid, *Metamorphoses*, ed. F.J. Miller (Loeb series); *Fasti*, ed. J.G. Frazier (Loeb series); *Livy*, ed. B.O. Foster (Loeb series).

10. Charitonis Aphrodisiensis de Chaerea et Callirhoe   s). amatoriarum Narrationum Libri Octo, ed. William E. Blake, Oxford, 1938.

11. *M. Tulli Ciceronis scripta quae manserunt omni*, ed. K. Ziegler (Teubner series) fasc. 39, Leipzig, 1969.

12. A. Erman, "Obelisken römischer Zeit," *Deutsches archäologisches Institut, römische Abteilung*, mitteil. 19; 1896. For text of Clement of Alexandria, see O. Stählin, *Clemens Alexandrinus* (*Griechische christliche Schriftsteller*), 1936; reprinted in Βιβλιοθήκη πατέρων ἑλλήνων, vol. VIII, p. 42f.

13. L. Vaganay, *L'évangile de Pierre*, Paris, 1930.

14. R.A. Lipsius, M. Bonnet, *Acta Apostolorum Apocrypha* II.2, Darmstadt, 1959.

15. See #5.

16. See #11.

17. See #6.

18. See #35.

19. W.C. Till, *Das Evangelium nach Philippos*, Leiden, 1963.

20. See #53.

21. See #54.

62. See #5.

63. See #11.

64. See #6.